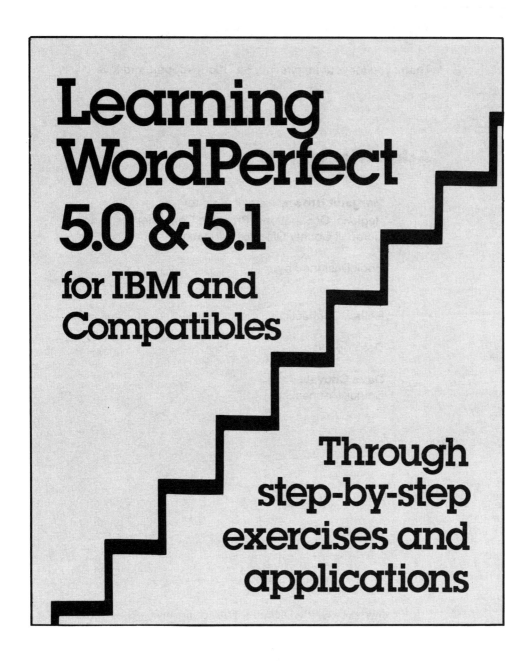

Learning WordPerfect 5.0 & 5.1
for IBM and Compatibles

Through step-by-step exercises and applications

Iris Blanc

Dictation Disc Company

TO MY FAMILY   Alan, Pamela and Jaime

Thank you for your Inspiration, devotion, support and love.

Acknowledgments

Margaret Brown, Technical Editor
Regional Occupational Program Computer Instructor,
Humbolt County Office of Education,

Book Designed by:

Irwin Bag
Bethel, Connecticut

Desktop by:

Dave Chuvala
Bethel, Connecticut

First Dictation Disc printing

ISBN: 1-56243-046-7

10 9 8 7 6 5

Printed in the United States of America

TABLE OF CONTENTS

continued...

TABLE OF CONTENTS

INTRODUCTION

ABOUT THIS BOOK

**LEARNING WORDPERFECT THROUGH APPLI-
CATIONS AND EXERCISES** will enable you to
learn how to use WordPerfect 5.0 or 5.1 word
processing software on an IBM PC or compatible
computer. Each lesson in this book will explain
WordPerfect concepts, provide numerous exercises
to apply those concepts, and illustrate the necessary keystrokes to complete the applications.
Summary exercises are provided to challenge and
reinforce the concepts you have learned. Proper
formatting of various documents will be presented
and reviewed. (See Directory of Document Formats,
page I)
After completing the 125 exercises in this book, you
will be able to use WordPerfect software with ease.

HOW TO USE THIS BOOK

Before you begin working on the exercises in
Lesson 1, you will need to read the first chapter on
"Introductory Basics." This chapter will explain the
basic differences between WordPerfect 5.0 and 5.1,
the WordPerfect screen, how to get help and other
necessary preliminary information.

Each exercise contains four parts:

- The "Notes" - explain the WordPerfect
  concept being introduced.
- The "Exercise Directions" - tell how to complete the exercise.
- Exercises - apply the concept that was
  introduced.
- Keystroke Procedures - outline the keys to
  use to complete the exercise.

The keystrokes are provided only when a new
concept is introduced. Therefore, if you forget the
keystroke procedures for completing a task, you
can use the Help Feature (explained in the "Introductory Basics" section), or you can use the book's
keystroke index to refer you to the page where the
keystroke procedures are located. (See Appendix
C, pages 295-297.)

To test your knowledge of the lesson concepts, you
may complete the two summary exercises at the
end of each lesson. Final versions of exercises can
be found in the separate solutions booklet which
accompanies this book. Because of the variety of
printers that are available, your line and page
endings may vary with the exercises illustrated
throughout the book.

A summary of WordPerfect commands can be
found in Appendix D, pages 298.

WORDPERFECT BASICS

WORDPERFECT 5.0/WORDPERFECT 5.1 BASIC DIFFERENCES

WordPerfect 5.1 has two significant additions not found in WordPerfect 5.0:

1. **Mouse feature**. The "mouse" is a device which sits on a table and may be used to select features and options from pull-down menus and block text. When the mouse is moved, the cursor moves in the same direction across the screen.

2. **Pull-down menus**. While this feature is optional, it may be used to access commands listed at the top of the screen. Once the command is selected, a "pull-down menu bar" appears listing additional options.

Keyboard vs. Mouse

WordPerfect 5.1 users can select pull-down menu commands by using either the keyboard keys or the mouse. Mouse actions will not be covered in this book. See WordPerfect 5.1 software information on mouse support.

Menu selections may be made either by letter or number. The keystrokes in this book are indicated by letter, not number.

Other differences in the two versions are noted throughout this book.

THE WORDPERFECT SCREEN

When WordPerfect is accessed, the following screen appears:

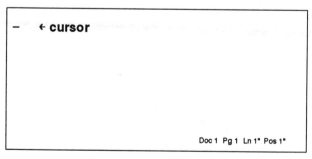

```
—   ← cursor




                              Doc 1  Pg 1  Ln 1"  Pos 1"
```

The **cursor** is the blinking marker that appears in the upper left hand corner when the WordPerfect screen is accessed. It indicates where the next character to be keyed will appear.

The **status line** appears at the bottom right-hand corner of the screen and displays the document number (Doc 1), the page number (Pg 1), the line position (Ln 1") and the position of the cursor (Pos 1"). "Ln" and "Pos" display the position of the cursor in relation to the paper on which the document will be printed. As you work, the status line will sometimes display messages and warnings.

DEFAULT/INITIAL SETTINGS

Default or initial settings are preset conditions created by the manufacturer of the software. For example, when you begin working on WordPerfect, margins have already been set for you. WordPerfect assumes you are working on a standard 8 1/2" x 11" sheet of paper. The line and position indicators on the status line are defaulted to inches. When you begin working on a WordPerfect document, the cursor is defaulted to begin at Line 1", giving you a 1" top margin on a standard sheet of paper. Margins are preset at 1" on the left and right. Consequently, the "Pos" indicator will start at 1" to reflect the 1" left margin. (Margin changes are covered in Lesson 4).

Other defaults include tabs, which are set 1/2" apart and full justification (WP5.1)/justification (WP5.0), which prints documents with an even right-hand margin. (Justification changes are covered in Lesson 5).

THE KEYBOARD

In addition to the character keys found on most typewriters, computers contain additional keys:

FUNCTION KEYS - located at the left of a Standard PC keyboard and across the top of an Enhanced PC keyboard, these keys perform special functions. A standard keyboard contains 10 function keys (F1, F2, etc.); while the enhanced keyboard contains 12 function keys. A list of function keys and WordPerfect Functions appears on next page. (See Template section)

continued...

WORDPERFECT BASICS

NUMERIC KEYS - located on the right side of either keyboard, these keys allow the user to enter numbers quickly when the "Num Lock" key (located above the 7/Home key) is depressed. When "Num Lock" is not on, the arrow keys and other application keys found on the numbers are activated.

ENTER/RETURN - located to the right of the home row, (contains an arrow) this key is known as the "Enter" or "Return" key. An "Enter/Return" key is also located to the right of the numeric keypad on enhanced keyboards. This key is used to force the cursor to the next line (hard return) or to complete a keystroke action.

CTRL/ALT/SHIFT - located on the left and right sides of the enhanced keyboard, (there are two of each), these keys are used in conjunction with other keys to select certain features. The standard keyboard has only one CTRL and ALT key, but contains two shift keys. (See template section below.)

THE WORDPERFECT TEMPLATE

To use a control key (**Shift, Alt** or **Ctrl**) with a function key, you must depress the control key and <u>tap</u> the function key. To assist you in remembering the keystroke combinations, WordPerfect provides a keyboard "template" with the purchase of the software. This template fits over the function keys on a standard or on an enhanced keyboard.

    A copy appears here.

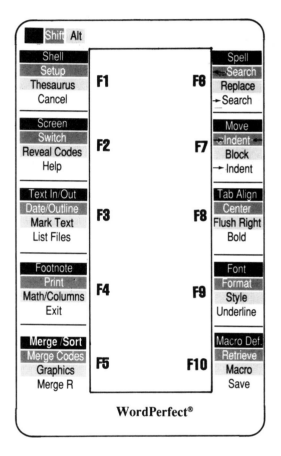

Shift	Alt					
Shell				Spell		
Setup		F1		Search		F8
Thesaurus				Replace		
Cancel				Search		
Screen				Move		
Switch		F2		Indent		F7
Reveal Codes				Block		
Help				Indent		
Text In/Out				Tab Align		
Date/Outline		F3		Center		F8
Mark Text				Flush Right		
List Files				Bold		
Footnote				Font		
Print		F4		Format		F9
Math/Columns				Style		
Exit				Underline		
Merge /Sort				Macro Def.		
Merge Codes		F5		Retrieve		F10
Graphics				Macro		
Merge R				Save		

WordPerfect®

WordPerfect®	Shell	Spell	Screen	Move	Ctr.	Text In Out	Tab Align	Footnote	Font		Merge Sort	Macro Define		
	Thesaurus	Replace	Reveal Codes	Block	ALT	Mark Text	Flush Right	Columns/Table	Style	ALT	Graphics	Macro		
	Setup	Search	Switch	Indent	Shift	Date/Outline	Center	Print	Format	Shift	Merge Codes	Retrieve		
	Cancel	Search	Help	Indent		List	Bold	Exit	Underline		End Field	Save	Reveal Codes	Block
	F1	F2	F3	F4		F5	F6	F7	F8		F9	F10	F11	F12

continued...

WORDPERFECT BASICS

THE HELP FEATURE

The Help Feature displays information about a feature or the proper keystrokes to complete a task. To access Help, depress F3. Your document will be replaced with a Help screen which asks you to press any letter to get an alphabetic list of features. Depressing F3 two times will display a function-key template. To exit Help, press Enter or Spacebar.

IF YOU MAKE AN ERROR...

...The following keys will get you out of trouble:

F1	- Will cancel a command.
BACKSPACE	- Will erase characters to the immediate left of the cursor.
F3	- Will access "Help"
F3, F3	- Will produce a function key template.

LOG OF EXERCISES

continued...

LOG OF EXERCISES

DIRECTORY OF DOCUMENTS

continued...

DIRECTORY OF DOCUMENTS

continued...

DIRECTORY OF DOCUMENTS

DIRECTORY OF DOCUMENT FORMATS

> **LESSON 1:**
> SAVING AND EXITING A DOCUMENT; KEYBOARDING USING WORD WRAP;
> CURSOR MOVEMENTS; CREATING A BUSINESS LETTER; BACKSPACING
> FOR CORRECTIONS; USING THE DATE FEATURE; USING ALL CAPS;
> PRINTING; ACCESSING "LIST FILES"

SAVING AND EXITING A DOCUMENT

Notes:

- As you type, the "Pos" indicator on the bottom right of the screen will change. As text advances to another line, the "Ln" indicator will also change. The "Pos" indicator shows you where you are horizontally on the page while the "Ln" indicator shows you where you are vertically on a page.

- As text is typed, it will automatically advance to the next line. This is called "word wrap" or "wraparound". It is only necessary to use the return key at the end of a short line or to begin a new paragraph.

- The backspace key may be used to correct immediate errors.

- Each document must be named when it is saved for future recall. A filename may contain a maximum of eight characters and may have an optional three-character file extension. The file extension may be used to further identify your document. The filename and extension are separated by a period. Example: travel.bos

   filename   extension

- Filenames are not case sensitive; they may be typed in either upper or lower case.

- After you name your document and press ENTER to save it, you will note the bottom left of your screen. The prompt line will ask, "Exit WP?" Typing "N" for (No) will clear your screen, while typing "Y" for (Yes) will exit you from the WordPerfect program and return you to the DOS prompt.

- IF YOU MAKE A MISTAKE AND WOULD LIKE TO BEGIN AGAIN, FOLLOW KEYSTROKES ON THE RIGHT **"TO EXIT WITHOUT SAVING"**.

Exercise Directions:

1. Keyboard the paragraphs on the right, allowing the text to "word wrap" to the next line.

2. Begin the exercise at the top of your screen; press the return key twice to begin a new paragraph.

3. Correct only immediate errors by using the backspace key.

4. Save the exercise; name it **TRY**.

5. Clear your screen.

As you type, notice the "Pos" indicator on your format line change as the position of your cursor changes.

The wraparound feature allows the operator to decide on line endings, making the use of the return unnecessary except at the end of a paragraph or short line. Each file is saved on a disk or hard drive for recall. Documents must be given a name for identification.

TO SAVE AND CLEAR SCREEN

NOTE: Watch the prompt line on the bottom left of your screen as you complete the procedures below.

1. Press **F7**..................................**F7**
2. Type **Y** (Yes)............................**Y**
3. Type document name.*
4. **ENTER**....................................↵
   to save
5. Type **N** (No).............................**N**
   to clear

*If saving on a floppy disk, indicate the drive where the disk resides before entering the document name.
Example: A:FIRST
If saving on a hard drive, it is only necessary to enter the document name.

TO EXIT WITHOUT SAVING

1. Press **F7**..................................**F7**
2. Type **N**....................................**N**
3. Type **N**....................................**N**

TO EXIT WORDPERFECT PROGRAM

1. Press **F7**..................................**F7**
2. Type **N**....................................**N**
3. Type **Y**....................................**Y**

3

SAVING AND EXITING A DOCUMENT

Notes:

- The way your document is laid out on a page is called the **format**.

- Format settings such as margins, tabs, and line spacing are automatically set by the WordPerfect program. Anything that is preset within the program is a "**default.**"

- The default margins are set for one inch on the left and the right. When the cursor is at the left margin, the "Pos" indicator displays 1", indicating a 1" left margin. Each time the tab key is pressed, the cursor will advance 1/2". Therefore, when the cursor is at the left margin and the tab key is pressed once, the "**Pos**" indicator will show 1.5".

- Line spacing is set for single space.

- Defaults may be changed at any time and as many times as desired throughout a document. For example, if you wanted to tab .8" instead of .5", this could be done. Defaults may be changed to affect <u>all</u> documents or <u>individual</u> documents. (Changing defaults will be covered in a later lesson.)

Exercise Directions:

1. Start with a clear screen.

2. Keyboard the paragraphs on the right allowing the text to "word wrap" to the next line.

3. Begin the exercise at the top of your screen.

4. Press the return key twice to begin a new paragraph and <u>press the tab key once to indent the paragraph</u>.

5. Correct only immediate errors by using the backspace key.

6. Save the exercise; name it **TRYAGAIN**.

7. Clear your screen.

TAB→ WordPerfect is simple to use since you can begin typing as soon as you enter the program. 2x↓

TAB→ The way text will lay out or "format" on a page is set by the WordPerfect program. For example, margins are set for 1" on the left and 1" in on the right; line spacing is set for single space; tabs are set to advance the cursor 1/2 inch each time the tab key is pressed. Formats may be changed at any time and as many times throughout the document.

TO TAB

1. Press **Tab**................................**TAB**

SAVING AND EXITING A DOCUMENT; CURSOR MOVEMENTS

Notes:

- This exercise will give you more practice typing in wraparound, using the tab key, and saving the document. Be sure to keyboard it exactly as shown since it will be used in a later exercise for additional editing practice.

- After typing this and the next few exercises, you will practice moving the cursor through the document. This is essential when you are ready to correct errors.

- The arrow keys on the numeric keypad or (depending on your keyboard) the separate arrow keys located to the left of the keypad move the cursor in the direction indicated by the arrow. The cursor will only move through text, spaces or codes. The cursor stops moving when the end or beginning of your document is reached.

- To quickly move the cursor from one point in the document to another, you may use "express" cursor movements. Note the keystroking procedures carefully. <u>If keystrokes are separated by a comma, tap each one separately; if keystrokes are separated by a plus (+), hold down the first key while you press the next.</u> For example, if the keystroke procedure looks like: Home, Home, ↑ you are to tap the "Home" key twice and then tap the up arrow key once. If the keystroke procedure looks like: Ctrl + ← you are to hold down the "Ctrl" key while you tap the left arrow key.

- Additional express movement keys will be covered in later exercises.

Exercise Directions:

1. Start with a clear screen.

2. Keyboard the exercise on the right <u>exactly as shown.</u>

3. Begin the exercise at the top of your screen.

4. Press the return key twice between paragraphs and <u>press the tab key once to indent first line of the paragraphs indicated</u>.

5. Correct only immediate errors by using the backspace key.

6. After you complete the exercise, move the cursor through the document as follows:
   - one line up/down
   - one character right/left
   - previous word
   - next word
   - top of screen
   - end of screen
   - beginning of line
   - end of line

7. Save the exercise; name it **DIVE**.

8. Clear your screen.

```
DIVING VACATIONS
DIVING IN THE CAYMAN ISLANDS

     Do you want to see sharks, barracudas and huge stingrays?  Do
you want to see gentle angels, too?

     The Cayman Islands were discovered by Christopher Columbus in
late 1503.  The Cayman Islands are located just south of Cuba.  The
Caymans are the home to only about 125,000 year-around residents.
However, they welcome approximately 200,000 visitors each year.
Each year more and more visitors arrive.  Most visitors come with
colorful masks and flippers in their luggage ready to go scuba
diving.

     Because of the magnificence of the coral reef, scuba diving
has become to the Cayman Islands what safaris are to Kenya.  If you
go into a bookstore, you can buy diving gear.

     Now, you are ready to jump in!

Recommendations for Hotel/Diving Accommodations:

Sunset House, Post Office Box 4791, George Towne, Grand Cayman;
(800) 854-4767.

Coconut Harbour, Post Office Box 2086, George Towne, Grand Cayman;
(809) 949-7468.

     Seeing a shark is frightening at first; they seem to come out
of nowhere and then return to nowhere.  But as soon as the creature
disappears, you will swim after it.  You will just want to keep
this beautiful, graceful fish in view as long as you can.
```

CURSOR MOVEMENTS
WITHIN A DOCUMENT

TO MOVE:	PRESS:
One Char left	←
One Char right	→
One line up	↑
One line down	↓
Previous word	Ctrl + ←

TO MOVE:	PRESS:
Next word	Ctrl + →
Top of screen	Home + ↑
Bottom of screen	Home + ↓
Beginning of document	Home , Home , ↑
End of document	Home , Home , ↓

TO MOVE:	PRESS:
Top of page	Ctrl + Home , ↑
Bottom of page	Ctrl + Home , ↓
Beginning of line	Home , ←
End of line	End
Top of previous page	Pg Up
Top of next page	Pg Dn

CREATING A BUSINESS LETTER

Notes:

- There are a variety of letter styles for business and personal use.

- The parts of a business letter and the vertical spacing of letter parts are the same regardless of the style used. A business letter is comprised of eight parts: 1. **date** 2. **inside address** (to whom and where the letter is going) 3. **salutation** 4. **body** 5. **closing** 6. **signature line** 7. **title line** 8. **reference initials** (the first set of initials belongs to the person who wrote the letter; the second set of initials belongs to the person who typed the letter). Whenever you see "yo" as part of the reference initials in an exercise, substitute "your own" initials.

- The letter style illustrated in this exercise is a "modified block" business letter, since the date, closing, signature and title lines begin at the center point of the paper (4.5"). Most business letters are printed on letterhead paper.

- In the inside address, there are two spaces between the state abbreviation and the zip code.

- A letter generally begins 15 lines down from the top of a page or 2.5" in WordPerfect. (There are 6 vertical lines to one inch.) If the letter is long, it may begin 12 lines down or 2" from the top. If the letter is short, it may begin beyond 2.5".

- Margins and the size of the characters (pitch) may also be adjusted to accommodate longer or shorter correspondence. Changing margins and pitch size will be covered in a later lesson.

Exercise Directions:

1. Start with a clear screen.

2. Keyboard the letter on the right as directed.

3. Use the default margins and tabs.

4. With your cursor at the top of the screen, press the return key 9 times to begin the date on line (Ln) 2.5".

5. Press the tab key 7 times to begin the <u>date</u> and <u>closing</u> at position (Pos) 4.5" on the page.

6. Press the return key between parts of the letter as directed in the exercise.

7. Correct only immediate errors by using the backspace key.

8. After completing the exercise, move cursor to the top of your screen (HOME), ↑ and back to the bottom of the document.

9. Save the exercise; name it **LETTER**.

10. Clear your screen.

↓ 9 returns – 2.5"

TAB→ TAB→ TAB→ TAB→ TAB→ TAD→ TAB→ **4.5"**
October 1, 199-

↓ 4 returns

INSIDE ADDRESS { Ms. Renee S. Brown
54 Williams Street
Omaha, NE 68101

↓ 2 returns

SALUTA-TION { Dear Ms. Brown:

↓ 2 returns

Thank you for your $ 150 contribution to the American Art Institution. This contribution automatically makes you a member in our arts program.

↓ 2 returns

As an active member, you can participate in our many educational activities.

↓ 2 returns

BODY

For example, you can take part in our monthly art lectures, our semi-annual auctions and our frequent art exhibits. Admission to all these events is free.

↓ 2 returns

We look forward to seeing you at our next meeting. We know you will enjoy speaking with our other members and participating in very stimulating conversation.

↓ 2 returns

TAB→ TAB→ TAB→ TAB→ TAB→ TAB→ TAB→ Sincerely, } **CLOSING**

↓ 4 returns

TAB→ TAB→ TAB→ TAB→ TAB→ TAB→ TAB→ Alan Barry } — **SIGNATURE LINE**
President } — **TITLE LINE**

↓ 2 returns

REFERENCE INITIALS { ab/yo

TO EXPRESS MOVE CURSOR

Beginning of Document..... Home , Home , ↑
End of Document............... Home , Home , ↓

9

USING THE DATE FEATURE

Notes:

• This exercise requires you to prepare another modified-block letter. See if you remember how to format it. If you are not certain, refer to Exercise 4. This time, however, when you type the date, you will use WordPerfect's date feature.

• WordPerfect's date feature enables you to insert the current date into your document automatically. You also have the option of inserting a Date Code which will automatically update the date whenever you retrieve or print the document. The date is pulled from the computer's memory. Use the date feature in this exercise; use the Date Code in subsequent exercises.

• Be sure to **hold down** the Shift key while the F5 key is tapped. DO NOT press the keys simultaneously. This procedure must be followed for keystrokes where Alt, Shift or Control (Ctrl) are used in conjunction with other keys.

Exercise Directions:

1. Start with a clear screen.

2. Keyboard the letter on the right.

3. Use the date feature to insert the date.

4. Correct only immediate errors by using the backspace key.

5. After completing the exercise, move the cursor to the end of the last line in the first paragraph. Then, express move the cursor to the beginning of that line.

6. Save the exercise; name it **GOODJOB**.

7. Clear your screen.

Today's Date *} use Date feature*

Mr. Wallace Redfield
23 Main Street
Staten Island, NY 10312

Dear Mr. Redfield:

You are to be commended for an outstanding job as convention chair.
The computer convention held last week was the best I attended.

The choices you made for lecturers were excellent. Every seminar
I attended was interesting.

Congratulations on a great job.

                          Sincerely,

                          Adam Howard
                          President

ah/yo

TO INSERT CURRENT DATE

1. Press **Shift + F5**........ `Shift` + `F5`
2. Press **T** (Date Text) .... `T`

TO INSERT DATE CODE

NOTE: This will update the date each
time document is printed or revised.

1. Press **Shift + F5** .... `Shift` + `F5`
2. Press **C** (Date Code) .... `C`

TO EXPRESS MOVE CURSOR

- Left:
Press **Home**, ← .... `Home` , `←`
- Right:
Press **End** .... `End`

PRINTING A DOCUMENT

Notes:

- The letter style in this exercise is called "block." This style is very popular because all parts of the letter begin at the left margin and there is no need to tab the date and closing. The spacing between parts of a block-style letter is the same as the modified-block letter.

- WordPerfect allows you to print <u>part</u> or <u>all</u> of a document that is in the screen work area. You can print a page of the document, the full document, selected pages of a document, or one or more block(s) of text within the document. A document may also be printed from the disk, without retrieving it to the screen.

- Check to see that the printer is turned on and paper is loaded.

- When you are ready to print, be sure to hold down the Shift key while the F7 key is tapped. DO NOT press the keys simultaneously. This procedure must be followed for keystrokes where Alt, Shift or Control (Ctrl) are used in conjunction with other keys.

- You will notice that your printed document will have a right-justified or flush right margin. Justification causes large gaps between words to occur. WordPerfect is defaulted to right-justify text. Justification is one of the few formatting features that is **not** shown on the screen. Turning off the justification feature will be covered in a later lesson.

- Pressing the "Caps Lock" key once will enable you to type ALL CAPITAL LETTERS without pressing the shift key. Only letters are changed by "Caps Lock." When the "Caps Lock" key has been pressed, the "Pos" indicator will change to an all caps "POS." Pressing the Caps Lock key again will end the upper-case mode.

Exercise Directions:

1. Start with a clear screen.

2. Keyboard the letter on the right.

3. Use the default margins.

4. With your cursor at the top of the screen, begin the date on line (Ln) 2.5". <u>Use the date feature to insert today's date.</u>

5. Press the return key between parts of the letter as directed in the exercise.

6. Correct only immediate errors by using the backspace key.

7. Print one copy of the exercise.

8. Save the exercise; name it **BLOCK**.

9. Clear your screen.

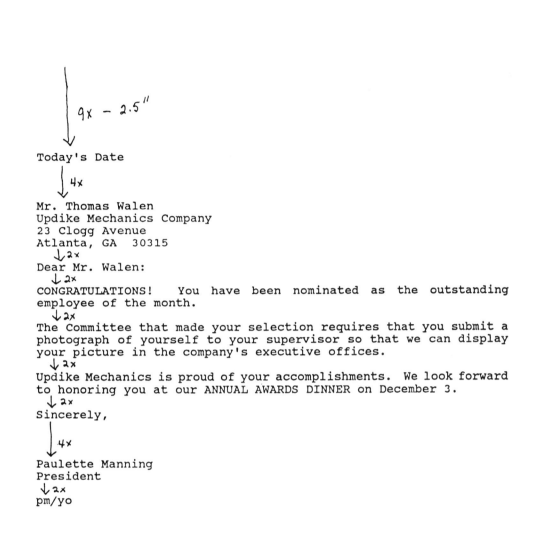

9x — 2.5"

Today's Date

4x

Mr. Thomas Walen
Updike Mechanics Company
23 Clogg Avenue
Atlanta, GA 30315
2x
Dear Mr. Walen:
2x
CONGRATULATIONS!   You have been nominated as the outstanding
employee of the month.
2x
The Committee that made your selection requires that you submit a
photograph of yourself to your supervisor so that we can display
your picture in the company's executive offices.
2x
Updike Mechanics is proud of your accomplishments. We look forward
to honoring you at our ANNUAL AWARDS DINNER on December 3.
2x
Sincerely,

4x

Paulette Manning
President
2x
pm/yo

TO CAPITALIZE

1. Press **Caps Lock** key......................**Caps Lock**

    NOTE: "Pos" changes to "POS" on status line.

2. Type text.

3. Press **Caps Lock** key......................**Caps Lock**
    to end upper case.

TO PRINT - Document on Screen

1. Press **Shift + F7**.........................**Shift** + **F7**
2. Press **P** (Page) *............................**P**

    * If you hear a beep and see a message
      your WordPerfect program has been set
      for "manual paper" feed. Do the following:

    Press **Shift + F7** ....**Shift** + **F7**

    Press **C** ....**C**

    Select **G** (Go) ....**G**

    Press **F7**...**F7**

PRINTING A SAVED DOCUMENT

Notes:

• The entire document or selected pages may be printed from the disk without bringing it to the screen. Printing selected pages will be covered in a later lesson.

• This exercise assumes you know the name of the document you wish to print.

Exercise Directions:

1. Print one copy of **LETTER** which you saved in Exercise 4.

2. Print one copy of **GOODJOB** which you saved in Exercise 5.

TO PRINT - A Saved Document

1. Press **Shift F7**............ `Shift` + `F7`
2. Press **D**.................................... `D`
3. Type document name.

   NOTE: It may be necessary to indicate drive and/or directory where file is located when typing document name. **Example: A:LETTER**

4. **ENTER**...................................... `↵`
5. **ENTER** .... `↵`
   to print entire document.*

---

* If WordPerfect is set to "manual feed" you will hear a beep. Do the following:

- Press **C** .... `C`
- Select **G** (Go) .... `G`
6. Press **F7** .... `F7`
   to exit printer menu.

TO CANCEL PRINT JOB

- Before printing begins

1. Press **Shift + F7**.......... `Shift` + `F7`
2. Select **C**.................................... `C`
3. Select **C**.................................... `C`
4. Type job number to cancel.
5. **ENTER**...................................... `↵`
6. Press **F7**.................................... `F7`

- Interrupt and resume printing

1. Press **Shift + F7**.......... `Shift` + `F7`
2. Select **C**.................................... `C`
3. Select **S**.................................... `S`
4. Make any changes to printer.
5. Select **G** (go - start printer)........ `G`

PRINTING FROM THE DIRECTORY

Notes:

- Exercise 5 assumed you knew the name of the document you wished to print. However, sometimes you might be unsure of the document name. Then, it becomes necessary to "List Files" or view the "directory" which will display the contents of the disk.

- List Files is an important feature for working with and organizing files.

- WordPerfect allows you to print from the directory menu, but you also have other options. These options will be covered in a later lesson.

- The List Files Screen includes other information. An illustration appears on the right. Note the following:

  - the header includes the current date, time of day, directory name, the size of the document on your screen (if a document is on your screen when you access the directory), the number of files created and the space available on the disk.

  - **all files appear in alphabetical order.**

  - next to each filename, the size of the file (indicated in bytes, which is equivalent to characters), and the date and time the file was last saved appears.

- You may print any file from the directory even though you might be working on another document at the time.

- You may print a copy of the List Files Screen if you desire a hard copy of your files. (Shift + Print Screen.)

Exercise Directions:

1. Assuming you forgot the name of the document you wish to print, access the directory.

2. Using the arrow keys, highlight the document **TRYAGAIN.**

3. Print one copy.

LIST FILES SCREEN

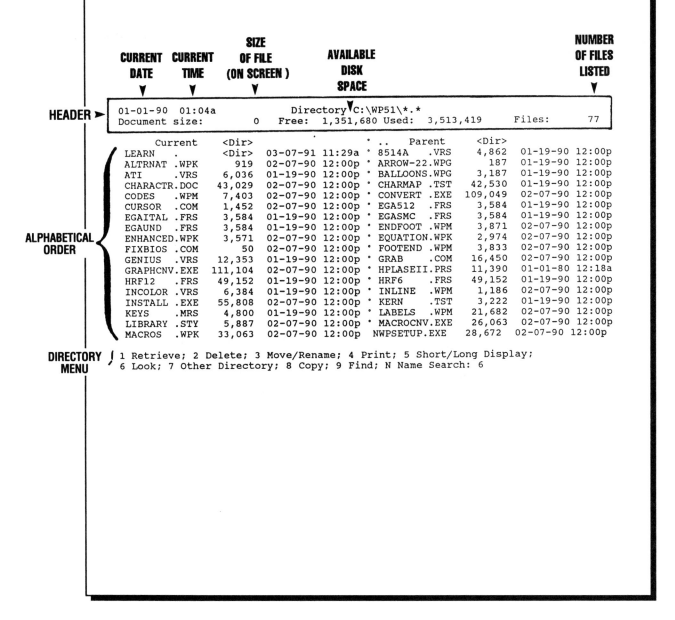

CURRENT DATE	CURRENT TIME	SIZE OF FILE (ON SCREEN)	AVAILABLE DISK SPACE	NUMBER OF FILES LISTED

HEADER ▶

```
01-01-90  01:04a              Directory▼C:\WP51\*.*
Document size:        0   Free:  1,351,680 Used:   3,513,419      Files:       77
```

ALPHABETICAL ORDER {

```
        Current    <Dir>        .              ..    Parent     <Dir>
      LEARN   .     <Dir>   03-07-91 11:29a * 8514A   .VRS    4,862   01-19-90 12:00p
      ALTRNAT .WPK     919   02-07-90 12:00p * ARROW-22.WPG      187   01-19-90 12:00p
      ATI     .VRS   6,036   01-19-90 12:00p * BALLOONS.WPG    3,187   01-19-90 12:00p
      CHARACTR.DOC  43,029   02-07-90 12:00p * CHARMAP .TST   42,530   01-19-90 12:00p
      CODES   .WPM   7,403   02-07-90 12:00p * CONVERT .EXE  109,049   02-07-90 12:00p
      CURSOR  .COM   1,452   02-07-90 12:00p * EGA512  .FRS    3,584   01-19-90 12:00p
      EGAITAL .FRS   3,584   01-19-90 12:00p * EGASMC  .FRS    3,584   01-19-90 12:00p
      EGAUND  .FRS   3,584   01-19-90 12:00p * ENDFOOT .WPM    3,871   02-07-90 12:00p
      ENHANCED.WPK   3,571   02-07-90 12:00p * EQUATION.WPK    2,974   02-07-90 12:00p
      FIXBIOS .COM      50   02-07-90 12:00p * FOOTEND .WPM    3,833   02-07-90 12:00p
      GENIUS  .VRS  12,353   01-19-90 12:00p * GRAB    .COM   16,450   02-07-90 12:00p
      GRAPHCNV.EXE 111,104   02-07-90 12:00p * HPLASEII.PRS   11,390   01-01-80 12:18a
      HRF12   .FRS  49,152   01-19-90 12:00p * HRF6    .FRS   49,152   01-19-90 12:00p
      INCOLOR .VRS   6,384   01-19-90 12:00p * INLINE  .WPM    1,186   02-07-90 12:00p
      INSTALL .EXE  55,808   02-07-90 12:00p * KERN    .TST    3,222   01-19-90 12:00p
      KEYS    .MRS   4,800   01-19-90 12:00p * LABELS  .WPM   21,682   02-07-90 12:00p
      LIBRARY .STY   5,887   02-07-90 12:00p * MACROCNV.EXE   26,063   02-07-90 12:00p
      MACROS  .WPK  33,063   02-07-90 12:00p  NWPSETUP.EXE   28,672   02-07-90 12:00p
```

DIRECTORY MENU {

```
1 Retrieve; 2 Delete; 3 Move/Rename; 4 Print; 5 Short/Long Display;
6 Look; 7 Other Directory; 8 Copy; 9 Find; N Name Search: 6
```

TO PRINT - From the directory

1. Press **F5** .... `F5`

   NOTE: It may be necessary to indicate drive/directory where files are located. **Example: A:**

2. **ENTER** .... `↵`

3. Press arrow keys to highlight document to be printed.

   `→` `↑` `↓` `←`

NOTE: Be sure your "Num Lock" key is off; otherwise, the arrow keys will lock and you will not be able to move the highlight.

4. Select **P** .... `P`

5. **ENTER*** .... `↵`
   to accept Page(s): (ALL)

   * If WordPerfect is set to "manual feed" you will hear a beep. Do the following:

Press **Shift + F7** ..... `Shift` + `F7`

Press **C** .... `C`

Select **G** (Go) .... `G`

6. Press **F7** .... `F7`
   to return to work screen.

Lesson 1
Summary Exercise A

Exercise Directions:

1. Keyboard the letter below in **modified-block** style. (A double slash (//) indicates a new paragraph; a single slash (/) indicates a return.)
2. Use the default margins.
3. Use the date feature.
4. Correct only immediate errors by using the backspace key.
5. Print one copy.
6. Save the exercise; name it **OPEN.**
7. Clear your screen.

Today's date/Mr. Martin Quincy/641 Lexington Avenue/New York, NY 10022/Dear Mr. Quincy://We are pleased to announce the opening of a new subsidiary of our company. We specialize in selling, training and service of portable personal computers.//This may be hard to believe, but we carry portable personal computers that can do everything a conventional desktop can. Our portables can run all of the same applications as your company's conventional PCs. With the purchase of a computer, we will train two employees in your firm on how to use an application of your choice.//For a free demonstration, call us at 212-456-9876 any business day from 9:00 a.m. to 5:00 p.m./Sincerely,/ Theresa Mann/President/tm:yo

Exercise Directions:

1. Keyboard the letter below in **block** style.
   (A double slash (//) indicates a new paragraph; a single slash (/) indicates a return.)
2. Use the default margins.
3. Use the date feature.
4. Correct only immediate errors by using the backspace key.
5. Print one copy.
6. Save the exercise; name it **REGRETS.**
7. Clear your screen.

```
Today's date/Ms. Kristin Paulo/765 Rand
Road/Palatine, IL 60074/Dear Ms. Paulo://
Thank you for your inquiry regarding employ-
ment with our firm.//We have reviewed your
qualifications with several members of our
firm.  We regret to report that we do not
have an appropriate vacancy at this time.//
We will retain your resume in our files in
the event that an opening occurs in your
field.//Your interest in our organization is
very much appreciated.  We hope to be able
to offer you a position at another time./
Very truly yours,/Carol B. Giles/PERSONNEL
MANAGER/cbg:yo
```

> **LESSON 2:**
> RETRIEVING A DOCUMENT: USING EXPRESS MOVEMENT KEYS, INSERT-
> ING; TYPING OVER TEXT; DELETING; UNDELETING; UPDATING.

RETRIEVING A DOCUMENT; INSERTING/TYPING OVER TEXT

Notes:

- Before a file can be revised or edited, it must be retrieved from the disk to the screen.

- A document is revised when corrections need to be made. **Proofreader's marks** are markings on a document that indicate errors to be corrected. These markings are often abbreviated in the form of symbols. As each proofreader's mark is introduced in an exercise, it is explained and illustrated. A summary list of all proofreader's symbols and their meanings appear in Appendix B.

- Documents containing proofreader's symbols are often referred to as a "rough-draft" copy. After all revisions are made, the completed document is referred to as a "final copy."

- When a file is retrieved and revisions are made, the revised or updated version must be resaved or "replaced." When a document is resaved, the old version is replaced with the new version.

- If the name of the document to be retrieved is known, the Shift + F10 procedure is used; if the document name is not known, the document may be retrieved through the directory. Retrieving from the directory will be covered in the next exercise.

- To make corrections, it is necessary to move through the document to the point of correction using the cursor movement keys including the end, home, page up and page down keys. You practiced moving the cursor through your document in previous exercises.

- Text is inserted immediately before the cursor. When typing inserted text, the existing text moves to the right. When inserting a word, the space following the word must also be inserted.

- Another way to edit text is to "type over" the existing text with new text. To put WordPerfect in "Typeover" mode, you must press the "Ins" key once. In this mode, existing text does not move to the right; it is typed over.

- Text is automatically adjusted after insertions have been made.

- To create a new paragraph, place the cursor <u>on the first character</u> of the new paragraph and press the ENTER key twice.

- The proofreader's mark for insertion is: ∧

- The proofreader's mark for a new paragraph is: ⁋

Exercise Directions:

1. Start with a clear screen.

2. Retrieve **TRY**.

3. Make the indicated insertions.

4. Use the "typeover" mode to insert the word "determine" in the second paragraph.

5. Print one copy (See Exercise 6).

6. Resave your file.

7. Clear your screen.

As you type, ^you will notice the "Pos" indicator on your format line change as the position of your cursor changes.

The ^wraparound feature allows the ^computer operator to ~~decide on~~ determine line endings, making the use of the return unnecessary except at the end of a paragraph or short line. ¶ Each file is saved on a ^key disk or hard drive for recall. Documents must be given a name for (data) identification.

↑ or number

TO RETRIEVE

- If Document Name is Known

1. Press **Shift + F10** ..... `Shift` + `F10`

   NOTE: It may be necessary to indicate drive and/or directory where file is located when typing document name. **Example: A:Letter**

2. Type name of document to be retrieved.

3. **ENTER** .... `↵`

TO INSERT TEXT

1. Place cursor where text is to be inserted.

2. Type text.

TO TYPEOVER

1. Place cursor where text is to be overwritten.

2. Press "**Ins**" key .... `Insert`

3. Type text.

4. Press "**Ins**"........................... `Insert`
   key to exit **TYPEOVER** mode.

TO RESAVE

1. Press **F7** .... `F7`

2. **ENTER** .... `↵`

3. **ENTER** .... `↵`

4. Type **Y** .... `Y`
   to update with revisions.

5. **ENTER** to clear screen .... `↵`

RETRIEVING A DOCUMENT FROM THE DIRECTORY; INSERTING TEXT

Notes:

• As indicated earlier, a document may be retrieved from the directory if you forget the name
of your document.

• To insert "Computer Associates" place cursor
at the end of the line, "Mr. Wallace Redfield";
press the return key once, then type the insertion.

• The proofreader's mark for changing uppercase
to lower case is: / or l.c.

Exercise Directions:

1. Start with a clear screen.

2. Access the directory.

3. Retrieve **GOODJOB**.

4. Make the indicated insertions.

5. Use the "typeover" mode to change the upper
    case letters to lower case where indicated.

6. Print one copy.

7. Resave your file.

Today's Date

(Computer Associates)

Mr. Wallace Redfield
23 Main Street
Staten Island, NY 10312

Dear Mr. Redfield: (Person)

You are to be commended for an outstanding job as convention chair.
(As a result of your efforts,) The computer convention held last week was the best I attended.
The choices you made for lecturers were excellent.   have Every seminar
I attended was interesting. (Guest)   (in a long while)

(Again,) Congratulations on a great job. (and informative)

                                        Sincerely,

                                        Adam Howard
                                        President

ah/yo

TO RETRIEVE

- From Directory

1. Press **F5** .... `F5`

   NOTE: It may be necessary to
   indicate drive/directory where files
   are located. **Example: A:**

2. **ENTER** .... `↵`

3. Press arrow keys to highlight
   document to be retrieved.

4. Press **R** (Retrieve) .... `R`

RETRIEVING A DOCUMENT; INSERTING TEXT

Notes:

- This exercise will enable you to insert text from the top of the page and create a modified-block letter. To insert the date, it is necessary to press the return key enough times to bring the "Ln" indicator to 2.5"; then press the tab enough times to bring the "Pos" indicator to 4.5". You are now ready to type the date. Remember to use WordPerfect's date feature.

- After typing the date, you will continue inserting the inside address and salutation. Text will adjust as you continue creating the letter.

Exercise Directions:

1. Start with a clear screen.

2. Retrieve **TRYAGAIN**.

3. Make the indicated insertions. Follow the spacing for a modified-block letter illustrated in Exercise 4. <u>Use the date feature to insert today's date.</u>

4. Use the "typeover" mode to insert the word "start" in the second paragraph.

5. Print one copy.

6. Resave your file.

Today's date

insert Ms. Donna Applegate
Consultants Unlimited, Inc.
45 East 45 Street
New York, NY 10022

Dear Ms. Applegate:

In response to your inquiry about software programs,
I have outlined below some of the merits of WordPerfect.

WordPerfect is simple to use since you can ~~begin~~ start typing as
soon as you enter the program. *(When you begin typing)*

The way text will lay out or "format" on a page is set by the
WordPerfect program. For example, margins are set for 1" on the
left and 1" in on the right; line spacing is set for single space;
tabs are set to advance the cursor 1/2 inch each time the tab key
is pressed. # Formats may be changed at any time and as many times
throughout the document.

(as desired)

(automatically)

(automatically)

Yours truly,

Jerry O'brien
Sales Manager

insert

jo/40

RETRIEVING A DOCUMENT; DELETING TEXT

Notes:

• Procedures for deleting text vary depending on what is being deleted: a character, previous character, word, line, paragraph, page, remainder of page, or blank line.

• The proofreader's mark for deletion is ⟋ .

• The proofreader's mark for closing up space is ⌣ .

• The proofreader's mark for moving text to the left is ← or ⌐ .

• The backspace key may be used to delete characters and close up spaces to the left of the cursor.

• To delete a character or a space, place the cursor on the character or space to be deleted, then press the "Del" key (located to the right of your keyboard.)

• Blocks of text (words, sentences and paragraphs) may be deleted by highlighting them. Highlighting procedures for defining block(s) of text are outlined in this exercise.

• To combine two paragraphs into one, it is necessary to delete hard returns that separate the paragraphs. Place the cursor at the end of the paragraph after the period and depress the "Del" key twice, or as many times as necessary to bring the paragraphs together. Sometimes it is necessary to adjust the spacing between sentences by inserting two spaces.

• To delete a tab, place the cursor at the left margin (to the left of the indent) and press the "Del" key once.

• Note each deletion in the exercise and use the proper keystroke procedure outlined to accomplish it. Deleting a sentence may be accomplished by "Remainder of Line" or "Block Highlight" deleting procedures.

Exercise Directions:

1. Start with a clear screen.

2. Retrieve **DIVE** from your directory.

3. Using the procedures indicated, make the directed deletions.

4. Print one copy.

5. Resave your file.

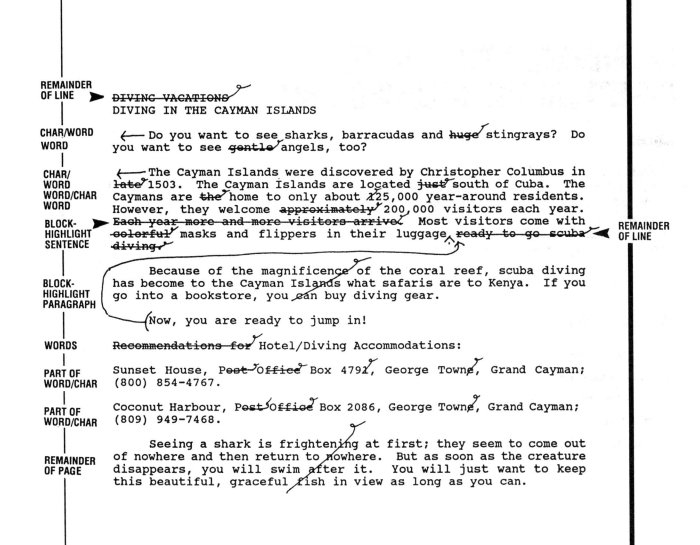

REMAINDER OF LINE ➤ ~~DIVING VACATIONS~~

DIVING IN THE CAYMAN ISLANDS

CHAR/WORD WORD ⟵ Do you want to see sharks, barracudas and ~~huge~~ stingrays? Do you want to see ~~gentle~~ angels, too?

CHAR/ WORD WORD/CHAR WORD ⟵ The Cayman Islands were discovered by Christopher Columbus in ~~late~~ 1503. The Cayman Islands are located ~~just~~ south of Cuba. The Caymans are ~~the~~ home to only about 25,000 year-around residents. However, they welcome ~~approximately~~ 200,000 visitors each year.

BLOCK- HIGHLIGHT SENTENCE ➤ ~~Each year more and more visitors arrive.~~ Most visitors come with ~~colorful~~ masks and flippers in their luggage, ~~ready to go scuba diving.~~ ◄ **REMAINDER OF LINE**

BLOCK- HIGHLIGHT PARAGRAPH Because of the magnificence of the coral reef, scuba diving has become to the Cayman Islands what safaris are to Kenya. If you go into a bookstore, you can buy diving gear.

Now, you are ready to jump in!

WORDS ~~Recommendations for~~ Hotel/Diving Accommodations:

PART OF WORD/CHAR Sunset House, ~~Post Office~~ Box 4792, George Towne, Grand Cayman; (800) 854-4767.

PART OF WORD/CHAR Coconut Harbour, ~~Post Office~~ Box 2086, George Towne, Grand Cayman; (809) 949-7468.

REMAINDER OF PAGE Seeing a shark is frightening at first; they seem to come out of nowhere and then return to nowhere. But as soon as the creature disappears, you will swim after it. You will just want to keep this beautiful, graceful fish in view as long as you can.

TO DELETE

- A Character

1. Place cursor on character or space to be deleted.
2. Press **Delete**............................ `Del`

- Previous Character

1. Press **Backspace** ...... `Backspace`

- A Word

1. Place cursor anywhere on word to be deleted.
2. Press **Ctrl + Backspace** .....

..... `Ctrl` + `Backspace`

- Remainder of Line

1. Place cursor on first character to be deleted.
2. Press **Ctrl+End**......... `Ctrl` + `End`

- Remainder of Page

1. Place cursor on first character to be deleted.
2. Press **Ctrl+PgDn**.... `Ctrl` + `Pg Dn`
3. Type **Y** to confirm deletion.......... `Y`

- Using Block Highlight

1. Place cursor on first character to be deleted.

2. Press **Alt+F4** (Block On)... `Alt` + `F4`

-or- F12 (enhanced keyboard).... `F12`

3. Highlight text to be defined:

                                 Press

one character to right................ `→`

one word right ....**spacebar**

one line down............................. `↓`

a sentence........**punctuation mark**

a paragraph................................. `↵`

4. Press **Delete** or **Backspace** ....

.... `Del` or `Backspace`

5. Type **Y** to delete block.............. `Y`

RETRIEVING A DOCUMENT; INSERTING AND DELETING TEXT

Notes:

• To bring the date and closing to the left margin (making this letter block style), place the cursor at the left margin on the same line as the date and press the "Del" key several times until the date moves to the margin. Do the same to bring the closing to the left margin.

Exercise Directions:

1. Start with a clear screen.
2. Retrieve **LETTER** from your directory.
3. Make the indicated deletions.
4. Print one copy.
5. Resave your file.

————————————————————————— October 1, 199-

Ms. Renee B. Brown
54 Williams Street
Omaha, NE 68101

Dear Ms. Brown:

Thank you for your $150 contribution to the American Art
Institution. This contribution ~~automatically~~ makes you a member
in our arts program.

As an active member, you can participate in our many ~~educational~~
activities.

For example, you can take part in ~~our~~ monthly art lectures, ~~our~~
semi-annual auctions and ~~our~~ frequent art exhibits. Admission to
~~all these~~ events is free.

We look forward to seeing you at our next meeting. ~~We know you
will enjoy speaking with our other members and participating in
very stimulating conversation.~~

————————————————————————(Sincerely,

————————————————————————(Alan Barry
                         President

ab/yo

RETRIEVING A DOCUMENT; DELETING TEXT; UNDELETING TEXT

Notes:

• Text may be restored after it has been deleted. WordPerfect remembers your last three deletions and allows you to restore them.

Exercise Directions:

1. Start with a clear screen.

2. Retrieve **TRYAGAIN.**

3. Make the indicated deletions.

4. After all deletions are made, restore or "undelete" the last deletion ("at any time and as many times").

5. Print one copy.

6. Resave your file.

January 10, 199-

Ms. Donna Applegate
Consultants Unlimited, Inc.
45 East 45 Street
New York, NY 10022

Dear Ms. Applegate:

In response to your inquiry about software programs, I have
outlined below some of the merits of WordPerfect.

WordPerfect is simple to use, since you can start typing as
soon as you enter the program.

The way text will ~~lay out or~~ format ~~on a page~~ when you begin
typing is automatically set by the WordPerfect program. For
example, margins are automatically set for 1" on the left and 1"
~~in~~ on the right; line spacing is set for single space; tabs are set
to advance the cursor 1/2 inch each time the tab key is
depressed.

Formats may be changed ~~at any time and as many times~~
as desired throughout the document.

                         Yours truly,

                         Jerry O'brien
                         Sales Manager

jo/yo

TO UNDELETE

1. Place cursor where deleted text will
   be inserted.

2. Press **F1**.................................**F1**

3. Select **R** ....**R**
   to restore last deletion
            or
   a. Select **P** ....**P**
      until desired deletion appears.

   b. Select **R** ....**R**
      to restore desired deletion.

RETRIEVING A DOCUMENT; INSERTING & DELETING TEXT

Notes:

- Bringing the date and closing to 4.5" (the center of the paper) will make this a modified-block letter. To do this, place the cursor on the first character of the line, and press the tab key as many times as necessary to bring the text to 4.5".

- To prevent two or more words from splitting during "word wrap" a **hard space** can be inserted between the words. This is particularly necessary when keyboarding first and last names, dates, equations and time.

- The proofreader's mark for moving text right is $\rightarrow$ or $\rceil$.

- The proofreader's mark for capitalization is ≡ .

Exercise Directions:

1. Start with a clear screen.
2. Retrieve **BLOCK**.
3. Make the indicated revisions.

4. After all revisions are made, restore the last deleted sentence.
5. Print one copy.
6. Resave your file.

October 14, 199- } ————————→ 4.5"

                    T.
Mr. Thomas Walen
Updike Mechanics Company
23 Clogg Avenue
Atlanta, GA 30315

Dear Mr. Walen: ↗ Mr. Walen

CONGRATULATIONS!   You have been nominated as ~~the~~ outstanding
employee of the month. # We made your selection based on the recommendations
   Selection   of your supervisors.
The Committee ~~that made your selection~~ requires ~~that~~ you submit a   to
photograph of yourself to your supervisor, ~~so that~~ we ~~can~~ display
your picture ~~in~~ the company's (executive offices.) ↗ Mr. Quinn.   will then
        throughout   immediate
Updike Mechanics is proud of your accomplishments. ~~We look forward~~
~~to honoring you at our ANNUAL AWARDS DINNER on December 3.~~

Sincerely,   )
                              }————————→ 4.5"
)
Paulette Manning   )
President   )

pm/yo

insert a
hard space

_____
Restore the last delete.

TO INSERT A HARD SPACE

1. Type first word.
2. Press **Home + Spacebar**.... **Home** + **Spacebar**
3. Type next word.

Exercise Directions:

1. Retrieve **REGRETS** from your directory.
2. Make the indicated revisions.
3. Print one copy.
4. Resave your file.

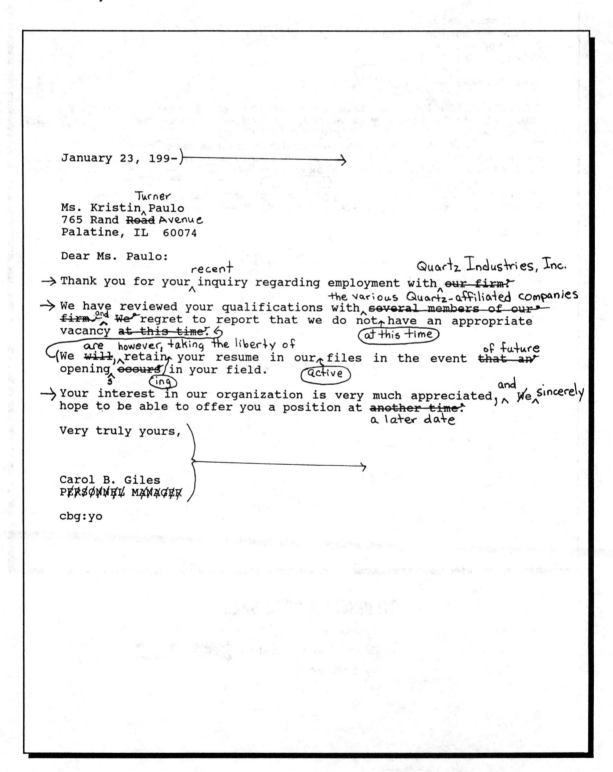

January 23, 199-

Ms. Kristin ⌃Turner Paulo
765 Rand ~~Road~~ Avenue
Palatine, IL 60074

Dear Ms. Paulo:

→ Thank you for your ⌃recent inquiry regarding employment with ~~our firm?~~ Quartz Industries, Inc.

→ We have reviewed your qualifications with ~~several members of our firm.~~ ⌃the various Quartz-affiliated companies and We regret to report that we do not⌃ have an appropriate vacancy ~~at this time.~~ (at this time)

(We ~~will~~, ⌃are however, taking the liberty of retain⌃ing your resume in our⌃ (active) files in the event ~~that an~~ of future opening ~~occurs~~ in your field.

→ Your interest in our organization is very much appreciated, ⌃and We⌃sincerely hope to be able to offer you a position at ~~another time?~~ a later date

Very truly yours,

Carol B. Giles
~~PERSONNEL MANAGER~~

cbg:yo

Lesson 2
Summary Exercise B

Exercise Directions:

1. Retrieve **OPEN**.
2. Make the indicated revisions.
3. <u>Change the letter style to block.</u>
4. Print one copy.
5. Resave your file.

January 22, 199-

(Arnco Industries, Inc.)
T.
Mr. Martin Quincy, President
641 Lexington Avenue - Suite 4001
New York, NY 10022

Dear Mr. Quincy:

We are very pleased to announce the opening of a new subsidiary of our company, We specialize in ~~selling~~, training and ~~service~~ of portable/personal computers. *service* *sales*
(COMPUSELLTRAIN.)
a full line of (All of)
~~This may be hard to believe, but~~ we carry portable personal computers that can do everything a conventional desktop can. Our (Computers) portables can run ~~all of~~ the same applications as your company's conventional PCs. With the purchase of a computer, we will train two employees in/your firm on ~~how to~~ use an application of your choice. (The graphics capabilities are outstanding.)

~~For a free demonstration, call us at 212-456-9876 any business day from 9:00 a.m. to 5:00 p.m.~~

The rep for your area is Ms. Sally Hansen. She will phone you to discuss your possible needs.

Very truly yours
~~Sincerely,~~

Theresa Mann
President

tm:yo

Restore the deleted paragraph.

35

> **LESSON 3:**
> HORIZONTAL AND VERTICAL CENTERING; CREATING A MEMORANDUM;
> USING SPELL CHECK; UNDERLINING; DOUBLE UNDERLINING; BOLDING;
> USING THE REPEAT KEY; VIEWING TEXT; DELETING CODES; USING
> ITALICS.

HORIZONTAL AND VERTICAL CENTERING

Notes:

- By using a special code, text can be horizontally centered between margins. Individual lines or blocks of text may be centered. This exercise will show you how to horizontally center individual lines of text.

- By using a special code, text may also be centered vertically on a page. If there are returns before or after the centered text, WordPerfect will include them in the vertical centering. Therefore, if you plan to vertically center text, be sure to start the text at the top of your screen.

- The proofreader's mark for centering is:] [

Exercise Directions:

1. Begin the exercise at the top of a clear screen.

2. Horizontaly center each line as indicated.

3. Vertically center the exercise.

4. Print one copy.

5. Save the exercise; name it **RSVP.**

```
                    Mr. and Mrs. George Lewis
                    requests the pleasure of your
                       company at a dinner
                           in honor of
                              ↓2x
                   The Honorable Abdul Shamsdeen
                              ↓2x
              on Friday, the twenty-first of April
                      at seven O'clock
                              ↓2x
                          Oak Room
                         Plaza Hotel
                        New York City

                              ↓3x

        R.S.V.P.
        25 Sutton Place South
```

TO HORIZONTALLY CENTER

- Before typing text

1. Place cursor at beginning of line.
2. Press **Shift + F6** .... `Shift` + `F6`
3. Type text.
4. **ENTER** .... `↵`
5. Repeat steps 1-4 for additional lines.

TO VERTICALLY CENTER

- A Page from top to bottom

NOTE: The text will not appear centered on the screen, but will print with vertically centered text .

1. Place cursor at beginning of page to be centered.
   Press **Home,** ↑ .... `Home` `↑`
2. Press **Shift + F8** .... `Shift` + `F8`

3. Select **P** .... `P`
4. Select **C** .... `C`

   WP5.1 Users:
   Press **Y** .... `Y`

5. Press **F7** .... `F7`

HORIZONTAL AND VERTICAL CENTERING; USING FLUSH RIGHT

Notes:

• The flush right feature allows you to align text flush against the right margin. This feature may be used when typing dates, creating invitations, or business headings.

• It is possible to make text flush right <u>before</u> or <u>after</u> typing.

Exercise Directions:

1. Begin the exercise at the top of a clear screen.

2. Horizontally center and make text flush right as indicated.

3. Vertically center the exercise.

4. Print one copy.

5. Save the exercise; name it **CONGRATS.**

```
                         MORITZ & CHASE
                              ↓2
                    Is Pleased to Announce that
                    the following Associates will
                    become members of the firm
                         January 1, 1992
                              ↓3

DENVER                                    Steven M. Jones
                                              ↓2
NEW YORK                                 Arthur J. Williams
                                              ↓2
SAN FRANCISCO                            Roberta W. Asher
                                           Donna Newman
                                         Michele T. McCabe
                                          Thomas C. Singh
                                        William B. Williams
                                              ↓2
WASHINGTON, D.C.                         Pamela T. Blanco
                                              ↓2
                     and that the following
                  Of Counsel will become members
                  of the firm on January 1, 1992
                                              ↓3

LONDON                                  Raymond T. Sedgewick
                                              ↓2
LOS ANGELES                              Angela Tsacoumis
                                          Roberto Vasquez
```

TO FLUSH RIGHT

- Before typing text

1. Press **Alt** + **F6** .... **Alt** + **F6**

2. Type text.

3. **ENTER** .... ↵

4. Repeat steps 1-3 for additional lines.

- Existing text

1. Place cursor at beginning of text to be made flush right.

2. Press **Alt** + **F4** .... **Alt** + **F4**

   -or- F12 (enhanced Keyboard)...... **F12**

3. Highlight text.

4. Press **Alt** + **F6** .... **Alt** + **F6**

5. Type **Y** .... **Y**

HORIZONTAL AND VERTICAL CENTERING; USING FLUSH RIGHT

Notes:

- It is possible to horizontally or vertically center text <u>before</u> or <u>after</u> typing.

- In this exercise, you will center individual lines of text and use the block feature to center and flush right text.

- To center or flush right a block of text, it is necessary to type the text at the left margin, highlight the block to be flush right or centered, and then insert the flush right or center code.

Exercise Directions:

1. Begin the exercise at the top of a clear screen.

2. Keyboard the first line, SOFTWARE COMPANIES, at the left margin as indicated.

3. Horizontally center each line in the first paragraph.

4. Keyboard the second and third paragraphs at the left margin as indicated.

5. Horizontally center the second paragraph as a block; flush right the third paragraph as a block.

6. Center the line, SOFTWARE COMPANIES (see keystrokes for centering "existing text").

7. Vertically center the entire exercise.

8. Print one copy.

9. Save the exercise; name it **COMPANY**.

```
SOFTWARE COMPANIES
                        ↓ 3 returns
             ⌐ ACCOUNTING & PERSONAL FINANCE ⌐
                    SOFTWARE COMPANIES
                          Astrix
                     Absolute Solutions
                    Check Mark Software
                    Computer Associates
                         Softview
                         Teleware
                 TimeSlips Corporation       ⌐
                   ↓ 3 returns
BUSINESS & PRESENTATION
SOFTWARE COMPANIES
ACIUS
AISB
Aldus
Ashton-Tate
CE Software
Fox Software
Microsoft
Power UP!
Satori
                   ↓ 3 returns
CALL 1-800-205-9831
ANY BUSINESS DAY
FOR INFORMATION
ABOUT
THE ABOVE COMPANIES
AND THEIR PRODUCTS
```

TO HORIZONTALLY CENTER

- Block of text

1. Place cursor at beginning of line to be centered.

2. Press **Alt + F4** .... **Alt** + **F4**

3. Highlight text.

4. Press **Shift + F6** .... **Shift** + **F6**

5. Type **Y** .... **Y**
   to center highlighted text.

- Existing text

NOTE: There must be a Hard Return at the end of the line that will be centered.

1. Place cursor at beginning of line to be centered.

2. Press **Shift + F6** .... **Shift** + **F6**

3. Press **down arrow** key.................. **↓**

CREATING A MEMORANDUM; CENTERING TEXT; USING SPELL CHECK

Notes:

- The "memo" is a written communication within a company. Many companies have preprinted memorandum forms. If a memorandum form is not available, it is necessary to create one.

- A memo should begin 1" from the top of the paper, which is the top of your screen. The word "MEMORANDUM" may be centered as illustrated or it may be omitted, if desired.

- Memorandums are usually prepared with all parts beginning at the left margin.

- Memorandums are generally <u>not</u> centered vertically.

- Double space between each part of the memorandum heading; the body of the memo begins a triple space below the subject line.

- If copies are to be sent to others, a copy notation may be indicated as the last item on a page.

- The WordPerfect Spelling feature will check the spelling of your document and look for double words. A word, page, or entire document may be checked for spelling errors. The speller compares the words in your document with the words in the WordPerfect dictionary.

- Special words may be added to the supplementary dictionary (to be covered in a later lesson).

- Spell check does not find errors in word usage; therefore, documents must still be proofread.

Exercise Directions:

1. Begin the exercise at the top of a clear screen.

2. Keyboard the memorandum on the right, centering text where indicated. (You may center each line or block center text).

3. After completing the exercise, spell check your document.

4. Print one copy.

5. Save the exercise; name it **MEMO**.

```
                    ]MEMORANDUM [
                          ↓3x
    TAB  TAB
TO: →   →   All Managers Attending Computer Expo
      TAB                    ↓2x
FROM: →   Robin McDonald
                     ↓2x
       TAB
DATE: →   December 10, 199-
                      ↓2x
         TAB
SUBJECT:→Hotels Offering Discounts to Computer Expo Attendees
                     ↓3x
The following San Francisco hotels have agreed to offer special
discounted rates to all attendees of Computer Expo:
                   ↓2x
               Fairmont Hotel
               Grand Hyatt
      Holiday Inn:  Civic Center
               Hyatt Regency
            King George Hotel
               Mark Hopkins
                  Nikko
              Villa Florence
           Westin St. Francis
                   ↓2x
When you call to make your reservation, mention that you're going
to the Computer Expo at the Convention Center.  There are only a
limited number of rooms available at preferred rates, so plan
early.
          ↓2x
rm
        TAB  ↓2x
c: →  Chad Wilkinson
   TAB  Julie Chen
```

TO SPELL CHECK A PAGE OR A DOCUMENT

1. With document on the screen,
   Press **Ctrl + F2**................................ `Ctrl` + `F2`
2. Select **P** (Page) or **D** (Document).......... `P` or `D`
3. When word is highlighted:
   Select letter of correctly-spelled word.
   *(If correctly-spelled word is not given,
   see "Select **4**" in next column.) **-or-**
   Select **1** (Skip once).. `1`
      to advance speller to next misspelling. **-or-**
   Select **2** (Skip).. `2`
      to ignore misspelling for rest of document. **-or-**

Select **4** (Edit)... `4`
   - retype word correctly.
   - Press **F7**... `F7`
      to exit speller.

TO SPELL CHECK A WORD:

1. Place cursor under word to be checked.
2. Press **Ctrl + F2**........................ `Ctrl` + `F2`
3. Select **W** (Word)....................................... `W`
4. Follow step 3 in left column.

PRESS F1 (CANCEL) AT ANY TIME TO STOP SPELL CHECK.

BOLDING AND UNDERLINING TEXT
Notes:

- Bolding, underlining, and double underlining are features which are used to enhance or emphasize text.

- It is possible to underline, double underline, and/or bold text <u>before</u> or <u>after</u> typing. In addition, you can decide whether or not to underline spaces and/or tabs. Double underline will be covered in a later exercise.

- In this exercise, you will underline and bold existing text as well as new text.

- The proofreader's mark for bold is: ~~~~

- The proofreader's mark for underline is: _____

Exercise Directions:

1. Start with a clear screen.
2. Retrieve **DIVE.**
3. Make the indicated revisions, bolding and underlining text where shown.
4. Print one copy.
5. Resave your file.

<u>DIVING IN THE CAYMAN ISLANDS</u>

Do you want to see sharks, barracudas and stingrays? Do you want
to see angels, too?

The Cayman Islands were discovered by Christopher Columbus in 1503 , and
~~The Cayman Islands~~ are located south of Cuba. The Caymans are home
to ~~only~~ about 25,000 year-around residents. However, they welcome
200,000 visitors each year. Most visitors come with masks and
flippers in their luggage. ~~Now, you are ready to jump in!~~

<u>Hotel/Diving</u> Accommodations:

<u>Sunset House</u>, <u>PO Box 479, George Town, Grand Cayman; (800) 854-</u>
<u>4767.</u>

<u>Coconut Harbour</u>, <u>PO Box 2086, George Town, Grand Cayman; (809) 949-</u>
<u>7468.</u>

<u>Red Sail Sports</u>, <u>PO Box 1588, George Town, Grand Cayman; (809) 979-7965.</u>

<u>Cayman Diving Lodge</u>, <u>PO Box 11, East End, Grand Cayman; (809)947-7555</u>

<u>Anchorage View</u>, <u>PO Box 2123, Grand Cayman; (809) 947-4209</u>

TO UNDERLINE/BOLD

- Before typing text

1. Press **F8** .... `F8`
   to begin underline.   **-or-**

-or- F6 .... `F6`
   to begin bold.

2. Type text.

3. Press **F8**.................................. `F8`
   to end underline.   **-or-**

-or- F6 .... `F6`
   to end bold.

- After typing text

1. Place cursor on first character to
   be underlined or bolded.

2. Press **Alt + F4** .... `Alt` + `F4`
   -or- F12 (enhanced keyboard)..... `F12`

3. Highlight text to be underlined or
   bolded.

4. Press **F8** .... `F8`
   to underline.   **-or-**

   -or- F6 .... `F6`
   to bold.

BOLDING, UNDERLINING, DOUBLE UNDERLINING, VIEWING TEXT

Notes:

- In this exercise, you will center and double underline "MEMORANDUM." If a word is to be centered <u>and</u> underlined/bolded, depress Shift + F6 to center; then follow steps to underline and/ or bold.

- Double underline may not display on the screen but will be included in the printed copy if your printer supports the feature.

- The **view document** feature allows you to see your formatted document before it is printed. Therefore, while you may not see the double underline on your screen, it will appear when you "view" your document. If the double underline is difficult to see, you can enlarge a portion of the page so that it is visible.

- The proofreader's mark for double underline is: ⹀

Exercise Directions:

1. Begin the exercise at the top of a clear screen.

2. Keyboard the memorandum to the right, bolding, underlining and double underlining where indicated.

3. After completing the exercise, spell check your document; proofread and correct any additional errors.

4. View your document.

5. Print one copy.

6. Save the exercise; name it **MEMONEWS**.

```
                        ] MEMORANDUM [

    TO:         The Staff

    FROM:       Sarah Walesk

    DATE:       December 9, 199-

    RE:         Computer Expo


    I strongly urge you to attend this year's Computer Expo.  In four
    days, you'll pick up all the latest computer news and discover new
    ways to put your computer to work -- in the office, in the lab, in
    the studio, in the classroom or in your home.

    Here are some of the events you can look forward to:

    Keynote Sessions.  These sessions will feature luminaries from the
    computer world who will offer you insights from industry.
    Application Workshops.  Join a series of two-hour learning sessions
    which will provide guidelines, tips and "how-to's" on popular
    software packages.
    Programmer/Developer Forums.  Veteran and novice computer users
    will brainstorm so you can learn about innovative advances and
    techniques.

    If you are interested in attending, see Derek Brennan.  He will
    pre-register anyone from our company who wishes to attend.  This
    will save you long lines at the show.

    sw
```

TO DOUBLE UNDERLINE

- Before typing text

1. Press **Ctrl + F8**.................... `Ctrl` + `F8`
2. Select **A**.. `A`
3. Select **D**.. `D`
4. Type text to be double underlined.
5. Press **right arrow** key............................. `→`

- After typing text

1. Place cursor on first character to be double underlined.
2. Press **Alt+F4**........................... `Alt` + `F4`
   -or- F12 (enhanced keyboard)........... `F12`

3. Highlight text to be double underlined.
4. Follow steps 1-3 in left column.

TO VIEW DOCUMENT

1. Press **Shift + F7**............. `Shift` + `F7`
2. Select **V**.. `V`
   Select   **1** (to enlarge 100%)........ `1`
   -or-   **2** (to enlarge 200%)........ `2`
   -or-   **3** (to view full page)........ `3`
3. Press **F7** to return to document... `F7`

USING ITALICS

Notes:

- Italics is right slanted text. It is used to enhance or emphasize the text. Italics may not display as slanted letters on the screen but will be included in the printed copy if your printer supports the feature. If your printer does not support italics, the printed copy will appear underlined. However, while you may not see italics on the screen, it will appear when you "view" your document.

- To insert and center the line, Sir Francis Drake, place the cursor at the end of the previous line, press the return key, and then enter the command to center (Shift + F6).

- Review cursor movements within a document (page 7) to assist with the editing of this document.

Exercise Directions:

1. Start with a clear screen.
2. Retrieve **MEMO.**
3. Make the indicated revisions.
4. View your document
5. Print one copy.
6. Resave your file.

MEMORANDUM

TO: ~~All~~ Managers Attending Computer Expo

FROM: Robin McDonald

DATE: December 10, 199-

SUBJECT: Hotels Offering Discounts to Computer Expo Attendees

The following San Francisco hotels have agreed to offer ~~special~~ discounted rates to all attendees of Computer Expo:

Fairmont Hotel
Grand Hyatt
Holiday Inn: Civic Center
Hyatt Regency
King George Hotel
~~Mark Hopkins~~
Nikko
Sir Francis Drake Villa Florence
Westin St. Francis

attending

When you ~~call to~~ make your reservation, mention that you're ~~going to~~ the Computer Expo at the Convention Center. ~~There are only~~ a limited number of rooms *are* available at preferred rates, so plan early. *All hotels listed in bold above are within 20 minutes of the Convention Center.*

rm

set to italics

c: Chad Wilkinson
     Julie Chen

TO SET ITALICS

- Before typing text

1. Press **Ctrl + F8** .... `Ctrl` + `F8`
2. Select **A** .... `A`
3. Select **I** .... `I`

4. Type text to be set to italics.
5. Press **right arrow** key .... `→`

- After typing text

1. Place cursor on first character to be set to italics.
2. Press **Alt + F4** .... `Alt` + `F4`
   or   or
   F12 (enhanced keyboard).......... `F12`
3. Highlight text to be set to italics.
4. Follow steps 1-3 in left column.

DELETING CODES

Notes:

- As a document is created in WordPerfect, codes are inserted that determine the document's appearance. These codes are not displayed on the screen, but can be revealed when necessary.

- When the "reveal codes" feature is selected, a "tab rule" is displayed by reversing the normal display of the screen. The codes that were inserted when you typed the document appear within the text below the tab rule. An example of this screen and its symbols appears below.

- It is necessary to reveal your codes to make certain edits. The document, DIVE, appears below with the codes displayed.

- To delete a code: move your cursor so that it sits on that code which appears before the word or sentence; then, press delete.

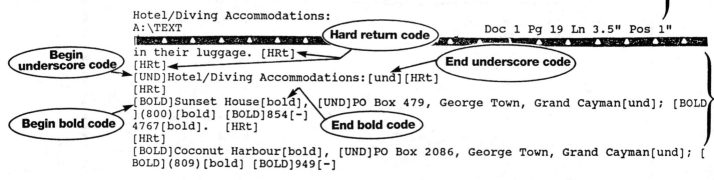

```
Do you want to see sharks, barracudas and stingrays?  Do you want
to see angels, too?

The Cayman Islands were discovered by Christopher Columbus in 1503
and are located south of Cuba.  The Caymans are home to about
25,000 year-around residents.  However, they welcome 200,000
visitors each year.   Most visitors come with masks and flippers
in their luggage.

Hotel/Diving Accommodations:
A:\TEXT                                      Doc 1 Pg 19 Ln 3.5" Pos 1"
```

Text without codes

Hard return code

Begin underscore code

End underscore code

Begin bold code

End bold code

```
in their luggage. [HRt]
[HRt]
[UND]Hotel/Diving Accommodations:[und][HRt]
[HRt]
[BOLD]Sunset House[bold], [UND]PO Box 479, George Town, Grand Cayman[und]; [BOLD
](800)[bold] [BOLD]854[-]
4767[bold].   [HRt]
[HRt]
[BOLD]Coconut Harbour[bold], [UND]PO Box 2086, George Town, Grand Cayman[und]; [
BOLD](809)[bold] [BOLD]949[-]

Press Reveal Codes to restore screen
```

Exercise Directions:

1. Start with a clear screen.
2. Retrieve **DIVE.**
3. Reveal your codes.
4. Delete the bold and underscore codes, and make the other indicated revisions.

5. View your document.
6. Print one copy.
7. Resave your file.

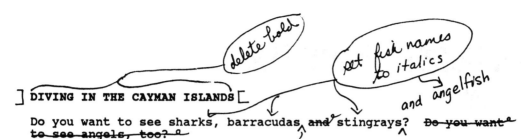

DIVING IN THE CAYMAN ISLANDS

Do you want to see sharks, barracudas, ~~and~~ stingrays? ~~Do you want to see angels, too?~~

The Cayman Islands were discovered by Christopher Columbus in 1503 and are located south of Cuba. The Caymans are home to about 25,000 year-around residents. However, they welcome 200,000 visitors each year. Most visitors come with masks and flippers in their luggage.

<u>Hotel/Diving Accommodations:</u>

Sunset House, <u>PO Box 479, George Town, Grand Cayman</u>; **(800) 854-4767.**

Coconut Harbour, <u>PO Box 2086, George Town, Grand Cayman</u>; **(809) 949-7468.**

Red Sail Sports, <u>PO Box 1588, George Town, Grand Cayman</u>; **(809) 979-7965.**

Cayman Diving Lodge, <u>PO Box 11, East End, Grand Cayman</u>; **(809) 947-7555.**

Anchorage View, <u>PO Box 2123, Grand Cayman</u>; **(809) 947-4209.**

TO REVEAL CODES (AND DELETE)

1. Press **Alt + F3**............... `Alt` + `F3`
   -or-
   -or- F11 (enhanced keyboard)... `F11`
   to reveal codes.

2. Place cursor on code to be deleted.

3. Press **Delete**................................ `Del`

4. Press **Alt + F3**.................. `Alt` + `F3`
   -or-
   -or- F11 (enhanced keyboard)..... `F11`
   to exit reveal codes.

DELETING CODES; USING THE REPEAT KEY

Notes:

- This exercise requires you to delete codes and to insert a horizontal double line after the subject line.

- The horizontal double line may be created by using the REPEAT VALUE function and the equal key. The Repeat Value will repeat a character or a WordPerfect feature a specified number of times. The repetition number is defaulted for 8 but can be changed at any time.

Exercise Directions:

1. Start with a clear screen.

2. Retrieve **MEMONEWS** from your directory.

3. Create the horizontal double line using the repeat value and the equal key. Set the repeat value for 65.

4. Make the indicated revisions.

5. Print one copy.

6. Resave your file.

<u>MEMORANDUM</u> *delete double underline*

TO: <u>The Staff</u>

Delete bold **FROM:**   Sarah Walesk

DATE: December 9, 199-   *underline*

RE: Computer Expo   *Draw a horizontal line using the equal key*
           ↓2x
↓2x
(wi) I strongly urge you to attend this year's <u>Computer Expo</u>. In four days, you'll pick up ~~all~~ the latest computer news and discover new ways to put your computer to work -- in the office, in the lab, in the studio, in the classroom, or in your home.

Here are some of the events you can look forward to:

Keynote Sessions. These sessions will feature luminaries from the computer world who will offer you insights from industry.
Application Workshops. Join a series of two-hour learning sessions which will provide guidelines, tips and "how-to's" on popular software packages.
Programmer/Developer Forums. Veteran and novice computer users will brainstorm so you can learn about innovative advances and techniques.

<u>If you are interested in attending, see</u> <u>Derek Brennan.</u> He will pre-register anyone from our company who wishes to attend. ~~This~~
delete underline ~~will save you long lines at the show.~~

sw

Restore the last sentence deleted

TO SET REPEAT VALUE

1. Place cursor where repeat value is to begin.

2. Press **Esc**.................................. **Esc**

3. Type a repetition number.

4. Type character to be repeated.

53

Lesson 3
Summary Exercise A

Exercise Directions:

1. Create the announcement below, using the center, underline, bold, italics, flush right and repeat key features.
2. Vertically center the exercise.
3. Spell check the document.
4. Print one copy.
5. Save the exercise; name it **INVEST**.

March 27, 199-

40,000,000 Shares

DACEENE

Quality Municipal Fund, Inc.

Common Stock

++

Price $12 Per Share

++

Copies of the Prospectus may be obtained from such
of the Underwriters as may legally offer these
securities in compliance with the securities laws of the
respective states.

ALEX, CROWN & SONS   LIDDER, PEABODY & CO.

ADVESTIN, INC.   THE ROBINSON-JEFFREY COMPANY

THE CHICAGO CORPORATION   FERRIS, QUAKER WATS & CO.

SOUTHEAST SECURITIES, INC.   RIDER INVESTMENTS, INC.

HUNTINGTON SECURITIES CORPORATION

Lesson 3
Summary Exercise B

Exercise Directions:

1. Create the memorandum below, centering, underlining, bolding and using italics where necessary.
2. Center, bold and double underline the word MEMORANDUM at the top of the document.

3. Spell check the document.
4. Print one copy.
5. Save the exercise; name it **BUSNEWS**.

TO: Caroline Herrara//FROM: Adam Varnet//SUBJECT: <u>Business News and Updates</u> Article//DATE: Today's//At our meeting on Friday, you indicated that you wanted me to provide you with suggestions of companies that you could write a feature story about in next month's issue of <u>Business News and Updates</u>.

I have done some research and found that the following companies are either announcing a new product, acquiring assets of another company, announcing a merger with another company, or announcing a new patent. You might want to do some preliminary interviews with their executives (I have listed the person to contact in italics) to learn more details and make a final determination as to which one would provide the best information for a feature article.

<u>**Abbott Laboratories**</u>
Located in Abbott Park, IL, this company makes hospital products and signed a long-term supply agreement with a foreign company. Contact: *George Richards*
<u>**Bank One Corp**</u>
Located in Columbus, OH, this company will acquire a commercial banking company in Springfield, IL. Contact: *Thomas Quinn*
<u>**Comshare, Inc.**</u>
Located in Ann Arbor, MI, this company purchased the assets and business of a Texas corporation. Contact: *Pamela Sutton*
<u>**Mesa Limited**</u>
Located in Amarillo, TX, this natural gas company agreed to sell part of its oil and gas interests to a Houston corporation. Contact: *Juan Perez*

You have done an outstanding job as feature editor, and I always look forward to receiving my copy. If you need any additional information, let me know.

yo

> **LESSON 4:**
> CREATING A ONE-PAGE REPORT; CHANGING LINE SPACING; INDENT-
> ING TEXT; CHANGING MARGINS; MOVING / COPYING TEXT; PREPAR-
> ING A RESUME.

CREATING A ONE-PAGE REPORT; CHANGING LINE SPACING; INDENTING TEXT

Notes:

- A report or manuscript generally begins 2" from the top of the paper and is prepared in double space. Tab each new paragraph once, to make a 5-space indention.

- Margins will vary depending on how the report will be bound. For an unbound report, margins of 1" on the left and right may be used.

- A line spacing change affects text from the cursor forward in the document. Remember, if your line spacing is set for double space, **two returns will result in four blank lines.**

- WordPerfect's <u>left</u> block indent feature sets a temporary left margin for paragraphs. WordPerfect's <u>left and right</u> block indent feature allows you to simultaneously indent paragraph text on the left and right. This feature is some-times called <u>double indent.</u>

- Paragraphs may be block indented <u>before</u> or <u>after</u> text is typed.

- Text is indented to a tab setting. Therefore, by depressing the indent feature once, text is indented five spaces to the right; by depressing it twice, text is indented ten spaces, etc. The same is true for the double indent feature: by depressing it once, text is indented five spaces on the left and right; by de-pressing it twice, text is indented ten spaces on the left and right, etc.

- The indent mode is ended by a hard return.

- The proofreader's symbol for indenting right is: ⌐

    left is: ⌐

Exercise Directions:

1. Start with a clear screen.

2. Keyboard the report on the right. Start the heading on Ln 2". Use the repeat value of 8 and the asterisk(*) before and after the heading.

3. Double space the first and last paragraphs; block indent and single space the middle paragraphs.

4. Use the default margins.

5. Spell check the exercise.

6. Print one copy.

7. Save the exercise; name it **BULLETIN**.

★★★ ★ ★ ★ ★ ELECTRONIC BULLETIN BOARDS *★ ★ ★ ★ ★ ★ ★ ★*

↓ 3 returns

Change line spacing *TAB →* Thousands of people across the nation are using computer

bulletin boards. Through their computer, they spend hours on

line "talking" with other users, "discussing" topics ranging from

zoology, finding information about taxes or taxis, completing

graduate courses to even exchanging wedding vows. Some

productive uses of bulletin boards are: *Return 1X*

change line spacing
Double Indent 2X
10

A system set up by a hospital in West
Virginia offers detailed answers to medical
questions for people who don't want to travel
great distances necessary to see a doctor.

A system created by a retired guidance
counselor in Atlanta provides current
information on scholarships and loans.

A system operated by a car expert in Las
Vegas lists thousands of collectors' cars. *Return 2x*

10

Change line spacing *TAB →* Besides the fee of subscribing to a bulletin board, the cost

of "talking" on your computer is the same as talking on your

phone, since phone lines are used for data transmission.

TAB → All you need to connect a bulletin board is a computer and a

modem connected to a telephone line. While most bulletin boards

are free, some of the largest are professional operations that

charge a fee.

TO CHANGE LINE SPACING

NOTE: Single spacing is the default.

1. Place cursor where line spacing change will occur.
2. Press **Shift + F8**..... `Shift` + `F8`
3. Select **L** (Line)........................... `L`
4. Select **S** (Line Spacing)............ `S`
5. Type desired spacing

Examples:
- **1.5** = one and one-half space
- **2** = double space
- **3** = triple space

6. **ENTER**.. `↵`
7. Press **F7**.................................... `F7`
   return to document.

TO BLOCK INDENT
- **Left Indent**
1. Press **F4**.................................... `F4`
   until cursor is at desired indention.

2. Type paragraph.
3. **ENTER**....................................... `↵`
   to end indent mode.

TO DOUBLE BLOCK INDENT
- **Left/Right Indent**
1. Press **Shift + F4**...... `Shift` + `F4`
   until cursor is at desired indention.
2. Type paragraph.
3. **ENTER**....................................... `↵`
   to end indent mode.

57

CREATING A ONE-PAGE REPORT; CHANGING LINE SPACING <u>and</u> (Left/ Right) MARGINS; INDENTING TEXT.

Notes:

* A margin change affects text from the cursor forward in the document. Therefore, the cursor should be placed at the beginning of the document, or the "home" position, before changing margins if you want to affect the entire document. This can be done quickly by pressing the home key twice, then pressing the up arrow key once.

* The left margin is measured from the left edge of the paper, and the right margin is measured from the right edge of the paper.

* Since text is centered between existing margins, you should change your margins before centering the title of the report.

* To indent numbered items (enumerations), tab once, type the number, then block indent the paragraph text.

Exercise Directions:

1. Start with a clear screen.

2. Set the left margin for 2" and the right margin for 1".

3. Keyboard the report on the right. Start the heading on Ln 2". Double space the first three paragraphs. Single space and block indent numbered paragraphs on the left.

4. Center, bold and underline as directed.

5. Spell check the exercise.

6. Print one copy.

7. Save the exercise; name it **OCR**.

] OPTICAL CHARACTER RECOGNITION AT WORK [

↓ 4x

Set double space →

Optical Character Recognition, or OCR, converts paper documents to digital format. Therefore, it is possible to have an OCR device "read" text and have it ~italics~ appear on the computer's screen, without rekeying copy.

Some OCR units have the ability to recognize a wide variety of fonts, reproduce tabs, text centering, and other formatting. Most OCR units process pages three or four times faster than the average typist's 70 words per minute.

Here are some interesting ways in which companies use Optical Character Recognition to ease their work loads:

TAB → 1. ⌐ INDENT ⌐ A Boston service bureau recently scanned and republished a client's large medical catalog, a project that would have been too time └ consuming to undertake.

TAB → 2. ⌐ INDENT ⌐ A New York-based newspaper plans to create data files of their back issues, many of which were └ published in 1845.

TAB → 3. ⌐ INDENT ⌐ A Maryland company needed to transfer files from an aging word processing system to a newer one. It discovered that printing the files from the old system and then scanning them into └ the new system was less expensive.

TO MOVE CURSOR "HOME"

1. Press **Home, Home,** ↑ ....
   .... `Home` , `Home` , `↑`

TO SET LEFT AND RIGHT MARGINS

1. Place cursor where margin change will occur.
2. Press **Shift + F8** ..... `Shift` + `F8`
3. Select **L (Line)** .... `L`
4. Select **M (Margin)** .... `M`

5. Type desired left margin.
6. **ENTER** .... `↵`
7. Type desired right margin.
8. **ENTER** .... `↵`
9. Press **F7** .... `F7`
   to return to document.

TO SET TOP/BOTTOM MARGINS

1. Place cursor where margin change will occur.

2. Select **P** .... `P`
3. Select **M** .... `M`
4. Type top margin.
5. **ENTER** .... `↵`
6. Type bottom margin.
7. **ENTER** .... `↵`
8. Press **F7** .... `F7`

MOVING TEXT; CHANGING MARGINS

Notes:

- The move feature allows you to move a block of text, a sentence, a paragraph, a page, or a column to another location in the same document or to another document. (Moving text to another document will be covered in a later lesson.)

- First, you must specify the text to be moved; then, you must give the "move" command. The text will temporarily disappear from the screen. The message in the status area will display: "Move cursor; press Enter to retrieve." You must then move your cursor to where you want the text to be reinserted and press Enter.

- To insure that the spaces following a sentence or a paragraph are also moved, use the procedure for "Moving a Sentence/Paragraph/ Page." If text was not reinserted at the correct point, it may be necessary to insert spaces, returns, or tabs after completing the move.

- This exercise requires that you move the middle paragraphs as indicated, indent the middle paragraphs, and insert and indent a new paragraph.

- If you indent the text and then move the indented paragraph, be sure the indent code to the left of the text is moved along with the paragraph. To insure that you do, reveal your codes and check to see that your cursor is sitting on the indent code before you move the paragraph.

- The proofreader's mark for moving text is

Exercise Directions:

1. Start with a clear screen.

2. Retrieve **MEMONEWS** from your directory.

3. Set the left and right margins for 1.5" below the horizontal line.

4. Make the indicated revisions.

5. Move paragraphs as directed.

6. Print one copy.

7. Resave your file.

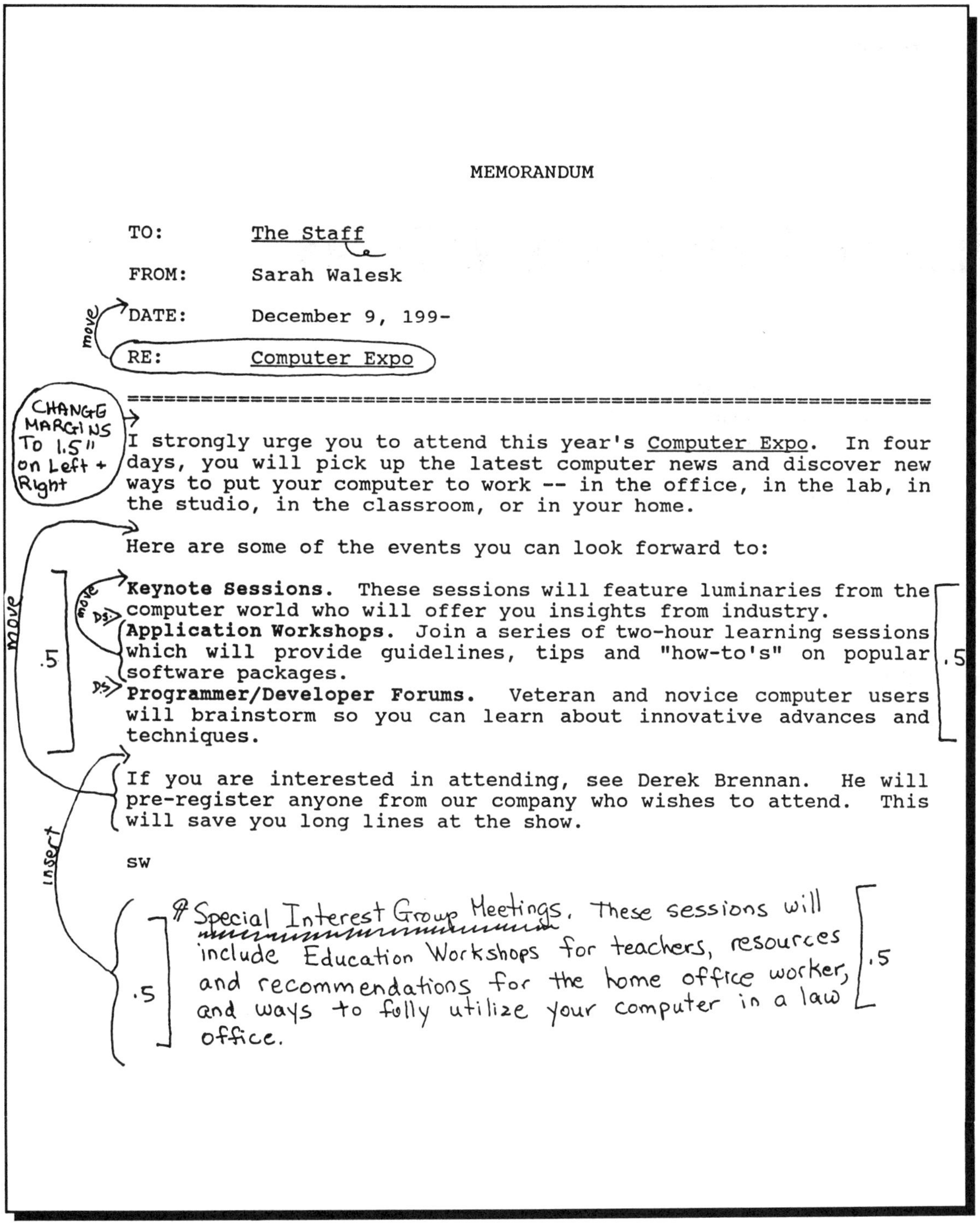

MEMORANDUM

TO: The Staff

FROM: Sarah Walesk

~~move~~ DATE: December 9, 199-

RE: Computer Expo

(handwritten note: CHANGE MARGINS TO 1.5" on Left + Right)

==

I strongly urge you to attend this year's Computer Expo. In four days, you will pick up the latest computer news and discover new ways to put your computer to work -- in the office, in the lab, in the studio, in the classroom, or in your home.

Here are some of the events you can look forward to:

(handwritten: move / .5 / DS / DS)

Keynote Sessions. These sessions will feature luminaries from the computer world who will offer you insights from industry.
Application Workshops. Join a series of two-hour learning sessions which will provide guidelines, tips and "how-to's" on popular software packages.
Programmer/Developer Forums. Veteran and novice computer users will brainstorm so you can learn about innovative advances and techniques.

(handwritten: .5)

If you are interested in attending, see Derek Brennan. He will pre-register anyone from our company who wishes to attend. This will save you long lines at the show.

sw

(handwritten insert:)
Special Interest Group Meetings. These sessions will include Education Workshops for teachers, resources and recommendations for the home office worker, and ways to fully utilize your computer in a law office.

(handwritten: .5 / .5)

TO MOVE

- a sentence/paragraph/page

1. Place cursor on the first character of text to be moved.
2. Press **Ctrl + F4**........ `Ctrl` + `F4`
3. Select:

    S (Sentence)........................ `S`
    -or-
    or-P (Paragraph)...................... `P`
    -or-
    or-A (Page)........................... `A`

4. Select **M** (Move)........................ `M`
5. Place cursor where text is to be reinserted.
6. **ENTER**.. `↵`

- a block of text

1. Place cursor on first character of text to be moved.
2. Press **Alt + F4**............. `Alt` + `F4`
    -or-
    -or- **F12** (enhanced keyboard)..... `F12`
3. Using cursor arrow keys, highlight text to be moved.

(See page 27 for other highlighting methods).

4. Press **Ctrl + F4**.......... `Ctrl` + `F4`
5. Select **B** (Block)........................... `B`
6. Select **M** (Move)........................... `M`
7. Place cursor where text is to be reinserted.

8. **ENTER**...................................... `↵`

TO INDENT AN EXISTING PARAGRAPH

1. Place cursor on first character of paragraph.
2. Press **F4**................................. `F4`
    to indent on left.
    -or-
    Press **Shift + F4**...... `Shift` + `F4`
    to double indent (left and right).

MOVING TEXT; CHANGING MARGINS

Notes:

- In this exercise you will move indented paragraphs. Reveal your codes and be sure your cursor is sitting on the indent code when you move the paragraph.

- The proofreader's mark for inserting a space is: #

Exercise Directions:

1. Start with a clear screen.

2. Retrieve **BULLETIN.**

3. Set the left and right margins for 1.5".

4. Move the paragraphs as directed.

5. Make the indicated revisions.

6. Print one copy.

7. Resave your file.

********ELECTRONIC BULLETIN BOARDS********

↓ 3✗

Thousands of people across the nation are using computer bulletin boards. Through their computer, they spend hours on line "talking" with other users, "discussing" topics ~~ranging~~ from zoology, finding information about taxes or taxis, completing graduate courses to even exchanging wedding vows. # Some productive uses of bulletin boards are:

#

move *move*

A system set up by a hospital in West Virginia offers detailed answers to medical questions for people who don't want to travel ~~great~~ *long* distances necessary to see a doctor.

A system created by a retired guidance counselor in Atlanta provides current information on scholarships and loans.

A system operated by a car expert in Las Vegas lists thousands of collectors' cars.

move

basic

Besides the fee of subscribing to a bulletin board, the cost of "talking" on your computer is the same as talking on your phone, since phone lines are used for data transmission.

move

All you need to connect a bulletin board is a computer and a modem connected to a telephone line. While most bulletin boards are free, some of the largest are professional operations that charge a fee.

COPYING and MOVING TEXT; CHANGING LINE SPACING and MARGINS

Notes:

• The copy feature allows you to leave text in its original location while placing it somewhere else, whereas the move feature removes the text from its original location and places it elsewhere.

• Be sure that the bold code is moved/copied along with the hotel information. To insure that you do, reveal your codes and check to see that your cursor is sitting on the bold code before you move/copy the paragraph.

Exercise Directions:

1. Start with a clear screen.

2. Retrieve **DIVE**.

3. Set the left and right margins for 1.5 ".

4. Insert paragraphs as indicated.

5. Double space the paragraphs; single space the hotel information.

6. Copy and move hotel information as directed.

7. Print one copy.

8. Resave your file.

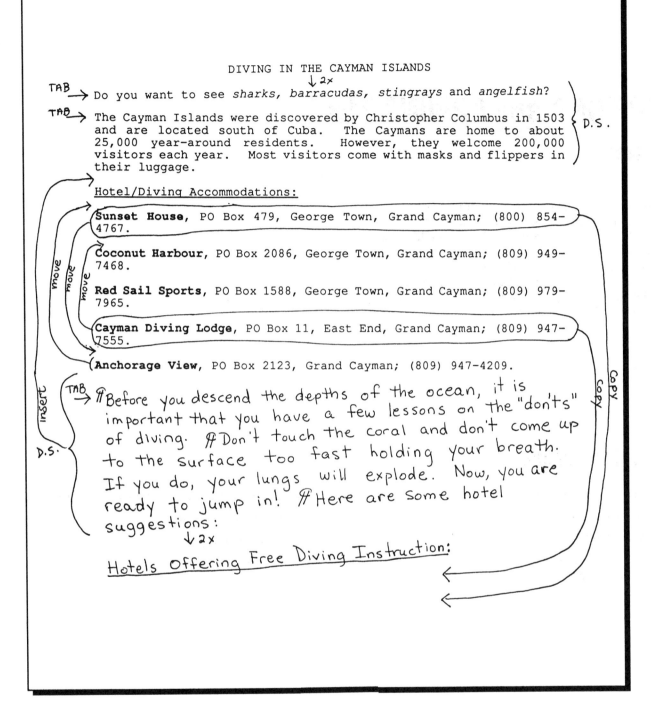

DIVING IN THE CAYMAN ISLANDS

TAB→ Do you want to see *sharks, barracudas, stingrays* and *angelfish*?

TAB→ The Cayman Islands were discovered by Christopher Columbus in 1503 and are located south of Cuba. The Caymans are home to about 25,000 year-around residents. However, they welcome 200,000 visitors each year. Most visitors come with masks and flippers in their luggage.

Hotel/Diving Accommodations:

Sunset House, PO Box 479, George Town, Grand Cayman; (800) 854-4767.

Coconut Harbour, PO Box 2086, George Town, Grand Cayman; (809) 949-7468.

Red Sail Sports, PO Box 1588, George Town, Grand Cayman; (809) 979-7965.

Cayman Diving Lodge, PO Box 11, East End, Grand Cayman; (809) 947-7555.

Anchorage View, PO Box 2123, Grand Cayman; (809) 947-4209.

¶Before you descend the depths of the ocean, it is important that you have a few lessons on the "don'ts" of diving. ¶Don't touch the coral and don't come up to the surface too fast holding your breath. If you do, your lungs will explode. Now, you are ready to jump in! ¶Here are some hotel suggestions:

Hotels Offering Free Diving Instruction:

TO COPY

- a sentence/paragraph/page

1. Place cursor on the first character of text to be copied.

2. Press **Ctrl + F4**........ **Ctrl** + **F4**

3. Select:

 S (Sentence)....................... **S**

 -or-

 or- **P** (Paragraph)................... **P**

 -or-

 or- **A** (Page).............................. **A**

4. Select **C** (Copy)...................... **C**

5. Place cursor where text is to be copied to.

6. **ENTER**................................. ↵

- a block of text

1. Place cursor on first character of text to be copied.

2. Press **Alt + F4**............. **Alt** + **F4**

 -or-

 -or- **F11** (enhanced keyboard).... **F12**

3. Using cursor arrow keys, highlight text to be copied.

*(See page 27 for other highlighting methods).

4. Press **Ctrl + F4**.......... **Ctrl** + **F4**

5. Select **B** (Block)......................... **B**

6. Select **C** (Copy)........................ **C**

7. Place cursor where text is to be copied to.

8. **ENTER**...................................... ↵

COPYING <u>and</u> MOVING TEXT

Notes:

* In this exercise, you will copy and move centered and bolded text. Use the copy procedure for "Copying a Block of Text." Be sure that the center and bold codes are moved/copied along with the hotel name. To insure that you do, reveal your codes and check to see that you highlight the begin and end center and bold codes before you move/copy.

Exercise Directions:

1. Start with a clear screen.

2. Retrieve **MEMO.**

3. Make the indicated revisions.

4. Create the horizontal line by using the repeat value and the asterisk (*). Set the repeat value for 65.

5. Copy and center hotel names as indicated.

6. View your document.

7. Print one copy.

8. Resave your file.

<u>MEMORANDUM</u> *delete double underscore*

delete underscores

TO: Managers Attending Computer Expo

FROM: Robin McDonald

DATE: December 10, 199-

SUBJECT: **Hotels Offering Discounts to Computer Expo Attendees** *delete bold subject line*

*insert a horizontal line of * (asterisks)*

The following San Francisco hotels have agreed to offer discounted *italics* rates to all attendees of Computer Expo: ←

Fairmont Hotel
Grand Hyatt *move*
Holiday Inn: Civic Center
Hyatt Regency
King George Hotel *move*
Nikko
Sir Francis Drake
Villa Florence
Westin St. Francis *move* *copy*

call to
When you make your reservation, ~~mention~~ *explain* that you are attending the
Computer Expo at the Convention Center. A limited number of rooms
are available at preferred rates, so plan early. *All hotels listed
in bold* ~~above~~ *are within 20 minutes of the Convention Center.*
below

rm

c: Chad Wilkinson
Julie Chen

¶ Hotels listed below will offer free overnight parking:
↓2x
≡ ←
↓2x

PREPARING A RESUME

Notes:

• A resume is a document which describes your background and qualifications. This document is used to gain employment. It is usually enclosed with a letter of application and sent to an employer or it may be given to the employer during an interview. Resume formats may vary depending on the extent of your education and work experience. Most resumes are one or two pages long. However, one page is preferable.

• Your education and work experience should be listed beginning with the most recent.

Exercise Directions:

1. Start with a clear screen.

2. Format the resume on the right, underlining, bolding and using italics as indicated. Begin the exercise on Ln 1".

3 Use the default margins.

4. Spell check the exercise.

5. View your document.

6. Print one copy.

7. Save the exercise; name it **RESUME.**

JODY ABBATO
7652 Shore Road
Statten Island, NY 10314
(718) 654-9870

↓3x   Indent

CAREER OBJECTIVE: ⌐ To secure a responsible management position in
                     ⌐ a leading hotel chain with opportunities for
                     ⌐ growth.
                          ↓2x

EDUCATION
        ↓2x   Indent
Sept. 1987-June 1991 ⌐ _Cornell University_, School of Hotel
                     ⌐ Administration, Ithaca, NY   14850.
                     ⌐ Received a Bachelor of Science degree in
                     ⌐ Hotel Administration with a 3.5 overall
                     ⌐ average.
                 Indent   ↓2x
Sept. 1983-June 1987 ⌐ _Tottenville High School_, 100 Luten Avenue,
                     ⌐ Statten Island, NY 10312
                          ↓2x

SKILLS
        ↓2x
Indent
→ IBM Personal Computer, knowledge of WordPerfect, Lotus and
  DBase III+ application software.
     ↓2x

EXPERIENCE
        ↓2x   Indent 2x
June 1988-Aug. 1988 → ⌐ **Holiday Inn**, Richmond Avenue, Statten
                     ⌐ Island, NY 10314. Duties: Worked in
                     ⌐ accounting department as assistant to
                     ⌐ manager.
              Indent 2x   ↓2x
June 1989-Aug. 1989 → ⌐ **Marriott Hotel**, Broadway, New York, NY
                     ⌐ 10012. Duties: Data entry operator in
                     ⌐ accounting department.
                          ↓2x

ACTIVITIES
     ↓2x
TAB → Vice President of Cornell University Management Society
TAB → Member of Cornell University Student Senate
TAB → Staff reporter for Cornell University _Management News_
                 ↓2x

REFERENCES
Indent   ↓2x
  ⌐ Dr. Stanley Simon, Professor of Management, Cornell
  ⌐ University, Ithaca, NY 14850 (325) 456-8765
Indent   ↓2x
  ⌐ Ms. Maria Lopez, Manager, Holiday Inn, Richmond Avenue,
  ⌐ Statten Island, NY 10314 (718) 876-3677

Exercise Directions:

1. Retrieve **RESUME** from your directory.
2. Set left and right margins to .5".
3. Make the indicated revisions.

4. View your document.
5. Print one copy.
6. Resave your file.

3 spaces

JODY ABBATO
7652 Shore Road
Statten Island, NY 10314
(718) 654-9870

CAREER OBJECTIVE: To secure a responsible management position in a leading hotel chain with opportunities for growth.

EDUCATION

Sept. 1987-June 1991   *Cornell University*, School of Hotel Administration, Ithaca, NY 14850. Received a Bachelor of Science degree in Hotel Administration with a 3.5 overall average.

Sept. 1983-June 1987   *Tottenville High School*, 100 Luten Avenue Statten Island, NY 10312

SKILLS

IBM Personal Computer, knowledge of WordPerfect, Lotus and DBase III+ application software.

EXPERIENCE

June 1988-Aug. 1988   *Holiday Inn*, Richmond Avenue, Statten Island, NY 10314. Duties: Worked in accounting department as assistant to manager.

June 1989-Aug. 1989   *Marriott Hotel*, Broadway, New York, NY 10012. Duties: Data entry operator in accounting department.

ACTIVITIES

Vice President of Cornell University Management Society
Member of Cornell University Student Senate
Staff reporter for Cornell University Management News

REFERENCES

Dr. Stanley Simon, Professor of Management, Cornell University, Ithaca, NY 14850 (325) 456-8765

Ms. Maria Lopez, Manager, Holiday Inn, Richmond Avenue, Statten Island, NY 10314 (718) 876-3677

HOBBIES

→ Skiing, Reading, Tennis

Lesson 4
Summary Exercise B

Exercise Directions:

1. Create a one-page report from the text below.

2. Set the left and right margins to .5".

3. Single space and double indent (left and right) the bolded bat species and their descriptions.

4. Spell check the exercise.

5. Print one copy.

6. Save the exercise; name it **BATS**.

BATS//Do bats get in your hair? Do vampire bats exist? How blind is a bat? These are questions you might ask yourself if you were ever near a cave, an attic or another sheltered place.//Bats are the only mammals that can fly. They usually stay in dark places, tend to live in colonies, come out only at night, and hang upside down when they are resting. As night approaches, they head for their feeding grounds. Bats have an excellent sense of smell and hearing and depend on these senses to navigate and find food at night. Bats eat large numbers of insects and are, therefore, valuable to people. //The following is a descriptions of several bat species://Vampire Bats. These mammals feed on blood of other animals and live in Central and South America. Vampire bats swallow about 1 tablespoon of blood a day. They leave their victims with a small wound which heals quickly, but these bats can carry rabies.//Brown Bats. They live in the United States in buildings and caves and have a wingspan of about 12 inches.//Free-Tailed Bats These brown bats have a wingspan up to 12 inches, live in colonies, mostly in caves in Southern United States and Mexico.//RED Bats. With a wingspan of 12 inches, these bats live alone in trees and fly south every winter. The male has bright red, white-tipped fur, while the female has a grayish red fur. // Now, to answer the questions asked earlier: Bats do not get tangled in people's hair. Bats tend to be frightened of people and will fly away. Bats are not blind. All species of bats can see, but they see very poorly, especially at night. But, vampire bats DO exist; They are one of several kinds of bat species which was described above.

> **LESSON 5:**
> CHANGING JUSTIFICATION; USING THESAURUS; SEARCHING AND
> REPLACING TEXT/CODES; HYPHENATING TEXT; OUTLINING.

CHANGING JUSTIFICATION/THESAURUS

Notes:

• When you printed your first document, you noticed that the left and right margins were even. WordPerfect 5.1 refers to an even right and left margin as "**full** justification," while WordPerfect 5.0 refers to an even right and left margin as "justification." Both versions of WordPerfect are defaulted to justify all printed text. (Justification does not display on the screen but may be seen by "viewing" the document.) It does this by expanding or compressing spaces between words and letters.

• The justification feature may be turned off by accessing the format menu and changing the setting from "yes" to "no" (for WordPerfect 5.0 users) or from "full" to "left" (for WordPerfect 5.1 users).

• A justification change affects text from the point where the justification code was entered.

• The thesaurus feature lists synonyms and antonyms of a desired word and also indicates the word's part of speech.

• You may replace a word in your document with a word listed in the thesaurus by selecting "Replace Word" and then indicating the letter next to the word you wish to use. It is sometimes necessary to edit the new word so that it fits properly in the sentence (example: singular/plural).

• In this exercise you will use the thesaurus feature to substitute the words marked in brackets. You will also unjustify the first two paragraphs and the last paragraph.

Exercise Directions:

1. Start with a clear screen.

2. Begin the exercise on Ln 1.5".

3. Keyboard the letter on the right as indicated.

4. Use the date feature.

5. Justify <u>only</u> the indented paragraphs.

6. Using the thesaurus feature, substitute the words marked in brackets. Be sure that the tense of the new word is the same as the one it replaces.

7. View your document.

8. Print one copy.

9. Save the exercise; name it **TOURS**.

Today's Date ↵ 1.5"

Ms. Christine Sabbio
876 North LaSalle Street
Chicago, IL 60601

Dear Ms. Sabbio:

add "ing" to replacement word

You called last week ⟨inquiring⟩ about horseback riding tours in the United States, particularly the eastern half of the country with English-style riding.

unjustify

Since I have been unable to ⟨reach⟩ you by phone, I am outlining in this letter some information about riding tours that I think will interest you.

EQUITABLE TOURS - This company offers riding tours of two to eight days and is located in Woodstock, Vermont. The cost ranges from $579 for four days to $1,229 for eight. They will arrange itineraries in Northern California and in Arizona.

.5 (left and right indent) .5

EQUESTRIAN RIDES - This company offers riding tours from inn to inn through the Sugarbush, Vermont area between the Green Mountains and Lake Champlain. There are five-day rides at $795 and six-day rides for $960.

HOOFBEATS INTERNATIONAL - This company is located in New Jersey and offers instruction. They will arrange riding tours in upstate New York where participants may ⟨mix⟩ lessons with trail rides and stay at the farm or a nearby inn. The ⟨cost⟩ varies according to the program.

While there are many other riding tours available, I have outlined what I believe to be the best three. If you ⟨desire⟩ more information about riding tours, please call me.

unjustify

Sincerely,

Paula Badar
Travel Agent

pb/yo

TO JUSTIFY/UNJUSTIFY

1. Place cursor at location for justification change.
2. Press **Shift + F8**..... **Shift** + **F8**
3. Select **L** (Line).............................. **L**
4. Select **J** (Justification)................ **J**
5. Select justification setting:

   WP5.0 USERS:
   Y (Yes).. **Y**
   or
   or N (No).. **N**

   O R

   WP5.1 USERS:
   F (Full).. **F**
   or
   or L (Left).. **L**
6. Press **F7**.. **F7**
   (to return to document)

TO USE THESAURUS

1. Place cursor on word to be looked up.
2. Press **Alt + F1**.............. **Alt** + **F1**
3. Select **1** (Replace Word).............. **1**
4. Type the letter preceding the desired replacement word.

   (If desired word is in the second column, press right arrow key to move the selection letters to next column.

SEARCHING TEXT/CHANGING JUSTIFICATION/THESAURUS

Notes:

- The **search** feature will scan your document, search for occurrences of specified text or codes. Once the desired text or code is found, it can be edited or replaced. WordPerfect searches in either a forward direction (from the cursor to the end of the document) or a reverse direction (from the cursor to the beginning of the document).

- In this exercise, you will search for the words shown in brackets. The search feature will quickly place the cursor on those words so you can edit them, using the thesaurus feature. You will also make two justification changes: one to unjustify the first two paragraphs and one to justify the indented paragraphs.

- To make the heading more attractive, you can "spread" the C A P I T A L letters by inserting a space between them.

Exercise Directions:

1. Start with a clear screen.

2. Retrieve **MEMONEWS**.

3. Unjustify the paragraphs indicated.

4. Using the Thesaurus feature, substitute the words marked in brackets. Be sure that the tense of the new word is the same as the one it replaces.

5. Print one copy.

6. Resave your file.

MEMORANDUM)spread cap

TO: The Staff

FROM: Sarah Walesk

RE: Computer Expo

DATE: December 9, 199-

==

I strongly ⟨urge⟩ you to attend this year's Computer Expo. [learn about]
In four days, you will ~~pick up~~ the latest computer news
and ⟨discover⟩ new ways to put your computer ~~to work~~ -- in [use]
the office, in the lab, in the studio, in the classroom,
or in your home.   *unjustify*

If you are interested in attending, see Derek Brennan.
He will pre-register anyone from our company who ⟨wishes⟩
to attend. This will save you long lines at the show.

Here are some of the events you can look forward to:

    Application Workshops. Join a series of two-
    hour learning sessions which will provide
    guidelines, tips and "how-to's" on popular
    software packages.

    Keynote Sessions. These sessions will feature
    ⟨luminaries⟩ from the computer world who will
    offer you insights from industry.   *make replacement words plural*

    Programmer/Developer Forums. Veteran and
    ⟨novice⟩ computer users will brainstorm so you
    can learn about innovative advances and
    ⟨techniques⟩.

    Special Interest Group Meetings. These
    sessions will include Education Workshops for
    teachers, resources and recommendations for
    the home office worker, and ways to fully
    ⟨utilize⟩ your computer in a law office.

sw

TO SEARCH TEXT/CODES

Search from cursor forward:

1. Press **F2**.................................. `F2`

   or   **or**

   Search from cursor backward:

   Press **Shift + F2**....... `Shift` + `F2`

2. Type **search word/code**.

3. Press **F2**.................................. `F2`

HYPHENATING TEXT; SEARCHING AND REPLACING TEXT

Notes:

- Hyphenating text produces a tighter right margin. If text is justified and hyphenated, the sentences will have smaller gaps between words.

- **WordPerfect 5.0 Users:** WordPerfect's hyphenation feature is set to "Off." When you change it to "On," you then have the option of selecting "Manual" or "Auto" hyphenation. **Manual** hyphenation prompts the operator to confirm hyphenation points. When the word to be hyphenated, along with the message, "Position hyphen; Press ESC," appears on the status line, you will press the left or right arrow keys to position the hyphen between desired syllables, then press ESC to hyphenate the word. If you do not want to hyphenate the word, press Cancel (F1). **Auto**matic hyphenation will insert hyphens according to WordPerfect's rules. If a word cannot be hyphenated according to the rules, WordPerfect will allow you to manually hyphenate the word.

- **WordPerfect 5.1 Users:** WordPerfect's hyphenation feature is set to "No." WordPerfect 5.1 uses automatic hyphenation and asks you to make a hyphenation decision only when it cannot find a good place to hyphenate according to its rules. When you change it to "Yes," WordPerfect will display

the word to be hyphenated along with the message, "Position hyphen; Press ESC" on the status line. Occasionally, you have the option to press the left or right arrow keys to position the hyphen between desired syllables, and press ESC to hyphenate the word. If you do not want to hyphenate the word, press Cancel (F1).

- As explained in Exercise 33, the **search** feature will scan your document and search for occurrences of text or codes. Once the desired text or code is found, it can be edited or replaced.

- If you enter lower case characters to be searched, WordPerfect will find <u>both</u> lower case and upper case. If you enter upper case characters to be searched, WordPerfect will match <u>only</u> upper case.

- If it is possible for the search word to be part of another word, spaces must be entered before and after the search word. For example, if you did not enter a space before and after the search word "cut," WordPerfect will stop at a word like "exe<u>cu</u>tive" because "cut" is within the word exe<u>cut</u>ive.

- The **replace** feature replaces occurrences of text or codes. WordPerfect gives you the option of replacing all occurrences of text or codes (global search and replace) or confirming each replacement (selective search and replace).

Exercise Directions:

1. Start with a clear screen.

2. Retrieve **BULLETIN**.

3. Unjustify the paragraphs indicated.

4. Hyphenate the <u>justified</u> paragraphs.

5. Using the thesaurus, replace words marked in brackets.

6. Search for the word "bulletin" and replace with "BULLETIN."

7. View your document.

8. Print one copy.

9. Resave your file.

   NOTE: Because of differences in printers, line endings and hyphenations may vary.

Globally search for "bulletin" and replace with "BULLETIN"

********ELECTRONIC BULLETIN BOARDS********

Thousands of people across the nation are using computer bulletin boards. Through their computer, they spend hours on line "talking" with other users, "discussing" topics from zoology, finding information about taxes or taxis, completing graduate courses to even exchanging wedding vows. While most bulletin boards are free, some of the largest are professional operations that ⟨charge⟩ a fee.   *}unjustify*

Some ⟨productive⟩ uses of bulletin boards are:

A system operated by a car expert in Las Vegas lists thousands of collectors' cars.

A system ⟨created⟩ by a retired guidance counselor in Atlanta provides current information on scholarships and loans.   *}hyphenate*

A system set up by a hospital in West Virginia offers detailed answers to medical questions for people who do not want to travel long distances necessary to see a doctor.

All you need to ⟨connect⟩ a bulletin board is a computer and a modem connected to a telephone line.

Besides the basic fee of subscribing to a bulletin board, the cost of "talking" on your computer is the same as talking on your phone, since phone lines are used for data transmission.   *}unjustify*

TO HYPHENATE

1. Place cursor where hyphenation is to begin.
2. Press **Shift + F8**...... `Shift` + `F8`
3. Select **L**.................................`L`
4. Select **Y** (Hyphenation)..............`Y`
5. Select hyphenation option:

WP5.0 USERS:
- Type **M** (Manual)....................`M`
  or   **or**
  Type **A** (Automatic)................`A`
  - Press **F7** ....`F7`
    to return to document

NOTE: When a word needs to be hyphenated, a beep will sound and a message will appear.

- Press **Left** or **Right Arrow**....
  ....`←` or `→` to select hypenation point.

- Press **Esc** ....`Esc`
  to hypenate word.
or   **or**
- Type **F** (Off)..........................`F`

WP5.1 USERS:
- Type **Y** (Hyphenation On)....`Y`
  - Press **F7** ....`F7`
    to return to document.

NOTE: When a word needs to be hyphenated, a beep will sound and a message will appear.

- Press **Left** or **Right Arrow**....
  ....`←` or `→` to select hypenation point.

- Press **Esc**............................`Esc`
  to hypenate word.
or   **or**
- Type **N** (Hyphenation Off)......`N`

- Press **F7** ....`F7`
  to return to document)

TO SEARCH & REPLACE TEXT/CODES

1. Press **Alt + F2**...........`Alt` + `F2`
2. Type **Y**...`Y`
   (to confirm replacement - SELECTIVE.)
   or   **or**
   Type **N**...`N`
   (to replace every occurrence without stopping to confirm - GLOBAL.)
3. Type search word/code.
4. Press **F2**....................................`F2`
5. Type replacement word/code.
6. Press **F2**....................................`F2`

HYPHENATING TEXT; SEARCHING AND REPLACING TEXT

Notes:

- In this exercise, you will search for a bolded "OCR" and replace it with an unbolded "Optical Character Recognition." When entering the search word, be sure to enter the begin and end bold codes as part of that word.

- To revise the indented paragraphs, reveal your codes (Shift + F3 or F11), delete the tab and indent codes, and reinsert left/right indent code (Shift + F4).

Exercise Directions:

1. Start with a clear screen.

2. Retrieve **OCR.**

3. Hyphenate the document.

4. Make the indicated revisions.

5. Using thesaurus, replace the words marked in brackets.

6. Search for the word "**OCR**" and replace with "Optical Character Recognition."

7. View your document.

8. Print one copy.

9. Resave your file.

search for OCR and replace with Optical Character Recognition

OPTICAL CHARACTER RECOGNITION AT WORK

Optical Character Recognition, or **OCR**, converts paper documents to digital format. Therefore, it is ⟨possible⟩ to have an **OCR** device *read* text and have it appear on the computer's screen, without rekeying copy.

Some **OCR** units have the ability to recognize a wide ⟨variety⟩ of fonts, reproduce tabs, text centering, and other formatting. Most **OCR** units process pages three or four times faster than the average typist's 70 words per minute.

Here are some interesting ways in which companies use Optical Character Recognition to ease their work loads:

1. A Boston service bureau recently scanned and republished a client's large medical catalog, a project that would have been too time consuming to ⟨undertake⟩.

2. A New York-based newspaper plans to create data files of their back issues, many of which were published in 1845.

3. A Maryland company needed to transfer files from an aging word processing system to a newer one. It discovered that printing the files from the old system and then scanning them into the new system was less ⟨expensive⟩.

indent .5

¶ at the supermarket checkout stand a laser beam "reads" the bar code on an item and ⟨gives⟩ the information — item, price, etc., — to the cash register.

OUTLINING

Notes:

- An outline is used to organize information about a subject for the purpose of making a speech or writing a report. There are two types of outlines: **a topic outline** and a **sentence outline**. A topic outline summarizes the main and subtopics in short phrases while a sentence outline uses complete sentences for each.
- WordPerfect's outline feature will insert outline characters automatically at the appropriate outline levels.
- When the outline feature is turned on, the message "Outline" is displayed in the lower left corner of your screen. When the feature is turned off, the message will disappear.
- An outline generally begins 2" from the top of the page and has a centered heading. A triple space follows the heading. The outline feature is then accessed.
- Press **Shift + Tab** to move backward through the levels.

Exercise Directions:

1. Start with a clear screen.
2. Center the heading on line (Ln) 2".
3. Using the outline feature, format the **topic outline** on the right.
4. Spell check the exercise.
5. View your document.
6. Print one copy.
7. Save the exercise; name it **CARS.**

80

PURCHASING VS. NOT PURCHASING A CAR

↓ 2ˣ

I.   Reasons for Purchasing a Car

↓ 2ˣ

    A.   Convenience
    B.   Prestige

↓ 2ˣ

II. Reasons for Not Purchasing a Car

↓ 2ˣ

    A.   Inconvenience
        1.   Expense of gasoline
        2.   Crowded roads
        3.   Parking problems
            a.   Expensive parking garages
            b.   Increasing tows
    B.   Hazards
        1.   Possibility of accidents
        2.   Unpredictable weather
    C.   Bad Financial Investment
        1.   High taxes
        2.   High interest rates
    D.   Continuing Costs
        1.   Fuel
        2.   Maintenance
            a.   Brakes
            b.   Oil
            c.   Filter
            d.   Tuneup
                (1)   Points
                (2)   Plugs
                (3)   Timing

TO OUTLINE

1. Place cursor where outline is to begin.
2. Press **Shift + F5**..... `Shift` + `F5`
3. **WP5.0 USERS:**
   Select O (Outline)...................... `O`
   O R   **or**
   WP5.1 USERS:
   Select O (Outline)...................... `O`
   Select O (On)........................... `O`
4. **ENTER**.................................... `↵`
   to reveal first outline level.
5. Press **F4** (Indent)................... `F4`

6. Type text.
7. **ENTER**.................................... `↵`
8. Press **Tab** to advance to an outline level.................................... `TAB`
   Optional:
   Press **Shift + Tab** to move back an outline level........ `Shift` + `TAB`
9. Press **F4**.................................. `F4`
10. Type text.
11. Repeat Steps 4-10 until outline is complete.

12. Press **Shift + F5**...... `Shift` + `F5`
   WP5.0 USERS
   Select O (Outline)........................... `O`
   O R
   WP5.1 USERS
   Select O (Outline)........................... `O`
   Select F (Off)................................. `F`

   NOTE: Shift + Tab (Margin Release) will move backward through the levels.

OUTLINING

Notes:

- In this exercise, you will prepare a sentence outline. The sentence outline is more difficult to write, but it has an important advantage: many of the sentences can be used within your report.

Exercise Directions:

1. Start with a clear screen.
2. Unjustify the document.
3. Using the outline feature, format the **sentence outline** on the right.
4. Begin the exercise on line (Ln) 2".
5. Spell check the exercise.
6. View your document.
7. Print one copy.
8. Save the exercise; name it **COLONY.**

BOLD ←

THE JAMESTOWN COLONY

↓ 2x

I.   The Jamestown colony was founded for two major reasons.
↓ 2x
     A.   The colonists hoped to find a treasure.
     B.   The colonists wanted to grow crops that could not be
          grown in England.
          1.   Soy beans and tobacco were two of the crops the
               colonists wanted to grow.
          2.   They were also eager to develop machinery to
               harvest these two crops.
↓ 2x
II. The settlers faced many hardships.
↓ 2x
     A.   The colonists were unaccustomed to the different
          weather in the new world.
     B.   The poor drinking water and bad diet caused many
          colonists to develop diseases and die.
     C.   Hostile Indians attacked the colony repeatedly.
↓ 2x
III. The Jamestown colony finally succeeded despite its many
     problems.
↓ 2x
     A.   A strong leadership helped the colonists overcome their
          hardships.
          1.   John Smith insisted that the colonists establish
               trade with the Indians.
               a.   The colonists and the Indians developed a
                    sense of trust as a result of trading.
               b.   The trading resulted in profits for both
                    groups.
          2.   Lord De La Warr arrived with new settlers and
               supplies in 1610.
     B.   Agriculture formed the basis for the colony's economy.

83

OUTLINING

Notes:

- In this exercise, you will prepare a letter which includes an outline. In order to center the outline, it is necessary to change your left and right margins to 2". After completing the outline, you must change your margins back to the default of 1" on the left and right. Double space before and after the outline.

- Be sure to turn the outline feature off before continuing with the letter.

Exercise Directions:

1. Start with a clear screen.

2. Format the letter on the right in **block** style beginning on Line (Ln) 1.5".

3. Unjustify the paragraphs.

4. Set the left and right margins for 2" before beginning the outline. Reset the margins to 1" for the remainder of the letter.

5. Spell check the exercise.

6. Print one copy.

7. Save the exercise; name it **CAREER.**

Today's date ←⌐ 1.5"

Mr. Ronald Mangano, Assistant Principal
New Dorp High School
465 New Dorp Lane
Staten Island, NY 10306

Dear Mr. Mangano:

(*italics*) I would once again like to make a presentation to your classes on
→ *Choosing and Planning a Career*. A brief outline of my planned
talk appears below:

set 2" →
left/right margins

      I. **CHOOSING AND PLANNING A CAREER**← (*bold*)
        ↓2x
        A. Discovering the World of Work
        B. Investigating Career Fields
           1. Medicine
           2. Business
              a. Marketing
              b. Brokerage
              c. Computer-related
                 (1) Technician
                 (2) Programmer
                 (3) Data Entry Operator
           3. Teaching
           4. Engineering
        ↓2x
     II. **GETTING A JOB** (*bold*)
        ↓2x
        A. Being Interviewed
           1. How to dress
           2. What to say
        B. Writing a Resume
        ↓2x

set
1" left/
right
margins

While I may not have enough time to include all the material in
my presentation, the outline will give you an overview of my
topic. I look forward to addressing your classes on March 31.

Sincerely,

Janice Waller

jw/yo

Lesson 5
Summary Exercise A

Exercise Directions:

1. Retrieve **RESUME.**
2. Make the indicated revisions.
3. Unjustify and hyphenate the document.
4. Search for "Statten" and replace with "Staten."
5. Using the thesaurus feature, substitute the words marked in brackets.
6. Print one copy.
7. Resave your file.

JODY ABBATO
7652 Shore Road
Statten Island, NY 10314
(718) 654-9870

CAREER OBJECTIVE: To ⟨secure⟩ a responsible management position in a leading hotel chain with opportunities for ⟨growth⟩.

EDUCATION

Sept. 1987-June 1991   *Cornell University*, School of Hotel Administration, Ithaca, NY 14850. Received a Bachelor of Science degree in Hotel Administration with a 3.5 overall average.

Sept. 1983-June 1987   *Tottenville High School*, 100 Luten Avenue Statten Island, NY 10312

EXPERIENCE

June 1988-Aug. 1988   **Marriott Hotel**, Broadway, New York, NY 10012. Duties: Data entry operator in accounting department.

June 1989-Aug. 1989   **Holiday Inn**, Richmond Avenue, Statten Island, NY 10314. Duties: Worked in accounting department as assistant to manager.

HOBBIES

    Skiing, Reading, Tennis

ACTIVITIES

    Vice President of Cornell University Management Society
    Member of Cornell University Student Senate
    Staff reporter for Cornell University Management News

SKILLS

    IBM Personal Computer, knowledge of WordPerfect, Lotus and DBase III+ application software.

REFERENCES

    Ms. Maria Lopez, Manager, Holiday Inn, Richmond Avenue, Statten Island, NY 10314 (718) 876-3677

    Dr. Stanley Simon, Professor of Management, Cornell University, Ithaca, NY 14850 (325) 456-8765

Lesson 5
Summary Exercise B

Exercise Directions:

1. Create the letter below, in any style, inserting the outline indicated. Reset margins, as desired, before and after creating the outline so that the outline appears indented on the left and right.

2. Unjustify and hyphenate your document.

3. Print one copy.

4. Save the exercise; name it **PRACTICE**.

Today's Date//Mr. Raymond Mangano/645 Avenue of Americas/New York, NY 10010/Dear Mr. Mangano:/In response to your inquiry, WordPerfect <u>does</u> contain an outline feature.//Each outline level is marked with a different character type which is specific to that level. Roman numerals are displayed for each Level 1 outline. Level 2 entries are marked with an uppercase letter, Level 3 entries are marked with an Arabic number, etc. Note the sample topic outline below://

I. WHAT IS A FLOOD A. Its Extent B. Its Effects 1. Bad effects a. Destroys property and homes b. Carries off topsoil c. Causes injuries and deaths 2. Good effects a. Creates fertile regions b. Transports soil (1) Nile Valley

(2) Mississippi Valley II. KINDS OF FLOODS
A. River Floods B. Seacoast Floods 1. Causes
2. Great Floods//

I think the above illustration should clarify outline levels. If you have any further questions, call me or check WordPerfect's reference manual.//Yours truly,/Crystal Williams/Marketing Director/cw/yo

LESSON 6:
MULTIPLE-PAGE DOCUMENTS: FOOTNOTING/ENDNOTING; INSERT-
ING HEADERS, FOOTERS AND PAGE NUMBERS; WIDOW AND OR-
PHAN PROTECTION; MOVING TEXT FROM ONE PAGE TO ANOTHER;
USING SUPERSCRIPTS AND SUBSCRIPTS.

MULTIPLE-PAGE DOCUMENTS: Creating a Two-Page Letter

Notes:

- WordPerfect assumes you are working on a standard sheet of paper measuring 8 1/2" wide x 11" long. Remember, WordPerfect is defaulted to leave a 1" top and 1" bottom margin. Therefore, there are exactly 9" of vertical space on a standard sheet of paper for entering text.

- The "Ln" indicator indicates how far you are from the top of the page. Therefore, when you enter text beyond 9.83" (the last line of the 9 inches), WordPerfect will automatically insert a dashed horizontal line across the screen to indicate the end of one page and the start of another. When WordPerfect ends the page, this is referred to as a "soft page break." Once the cursor is below the horizontal line, you will note that the "Pg" indicator on the status line displays "Pg 2."

- If you wish to end the page before 9.83," you can do so. When you force the end of a page, this is referred to as a "hard page break." A hard page break is indicated by a double horizontal line across the screen.

- A hard page break may be deleted, which will allow text below the hard page break to flow into the previous page, as room allows.

- A multiple-page letter requires a heading on the second and succeeding pages. The heading should begin at 1" and include the name of the addressee (to whom the letter is going), the page number, and the date.

- In this exercise, allow WordPerfect to insert the page break for you.

- When printing, it is necessary to indicate that you are printing a "Full Document," not a "Page." Therefore, after pressing Shift + F7 to access printing, select F(ull Document) as your print option. Your cursor may be on any page in the document when making this selection.

Exercise Directions:

1. Start with a clear screen.

2. Format the letter on the right in **block** style beginning on Line (Ln) 2.5".

3. Unjustify your document for WordPerfect 5.0; (left justify for WP5.1).

4. Include the second-page heading immediately after WordPerfect inserts the page break.

5. Spell check the exercise.

6. Print one copy.

7. Save the exercise; name it **NYC**.

Today's date

Mr. Brendon Basler
54 West Brook Lane
Fort Worth, TX 76102-1349

Dear Mr. Basler:

I am so glad to hear that you might be moving to Manhattan. You asked me to write and tell you what it is like living in Manhattan. Since I have been a New Yorker for most of my life and love every minute of it, I will describe to you what it might be like for you to live here.

If you move to an apartment in Manhattan with a view, you might see the Empire State Building, the Metropolitan Life Tower, the Chrysler Building or even the Citicorp Center. Depending on where your apartment is located, you might even see the twin towers of the World Trade Center. The Brooklyn and Manhattan Bridges are off to the east and on a clear day you can see the Hudson River.

Traffic in New York as well as waiting in long lines at the post office and the movie theaters can be very frustrating. However, after you have lived here for a short while, you will know the best times to avoid long lines.

It is absolutely unnecessary and <u>very</u> expensive to own a car in Manhattan. The bus and subway system are excellent means to travel within the City.

There is always something to do here. If you love the opera, ballet, theater, museums, art galleries, and eating foods from all over the world, then New York is the place for you.

Before you actually make the move, I suggest that you come here for an extended visit. Not everyone loves it here.

You mentioned that you would be visiting some time next month. I have listed on the next page some of the hotels (and their phone numbers) you might want to consider staying at while you are visiting. I have included those that would be in walking distance to your meeting locations. And, while you are attending

continued...

Mr. Brendon Basler
Page 2
Today's date
↓3x

your meetings, your family can take advantage of some of the
sights and shopping near your hotel. I have called the hotels to
be certain they can accommodate you and your family. They all
seem to have availability at the time you are planning to visit.

TAB   Indent
—→ 1. —→ **Plaza Hotel** - located at 59th Street and Central Park
            South at the foot of Central Park. 1-800-228-3000

       2.   **The Pierre Hotel** - located at 61st Street and Fifth
             Avenue across the street from Central Park. 1-800-332-
             3442

       3.   **The Drake Swissotel** - located at 56th Street and Park
             Avenue. 212-421-0900

Of course, you realize that there are many other hotel options
available to you. If these are not satisfactory, let me know and
I will call you with other recommendations.

Good luck with your decision. When you get to New York, I will
show you some of the sights and sounds of the City. Hopefully,
you will then be able to decide whether or not New York City is
the place for you.

Sincerely,

Pamela Davis

pd/yo

continued...

TO PRINT A MULTIPLE-PAGE DOCUMENT

- from Screen

1. Press **Shift + F7**..... `Shift` + `F7`
2. Select **F** (Full Document).......... `F`

- if Using Manual Paper Feed

• Press **Shift + F7**..... `Shift` + `F7`
• Select **C**.................................... `C`
• Type **G**.................................... `G`
• Press **F7**.................................... `F7`

- from Directory

1. Press **F5**.................................... `F5`

   NOTE: If necessary, specify drive and/or directory to access files.

2. **ENTER**.................................... `↵`
3. Highlight document to be printed.
4. Select **P**.................................... `P`

5. **ENTER**.................................... `↵`
   to print entire document.

OR

• Type selected page(s) with commas and dashes.

   Examples: 1-3..... pages 1-3
              2,5   page 2 and 5
              4-9   pages 4-9
              6-   page 6 to last page

• Enter.................................... `↵`

6. Press **F7**.................................... `F7`
   to exit List Files.

TO PRINT NUMBER OF COPIES

1. Press **Shift + F7**....... `Shift` + `F7`

2. Select **N**.................................... `N`
3. Type number of copies to be printed.
4. **ENTER**.................................... `↵`
5. Select Print option:

   • **F** (Full document)............... `F`
   • **P** (Page).................................... `P`

TO PRINT SELECTED PAGES

1. Press **Shift + F7**....... `Shift` + `F7`
2. Select **M**.................................... `M`
3. Type selected page(s) with commas and dashes.

   Examples: 1-3..... pages 1-3
              2,5   page 2 and 5
              4-9   pages 4-9
              6-   page 6 to last page

4. **ENTER**.................................... `↵`

MULTIPLE-PAGE DOCUMENTS: Creating a Two-Page Letter with Special Notations

Notes:

• Some letters may include special parts in addition to those you have learned thus far. The letter in this exercise contains four special letter parts: a mailing notation, a subject line, an enclosure notation and a copy notation.

• When a letter is sent by a special mail service such as EXPRESS MAIL, REGISTERED MAIL, CERTIFIED MAIL or BY HAND (via a messenger service), it is necessary to include an appropriate notation on the letter. This notation is placed a double space below the date. The type of mail service is usually typed in all caps.

• A subject line identifies or summarizes the main theme of the letter. It is typed a double space below the salutation. A double space also follows it. The subject line may then be typed at the left margin or centered. The word "Subject" may be typed in all caps or in upper and lower case.

• If something else besides the letter is included in the envelope, it is necessary to indicate that there is an enclosure or an attachment. The enclosure or attachment notation is typed below the reference initials and may be typed in several ways:

> ENC.
> Enc.
> Encl.
> Enclosure
> Encls.
> Encls. (2)
> Enclosures (2)
> Attachment
> Attachments (2)

• If copies of the document are to be sent to others, a copy notation should be typed a double space below the enclosure/attachment notation or the reference initials if there is no enclosure/attachment. A copy notation may be typed in several ways:

> Copy to:
> Copy to
> c:
> pc: (photocopy)
> cc: (carbon copy)*

* While carbon copies are infrequently used in an office today, this notation is often used nonetheless to indicate a copy sent to others.

Exercise Directions:

1. Start with a clear screen.

2. Format the letter on the next page as indicated. Begin on Ln 2.5".

3. Unjustify (for WP5.0) or left justify (for WP5.1) and hyphenate the document.

4. Indent the paragraphs on the left and right 1". (Use "double indent" --**Shift** + **F4**-- two times.)

5. Insert a hard page break as indicated and include the second-page heading.

6. Spell check the exercise.

7. Print one copy.

8. Save the exercise; name it **PREVIEW.**

Today's date
↓2×

REGISTERED MAIL
↓2×
Ms. Elizabeth DeKan
Broward College
576 Southfield Road
Marietta, Ga 30068

Dear Ms. DeKan:
↓2×
Subject: Educational Films for High Schools and Colleges
↓2×
Thank you for your interest in the films that we have available
for high school and college students. We are pleased to send you
the enclosed flyer which describes the films in detail. Also
enclosed is a summary of those films that have recently been
added to our collection since the publication of the flyer.

There have been many positive reactions to our films. Just three
weeks ago, a group of educators, editors and vocational experts
was invited to view the films at the annual EDUCATOR'S CON-
FERENCE.   Here are some of their comments:

We will be sure to send the films in time for you to preview
them. Please be sure to list the date on which you wish to
preview the film.

Mr. William R. Bondlow, Jr., president of the National Vocational
Center in Washington, D.C. and editor-in-chief of Science Care-
ers, said,

> 1"   I like the films very much. They are in-   1"
>   novative and a great benefit to all those
>   interested in the earth sciences as a profes-
>   sional career. Furthermore, they have cap-
>   tured the objects on film so true to life
>   that anyone watching them is captivated.

Ms. Andra Burke, a leading expert presently assigned to the
United States Interior Department, praised the films by saying
that,

continued...

Ms. Elizabeth DeKan
Page 2
Today's date

↓ 3×

⌐1"⌐ They are a major educational advance in ca- ⌐1"⌐
|1"| reer placement, which will serve as a source |1"|
_⌐ of motivation for all future geologists. _⌐

A member of the National Education Center, Dr. Lawrence Pilgrim,
also liked the films and said,

⌐1"⌐ I will institute a program which will make ⌐1"⌐
|1"| schools throughout the country aware of their |1"|
_⌐ vocational potential. _⌐

These are just some of the reactions we have had to our films.
We know you will have a similar reaction.

We would very much like to send you the films that you would like
during the summer session. You can use the summer to review
them. It is important that your request be received quickly
since the demand for the films is great, particularly during the
summer sessions at colleges and universities throughout the
country.

                    Cordially,

                    William DeVane
                    Executive Vice President
                    Marketing Department

wd/yo
Enclosures (2)
 ↓ 2×
Copy to Robert R. Redford
        Nancy Jackson

TO <u>INSERT</u> HARD PAGE BREAK

1. Place cursor where new page is to begin.
2. Press **Ctrl + ENTER**... **Ctrl** + **↵**

TO <u>DELETE</u> HARD PAGE BREAK

1. Place cursor immediately after the Hard Page break line.
2. Press **Backspace**........ **Backspace**

MULTIPLE-PAGE DOCUMENTS: Creating a Two-Page Letter; Saving as a New file

Notes:

- In this exercise, you will retrieve the document DIVE, create a modified-block letter from the text, and save it under a new file name.

- When a document is saved under a new file name, the original document remains intact.

Exercise Directions:

1. Start with a clear screen.

2. Retrieve **DIVE.**

3. Create a **two-page, modified block**-style letter from the document on the right. (Check to see that your left and right margins are 1.5".) Begin the exercise on Ln 2.5".

4. Set to single spacing. (Reveal your codes and delete the double space code.)

5. Make the indicated revisions.

6. Spell check the exercise.

7. Print one copy.

8. Save the document as a <u>new</u> file; name it **DIVING.**

Insert {
Mr. Kenyatta Belcher
8.0 Avenue P
Cambridge, MA 02138
Dear Ken:

Today's date

SUBJECT: ~~DIVING IN THE CAYMAN ISLANDS~~
                      ↓2x

A Some hotels do not have a beach. Instead, they have a cliff from which you can make entry into the ocean. When the sun sets, you can see the incredible sights down below.

S.S. {   Do you want to see *sharks, barracudas, stingrays and angelfish?*

S.S. {   The Cayman Islands were discovered by Christopher Columbus in 1503 and are located south of Cuba. The Caymans are home to about 25,000 year-around residents. However, they welcome 200,000 visitors each year. Most visitors come with masks and flippers in their luggage.

S.S. {   Before you descend the depths of the ocean, it is important that you have a few lessons on the "don'ts" of diving.

S.S. {   Don't touch the coral and don't come up to the surface too fast holding your breath. If you do, your lungs will explode. Now, you are ready to jump in!

Here are some hotel suggestions:

Hotel/Diving Accommodations:

.5" **Anchorage View**, PO Box 2123, Grand Cayman; (809) 947-4209.
Cayman Diving Lodge, PO Box 11, East End, Grand Cayman; (809) 947-7555.
Coconut Harbour, PO Box 2086, George Town, Grand Cayman; (809) 949-7468.
Red Sail Sports, PO Box 1588, George Town, Grand Cayman; (809) 979-7965.
Sunset House, PO Box 479, George Town, Grand Cayman; (800) 854-4767.   .5"

Hotels Offering Free Diving Instruction

.5" **Cayman Diving Lodge**, PO Box 11, East End, Grand Cayman; (809) 947-7555.
Sunset House, PO Box 479, George Town, Grand Cayman; (800) 854-4767.   .5"

I am enclosing a brochure which will give you more details about the Cayman Islands. If you have any additional questions, please feel free to call me at any time.

Yours truly,
John Rogers
Travel Agent

jr/yo
enclosure

TO SAVE AS A NEW DOCUMENT

1. Press **F7**.............................. `F7`
2. Type **Y**...................................... `Y`
3. Type new document name.

4. **ENTER**.................................. `↵`
5. Type **N** to clear screen............. `N`

FOOTNOTING/ENDNOTING

Notes:

- A **footnote** is used in a document to give information about the source of quoted material. The information includes: the author's name, the publication, the date of the publication and the page number from which the quote was taken.

- A footnote is usually typed below the text on a page. A short horizontal line separates the footnote from the regular text on the page.

- A note or reference number appears immediately after the quote in the text and the corresponding footnote number or symbol appears at the bottom of the page.

- An **endnote** contains the same information as a footnote, but is typed on the last page of a report.

- WordPerfect's footnote/endnote feature automatically inserts the reference number after the quote, numbers the footnote/endnote, inserts the separator line, and places the footnote on the same page as the reference number. If you desire endnotes instead of footnotes, WordPerfect will compile the endnote information on a separate page.

- It is possible to have both footnotes and endnotes in the same document.

- The footnote does not display on the screen but may be seen by "viewing" the document. While the reference number will not appear as a superscript (a raised character) on your screen, it will print as a superscript, and may also be seen by viewing the document.

- In this exercise, you will create footnotes.

Exercise Directions:

1. Start with a clear screen.

2. Create the report on the right in <u>double space</u>. Begin on Ln 2".

3. Use the preset margins.

4. Unjustify (for WP5.0) or left justify (for WP5.1) the document.

5. Type until you reach each reference number; use the footnote feature to insert the reference number and the footnote.

6. Spell check the exercise.

7. View your document.

8. Print one copy.

9. Save the exercise; name it **SCORPION**.

THE SCORPION ⟵ 2"

What is the first thing you think of when you hear the word "scorpion"? Most people think of "sting," "unsightly insect" or "poisonous."

The scorpion is a small animal with a dangerous poisonous sting in its tail. The scorpion is <u>not</u> an insect. It belongs to a class of animals called <u>arachnids</u>, the same family that spiders, mites and ticks also belong. Scorpions live in warm countries in most parts of the world.

Scorpions eat large insects and spiders, and are most active at night. "Scorpions capture and hold their prey with their pedipalps, which have teeth. They then stab the prey with their stingers."[1] ⟵

The scorpion's sting is a curved organ in the end of its tail. Two glands at the base give out a poison that flows from two pores. "Of the more than forty species of scorpions found in the United States, only two are considered to be harmful to people."[2] While a scorpion's sting is painful, it does not usually cause death.

REFERENCE NUMBERS

FOOTNOTES

[1]Gottfried, et. al, <u>Biology</u>, (New Jersey: Prentice-Hall, Inc. 1983), p. 461

[2]<u>Ibid</u>., p. 461.

TO FOOTNOTE

1. Type to the first reference number
   or
   place cursor at the location of the first reference number.
2. Press **Ctrl + F7**........ `Ctrl` + `F7`
3. Select **F**...................................... `F`
4. Select **C**...................................... `C`
   (A blank screen appears with the reference number.)
5. Type footnote information.
6. Press **F7**.................................. `F7`
   to return to document.

FOOTNOTING/ENDNOTING

Notes:

- In this exercise, you will create endnotes.

- Type until you reach the reference number, then access the footnote feature. A blank screen with the first note number will appear. Then press the indent key once before typing the endnote information.

- The endnote feature requires additional steps to make the endnote information print on a separate page. Follow the keystroke procedures carefully.

Exercise Directions:

1. Start with a clear screen.

2. Create the report on the right in <u>double space</u>. Begin on Ln 2".

3. Use the preset margins.

4. Justify (for WP5.0) or full justify (for WP5.1) the document.

5. Use the <u>endnote</u> feature at each reference number.

6. Spell check the exercise.

7. View your document.

8. Print one copy.

9. Save the exercise; name it **COMPUTER.**

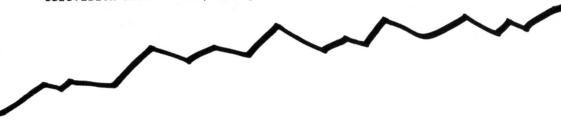

COMPUTERS **AND** TERMINALS

"A computer is an electronic or mechanical device used to perform high speed arithmetic and logical operations."[1] A computer system is composed of a computer (or computers) together with peripheral equipment such as disk drives, printers and terminals. "A terminal is an electronic device used by a person to send or receive information from a computer system."[2]

A terminal usually consists of a keyboard connected to a television monitor and/or a printer.

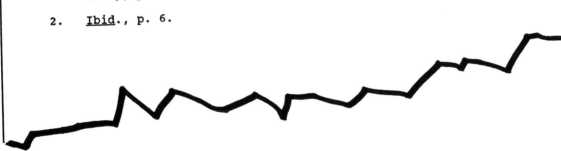

1. David Chandler, <u>Dialing for Data</u>, (New York: Random House 1984), p. 5.

2. <u>Ibid.</u>, p. 6.

TO ENDNOTE

1. Type to the first reference number
   or
   place cursor at the location of the first reference number.
2. Press **Ctrl + F7**.........**Ctrl** + **F7**
3. Select **E**.....................................**E**
4. Select **C**.....................................**C**
   (A blank screen appears with endnote number.)
5. Press **F4** (Indent).......................**F4**

6. Type endnote information.
7. Press **F7**.....................................**F7**
   to exit endnote screen.

   • Repeat Steps 1-7 for each endnote.

TO PLACE ENDNOTES ON SEPA-RATE PAGE:

8. Press **PgDn**..........................**Pg Dn**
   to place cursor at end of text.
9. Press **Ctrl + ENTER**....**Ctrl** + **↵**

10. Press **Ctrl + F7**............**Ctrl** + **F7**
11. Select **P**.......................................**P**
12. Select **N**.......................................**N**
    (endnote placement code appears followed by HPg)
13. Press **Backspace**............**Backspace**
    to delete last hard page so WordPerfect won't try to print a third, blank page.

MULTIPLE-PAGE DOCUMENTS: Creating a Report with HEADERS/FOOTERS/PAGE NUMBERS

Notes:

- A **header** is the same text appearing at the top of every page or every other one, while a **footer** is the same text appearing at the bottom of every or every other page.

- After typing the desired header or footer once, WordPerfect's header/footer feature will automatically insert it on every page or on specific pages of your document.

- The header is usually defaulted to print six lines (or 1") down from the top of the page; the footer is usually defaulted to print at 1" from the bottom of the page. However, the header/footer printing line may be changed, if desired.

- You can create up to two headers and two footers in a document (Header/Footer A and Header/Footer B).

- Headers, footers and page numbers usually appear on the second and succeeding pages of a report; they generally do not appear on the first page.

- Headers, footers and page numbers do not display on the screen but can be seen by "viewing" your document.

- On multiple-page documents, it is necessary to include page numbers. WordPerfect's page numbering feature will allow you to insert page numbers and indicate where on the printed page the page number should appear: upper or lower corner (left or right), centered on top or bottom of the page, on odd or even pages.

- If you plan to insert a header on the left side of your pages, insert page numbers on the top right side or bottom of your pages. Be sure that your header/footer text does not overlap or appear too close to the page number.

- Headers, footers and page numbers may be inserted after the document is typed.

communities without appreciating the nature of the
world these newcomers left."[2]

The rate of people leaving Ireland was extremely
high in the late 1840s and early 1850s due to
overpopulation and to the potato famine of 1846. "By
1850, there were almost one million Irish Catholics in
the United States, especially clustered in New York and
Massachusetts."[3]

Germans left their homeland d

Exercise Directions:

1. Start with a clear screen.

2. Create the report on the next page in <u>double space</u> (set DS where the body of the report begins) using the <u>footnote</u>, <u>header</u> with <u>page number</u> features. Begin the exercise on Ln. 2".

3. Set left and right margins for 1.5".

4. Unjustify the document (for WP5.0); (left justify for WP5.1).

5. Allow WordPerfect to break your pages (soft page breaks).

6. <u>Include the header, COMING TO AMERICA, and page number at the beginning of the document,</u> **<u>but suppress header and page number on the first page.</u>**

7. View your document.

8. Spell check the exercise.

9. Print one copy.

10. Save the exercise; name it **VOYAGE.**

NOTE: The exercise is illustrated in single space, but you are directed to set double space. Therefore, your printed document will result in three pages, and footnotes will appear on the same pages as reference numbers.

continued...

IMMIGRATION TO THE UNITED STATES
IN THE NINETEENTH CENTURY

The United States is sometimes called the "Nation of Immigrants" because it has received more immigrants than any other country in history. During the first one hundred years of US history, the nation had no immigration laws. Immigration began to climb during the 1830s. "Between 1830-1840, 44% of the immigrants came from Ireland, 30% came from Germany, 15% came from Great Britain, and the remainder came from other European countries."[1]

The movement to America of millions of immigrants in the century after the 1820s was not simply a flight of impoverished peasants abandoning underdeveloped, backward regions for the riches and unlimited opportunities offered by the American economy. People did not move randomly to America but emanated from very specific regions at specific times in the nineteenth and twentieth centuries. "It is impossible to understand even the nature of American immigrant communities without appreciating the nature of the world these newcomers left."[2]

The rate of people leaving Ireland was extremely high in the late 1840s and early 1850s due to overpopulation and to the potato famine of 1846. "By 1850, there were almost one million Irish Catholics in the United States, especially clustered in New York and Massachusetts."[3]

Germans left their homeland due to severe depression, unemployment, political unrest, and the failure of the liberal revolutionary movement. It was not only the poor people who left their countries, but those in the middle and lower-middle levels of their social structures also left. "Those too poor could seldom afford to go, and the very wealthy had too much of a stake in the homelands to depart."[4]

Many immigrants came to America as a result of the lure of new land, in part, the result of the attraction of the frontier. America was in a very real sense the last frontier--a land of diverse peoples that, even under the worst conditions, maintained a way of life that permitted more freedom of belief and action than was held abroad. "While this perception was not entirely based in reality, it was the conviction that was often held in Europe and that became part of the ever-present American Dream."[5]

---

[1]Lewis Paul Todd and Merle Curti, _Rise of the American National_ (New York: Harcourt Brace Jovanovich, Inc., 1972), p. 297.

[2]Bodner, John, _The Transplanted_ (Bloomington: Indiana University Press, 1985), p. 54.

[3]E. Allen Richardson, _Strangers in This Land_ (New York: The Pilgrim Press, 1988), p. 6.

[4]_Ibid._, p. 13.

[5]_Ibid._, p. 72.

TO CREATE HEADERS/ FOOTERS

1. Place cursor at the beginning of document.
2. Press **Shift + F8**...... `Shift` + `F8`
3. Select **P**...........................`P`
4. Select **H**(Header).......................`H`

   or

   or F (Footer)..............................`F`
5. Indicate the header/footer to be created:

   - Select **A** `A` and/or **B** `B`
6. Select how often header or footer will occur:

   - Type **P** (Every Page)...............`P`

   or

   or - Type **O** (Odd Pages)...............`O`

   or

   or - Type **V** (Even Pages)..............`V`
7. Type header/footer text.
   (If extra space is desired between header/footer and text, press **ENTER** for each extra line after typing the header or before typing the footer.)
8. Press **F7**...................................`F7`
   to exit header and return to format menu.

TO SUPPRESS HEADER/FOOTER/ PAGE NUMBER ON FIRST PAGE:

9. Select **U** (suppress this page only)....................................`U`
10. Select **A** (all)............................`A`
11. Press **F7**...................................`F7`
    to return to format menu
12. Press **F7**...................................`F7`
    to return to document.

TO INSERT PAGE NUMBERS

1. Place cursor at beginning of document or page.
2. Press **Shift + F8**...... `Shift` + `F8`
3. Select **P**...................................`P`
4. **WORDPERFECT 5.0 USERS:**
   - Select **P**...........................`P`

   WORDPERFECT 5.1 USERS:
   - Select **N**...........................`N`
   - Select **P**...........................`P`
5. Select a placement option:
   1 (top left)
   2 (top center)
   3 (top right)
   4 (top, alternating left/right)
   5 (bottom left)
   6 (bottom center)
   7 (bottom right every page)
   8 (bottom, alternating left/right)
6. Press **F7**...................................`F7`
   to return to document.

MULTIPLE-PAGE DOCUMENTS: Creating a Report with HEADERS/FOOTERS/PAGE NUMBERS; WIDOW/ORPHAN PROTECTION

Notes:

- In this exercise, you will prepare a report with footnotes, a header and page numbers that are centered at the bottom of the second and succeeding pages.

- When a quotation is longer than two sentences, it is single spaced and indented. In this exercise, you will indent the quoted material as directed.

- Sometimes after a multiple-page document is created, you may discover that the last line of a paragraph is printed by itself at the top of a page. This is called a **widow** line. Or, you may discover that the first line of a paragraph appears by itself on the last line of the page. This is called an **orphan** line. Widow and orphan lines should be avoided. WordPerfect contains a "widow/orphan line" protection feature to eliminate widows and orphans in a document.

Exercise Directions:

1. Start with a clear screen.

2. Create the report on the right in <u>double space</u> (set DS where the body of the report begins) using the <u>footnote</u>, <u>header</u> and <u>page numbering</u> features. Begin the exercise on Ln 2".

3. Set left and right margins for 1.5".

4. Unjustify the document (for WP5.0); (left justify for WP5.1).

5. Turn widow/orphan protection on.

6. Use the left/right indent feature and single space for indented text.

7. Allow WordPerfect to break your pages (soft page breaks).

8. <u>Include the header, BUILDING THE U.S.A. at the beginning of the document, but **suppress header and page number on the first page.**</u> Include page numbers at the bottom center of the second and succeeding pages.

9. View your document.

10. Spell check the exercise.

11. Print one copy.

12. Save the exercise; name it **USA.**

    NOTE: The exercise is illustrated in single space, but you are directed to set double space. Therefore, your printed document will result in three pages, and footnotes will appear on the same pages as reference numbers.

IMMIGRATION'S IMPACT IN THE UNITED STATES

The opportunity to directly transfer a skill into the American economy was great for newcomers prior to the 1880s. "Coal-mining and steel-producing companies in the East, railroads, gold- and silver-mining interests in the West, and textile mills in New England all sought a variety of ethnic groups as potential sources of inexpensive labor."[1] Because immigrants were eager to work, they contributed to the wealth of the growing nation. During the 1830s, American textile mills welcomed hand-loom weavers from England and North Ireland whose jobs had been displaced by power looms. It was this migration that established the fine-cotton-goods trade of Philadelphia. "Nearly the entire English silk industry migrated to America after the Civil War, when high American tariffs allowed the industry to prosper on this side of the Atlantic."[2]

Whether immigrants were recruited directly for their abilities or followed existing networks into unskilled jobs, they inevitably moved within groups of friends and relatives and worked and lived in clusters.

As the Industrial Revolution progressed, immigrants were enticed to come to the United States through the mills and factories who sent representatives overseas to secure cheap labor. An example was the Amoskeag Manufacturing Company, located along the banks of the Merrimack River in Manchester, New Hampshire. In the 1870s, the Amoskeag Company recruited women from Scotland who were expert gingham weavers. Agreements were set specifying a fixed period of time during which employees would guarantee to work for the company.[3]

In the 1820s, Irish immigrants did most of the hard work in building the canals in the United States. In fact, Irish immigrants played a large role in building the Erie Canal. American contractors encouraged Irish immigrants to come to the United States to work on the roads, canals, and railroads, and manufacturers lured them into the new mills and factories.

"Most German immigrants settled in the middle western states of Ohio, Indiana, Illinois, Wisconsin and Missouri."[4] With encouragement to move west from the Homestead Act of 1862, which offered public land free to immigrants who intended to become citizens, German immigrants comprised a large portion of the pioneers moving west. "They were masterful farmers and they built prosperous farms."[5]

---

[1]E. Allen Richardson, Strangers in This Land (New York: The Pilgrim Press, 1988), p. 67

[2]John Bodnar, The Transplanted (Bloomington: Indiana University Press, 1985), p. 54

[3]Ibid., p. 72.

[4]David A. Gerber, The Making of An American Pluralism (Chicago: University of Illinois, 1989), p. 124.

[5]Bodnar, op. cit., p. 86.

TO TURN WIDOW/ORPHAN PROTECTION ON

1. Place cursor at the beginning of the document.
2. Press **Shift + F8**....... Shift + F8
3. Select **L**............ L
4. Select **W**............ W
5. Select **Y**............ Y
6. Press **F7**............ F7

MOVING TEXT FROM ONE PAGE TO ANOTHER

Notes:

- The procedure for moving blocks of text from one page to another is the same as moving blocks of text on the same page. However, if text is to be moved from page one to another, the "go to" key (Ctrl + Home) may be used to quickly advance to the page where the text is to be reinserted.

- If a hard page break was inserted, delete the break, then move the text. WordPerfect will then insert a soft page break. If the soft page break is not in a satisfactory location, insert a hard page break in a desired location.

- After you move the paragraph in this exercise, it may be necessary to move the second-page heading appropriately.

Exercise Directions:

1. Start with a clear screen.
2. Retrieve **PREVIEW.**
3. Make the indicated revisions.
4. Using the thesaurus, replace words marked in brackets. Be sure replacement words maintain the same tense/endings as original words.
5. Print one copy.
6. Resave the file.

←——————————————————— Today's date

REGISTERED MAIL

Ms. Elizabeth DeKan
Broward College
576 Southfield Road
Marietta, Ga 30068

Dear Ms. DeKan:

<u>Subject</u>: Educational Films for High Schools and Colleges

Thank you for your interest in the films that we have available
for high school and college students. We are pleased to send you
the enclosed flyer which describes the films in detail. Also
enclosed is a ⟨summary⟩ of those films that have recently been
added to our collection since the publication of the flyer.

There have been many positive reactions to our films. Just three
weeks ago, a group of educators, editors and vocational experts
was invited to view the films at the annual EDUCATORS' CON-
FERENCE.   Here are some of their comments:

Move to next page Ⓐ We will be sure to send the films in time for you to preview
them. Please be sure to list the date on which you wish to
preview the film.

Insert Ⓑ Mr. William R. Bondlow, Jr., president of the National Vocational
Center in Washington, D.C. and editor-in-chief of <u>Science Care-
ers</u>, said,

> I like the films very much. They are in-
> novative and a great benefit to all those
> interested in the earth sciences as a profes-
> sional career. Furthermore, they have cap-
> tured the objects on film so true to life
> that anyone watching them is captivated.

Ⓒ Ms. Andra Burke, a ⟨leading⟩ expert presently assigned to the
United States Interior Department, praised the films by saying
that,

move to next page

continued...

Ms. Elizabeth DeKan
Page 2
Today's date

Insert ⓒ →

They are a major educational advance in career placement, which will serve as a source
of motivation for all future geologists.

Move to previous page →

A member of the National Education Center, Dr. Lawrence Pilgrim,
also liked the films and said,

Ⓑ   I will institute a program which will make
schools throughout the country aware of their
vocational potential.

These are just some of the (reactions) we have had to our films.
We know you will have a similar reaction.

INSERT Ⓐ →

We would very much like to send you the films that you would like
during the summer session. ~~You can use the summer to review
them.~~ It is important that your request be received ⟨quickly⟩
since the demand for the films is great, particularly during the
summer sessions, ~~at colleges and universities throughout the
country.~~

Cordially,

William DeVane
Executive Vice President
Marketing Department

wd/yo
Enclosures (2)

Copy to Robert R. Redford
       Nancy Jackson

TO MOVE TEXT FROM ONE PAGE TO ANOTHER USING "GO TO"

- a sentence/paragraph/page

1. Place cursor on the first character of text to be moved.
2. Press **Ctrl + F4**.......... `Ctrl` + `F4`
3. Select:

   S (Sentence).......................`S`

   or

   P (Paragraph).....................`P`

   or

   A (Page)...............................`A`
4. Select **M** (Move)......................`M`
5. Press **Ctrl + Home**.. `Ctrl` + `Home`

6. Type **page number** where text is to be reinserted.
7. **ENTER**.....................................`↵`
8. Place cursor where text is to be reinserted.
9. **ENTER**.....................................`↵`

- a block of text

1. Place cursor on first character of text to be moved.
2. Press **Alt + F4**.............. `Alt` + `F4`

   or **F12** (enhanced keyboard).........`F12`
3. Using cursor arrow keys, highlight text to be moved.

   * (See page 27 for other highlighting methods.)

4. Press **Ctrl + F4**............ `Ctrl` + `F4`
5. Select **B** (Block).........................`B`
6. Select **M** (Move).........................`M`
7. Press **Ctrl + Home**... `Ctrl` + `Home`
8. Type **page number** where text is to be reinserted.
9. **ENTER**.....................................`↵`
10. Place cursor where text is to be reinserted.
11. **ENTER**.....................................`↵`

TO "GO TO"

1. Press **Ctrl + Home**... `Ctrl` + `Home`
2. Type **page number**.
3. **ENTER**.....................................`↵`

MOVING TEXT FROM ONE PAGE TO ANOTHER

Notes:

- Moving paragraphs in this exercise will not affect footnote placement. WordPerfect will automatically readjust footnote placement.

Exercise Directions:

1. Start with a clear screen.
2. Retrieve **USA.**
3. Make the indicated revisions.
4. Using the thesaurus, replace words marked in brackets. Be sure replacement words maintain the same tense/endings as original words.
5. Print one copy.
6. Resave the file.

(justify and hyphenate entire document)

BOLD ←

IMMIGRATION'S IMPACT IN THE UNITED STATES

The opportunity to directly transfer a skill into the American economy was great for newcomers prior to the 1880s. *(Single space and indent quote)* Coal-mining and steel-producing companies in the East, railroads, gold- and silver-mining interests in the West, and textile mills in New England all sought a variety of ethnic groups as potential sources of inexpensive labor.[1] Because immigrants were eager to work, they contributed to the wealth of the growing nation. During the 1830s, American textile mills welcomed hand-loom weavers from England and North Ireland whose jobs had been displaced by power looms. It was this migration that established the fine-cotton-goods trade of Philadelphia. "Nearly the entire English silk industry migrated to America after the Civil War, when high American tariffs allowed the industry to prosper on this side of the Atlantic."[2]

Insert Ⓐ → Whether immigrants were recruited directly for

---

[1]E. Allen Richardson, Strangers in This Land (New York: The Pilgrim Press, 1988), p. 67.

[2]John Bodnar, The Transplanted (Bloomington: Indiana University Press, 1985), p. 54.

continued...

BUILDING THE U.S.A.

their abilities or followed existing networks into

unskilled jobs, they inevitably moved within⟨groups⟩of

friends and relatives and worked and lived in clusters.

> As the Industrial Revolution progressed,
> immigrants were enticed to come to the United
> States through the mills and factories who
> sent representatives overseas to secure cheap
> labor. An example was the Amoskeag
> Manufacturing Company, located along the
> banks of the Merrimack river in Manchester,
> New Hampshire. In the 1870s, the Amoskeag
> Company recruited women from Scotland who
> were expert gingham weavers. Agreements were
> set specifying a fixed period of time during
> which employees would guarantee to work for
> the company.[3]

(A)   In the 1820s, Irish immigrants did most of the

hard work in building the canals in the United States.

In fact, Irish immigrants played a large role in

building the Erie Canal. American contractors

[move to page 1]

encouraged Irish immigrants to come to the United

States to work on the roads, canals, and railroads, and

manufacturers⟨lured⟩them into the new mills and

factories.

"Most German immigrants settled in the middle

western states of Ohio, Indiana, Illinois, Wisconsin

and Missouri."[4] With encouragement to move west from

the Homestead Act of 1862, which offered public land

---

[3]_Ibid_., p. 72.

[4]David A. Gerber, _The Making of An American Pluralism_
(Chicago: University of Illinois, 1989), p. 124.

continued…

BUILDING THE U.S.A.

free to immigrants who intended to become citizens,
German immigrants ⟨comprised⟩ a large portion of the
pioneers moving west. "They were masterful farmers and
they built prosperous farms."[5]

---

[5]Bodnar, op. cit., p. 86.

USING SUPERSCRIPTS AND SUBSCRIPTS

Notes:

- **Superscripts** are characters that are printed a half-line above the normal typing line; **subscripts** are characters that are printed a half-line below the normal typing line.

- Superscripts and subscripts are commonly used in mathematical and scientific formulas. Superscripts are also used in footnoting.

- WordPerfect's footnote feature automatically creates the superscript when footnoting. Therefore, in order to raise or lower a character for any other purpose, it is necessary to use the superscript/subscript feature.

- Superscripts/subscripts do not display above or below the line on the screen. However, they will print (providing your printer supports this feature), and/or you may use the "view" feature to see them.

- If possible, single spacing should not be used when using superscripts/subscripts, because the characters will interfere with the lines above or below.

Exercise Directions:

1. Start with a clear screen.

2. Create the report on the right in <u>double space</u> (set DS where the body of the report begins) using the superscript and subscript features. Begin the exercise on Ln 2".

3. Set left and right margins for 1.5".

4. Justify the document (for WP5.0); (full justify for WP5.1).

5. Include a **bold**, flush right header, **SUPER-SCRIPT/SUBSCRIPT**, at the beginning of the document, but **suppress header and page number on the first page.**

6. View your document.

7. Spell check the exercise.

8. Print one copy.

9. Save the exercise; name it **UPNDOWN.**

USING SUPERSCRIPTS AND SUBSCRIPTS
IN ALGEBRA AND CHEMISTRY

Superscripts and subscripts are commonly used in mathematical equations and scientific formulas. In algebra, superscripts are primarily used, while in science, subscripts are primarily used. Let's look at a few examples.

Multiplication in Algebra - **Superscripts**

Multiplication in algebra is usually demonstrated by writing two or more expressions together without a multiplication symbol. Example: a x b is written *ab*. Sometimes you may see a formula that is written ab^4. The little, raised number is called the **exponent**. It indicates the number of times a quantity is multiplied by itself. Therefore, a x a is written a^2. This is called the square of a. It means that "a" is multiplied by itself. If you wanted to multiply a x a x a, the formula would be written a^3. This is called the cube of "a". If you wanted to multiply a x a x a x a, the formula would be written as a^4. A typical formula used to multiply an expression consisting of two or more terms by a single term or expression would look like this: $(5b^2c+2d)(3bd)$.

Chemical Compounds in Chemistry - **Subscripts**

In chemistry, chemical compounds have common names and are also represented by a formula. Many of the common names of chemical compounds are so familiar to us, yet the compound name sounds so scientific. For example, water is a chemical compound with which we are probably the most familiar. Its common name is "water" and it is represented by the formula H_2O. Laughing gas is another common name of a chemical compound. Its compound name is nitrous oxide and is represented by the formula N_2O. Baking soda, or sodium bicarbonate, is represented by the formula $NaHCo_3$. A compound which is not as familiar is ammonium hydroxide. However, when we look at the common name, it really is one we might have used: ammonia water. It is represented by the formula NH_4OH. Since you probably have used some of the compounds mentioned, you may be a chemist and not even know it!

TO SET SUPERSCRIPT/ SUBSCRIPT

1. Place cursor where **superscript/subscript** is to be inserted.
2. Press **Ctrl + F8**............ **Ctrl** + **F8**
3. Press **S**.................................**S**

4. Press **P** (superscript)................. **P**
   or
   or B (subscript).......................... **B**
5. Type text to be super/subscripted.
6. Press **Right Arrow**...................... **➡**
   to revert to normal text.

Lesson 6
Summary Exercise A

Exercise Directions:

1. Create a two-page letter from the document below in any style.
2. Use the preset margins; send the letter SPECIAL DELIVERY and include an appropriate subject line.
3. Tab and indent the enumerated items.
4. Unjustify (for WP5.0);(left justify for WP5.1) and hyphenate your document.
5. Spell check the exercise.
6. Print one copy.
7. Save the exercise; name it **CHOICES**.

Today's date/Ms. Tricia P. Blane/40 East 78 Street/New York, NY 10035/Dear Ms. Blane://I have received your letter requesting advice on how to make a wise decision in your purchase of a personal computer.//There are many factors you must consider when you are ready to purchase a PC, but those outlined below are the most significant://1. **The Microprocessor** - The heart of the machine is the microprocessor which is the most critical component to consider. The microprocessor controls the speed with which the computer responds. Certain software requires a specific speed to run. Therefore, you must decide what software you want to run and then ask the salesperson for a computer whose microprocessor will run your desired software.//2. **Random Access Memory** - Certain software programs require a certain amount of working memory, or RAM to operate; one megabyte is practically a minimum these days, and the smallest hard disk available is usually about 40 megabytes.//3. **The Screen & Graphics Card** - The color screens of a few years ago were difficult to view when doing word processing. But the color screens today are excellent and are a must if you intend to do desktop publishing or other graphics applications. An important factor in selecting a graphics card is their resolution, that is, how many dots make up the display on the screen vertically and horizontally. A VGA card, or "video graphics adaptor" generally displays 800 dots horizontally and 600 dots vertically. But you can purchase graphics cards with higher resolution, giving you 1,024 horizontal and 768 vertical dots.// You do realize, of course, that the cost of a computer depends upon the quality of the parts you assemble. Be sure to go to a reliable vendor. You might get a better price from a mail-order retailer, but if you need service -- you might have a problem.//I am enclosing an article from a recent PC magazine which compares several models. Stop by my office any time and I will show you my computer. I might also suggest that you try out different varieties. The more research you do, the better qualified you will be to make a purchasing decision.//Sincerely,/Rose Jaffe/Consultant/rj:yo/enclosure/copy to: Jabar Hammond, Paul Salow.

Lesson 6
Summary Exercise B

Exercise Directions:

1. Create the report below inserting footnotes where indicated.
2. Use left and right margins of 1.5".
3. Include a header, **LABOR IN COLONIAL AMERICA,** and a page number on the second and succeeding pages--in any style.

4. Justify your document.
5. Turn widow/orphan protection on.
6. Print one copy.
7. Save the exercise; name it **NUWORLD.**

LABOR IN COLONIAL AMERICA//Labor was a key issue in colonial America. The American labor force consisted of indentured servants, redemptioners from Europe, slaves from Africa and the colonists themselves.//Indentured servants were the first source of foreign labor to arrive in the new world. Scores came from England between 1698 and 1700. "Out of 3,257 people who left for America, 918 of them were on their way to Maryland, a major port of indentured servants and redemptioners."[1]//The new world offered much to the Europeans. Most European laborers desired the political and economic freedoms of America. The British capitalists offered those who wanted to come to America, but could not afford it, the opportunity to do so by having them agree to surrender a portion of their life to work as a laborer in return for having those expenses paid. This was the beginning of indentured servants.//Why were people so willing to enter into a life of servitude in a new country? Conditions in Europe during this period were poor. Political and economic problems existed. People were lured to the new world by its promise for religious freedom and an opportunity for a better life.//The colonists realized that in the development of a new country, labor is the most important element of production. They recognized the importance of a good labor supply. Because the supply of good white servants infrequently met the demand, more than half of all persons who came to America, south of England, were servants.//The contract of servitude was simple. Europeans who were unable to pay their own passage across the Atlantic become bond servants for a period of years to some colonial master who paid for them. "It was a legal contract by which the servant bound himself to serve the master in such employments as the master might assign for a given length of time usually in a specified plantation."[2] The contract included other clauses. A more skilled worker might collect wages and also be excluded from field labor. Education was included in a child's indenture. "Four years for each adult was the average time of servitude. Children usually worked until they were 21."[3]// Servitude was cruel; it subjected large numbers of people to a hard, laborious, and dangerous way of life. Many who came found the work too difficult; they were not ready for this type of life. "In the first few years, it killed fifty or seventy-five out of every hundred."[4]

---

[1]Emerson Smith, Colonists in Bondage, (New York: Holt Rinehart and Winston, Inc., 1975), p. 308.

[2]Ibid., p. 45.

[3]Ibid., p. 47.

[4]Percy Brackson and John Falcon, History of Agriculture in Northern United States, (New York: Alfred A. Knopf, Inc., 1974), p. 117.

> ### LESSON 7:
> MERGING; PREPARING ENVELOPES; DOCUMENT ASSEMBLY;
> APPENDING TEXT; CREATING MACROS.

MERGING TEXT - PREPARING THE <u>PRIMARY</u> FILE

Notes:

- WordPerfect's merge function allows the user to mass produce personalized documents by combining a form letter or other documents with a list of names and addresses and/or other variable information. Therefore, if you wanted to send the same letter or other documents to many different people, you would only need to type the document once, type a name and address list once and have WordPerfect print the letter with each individual name and address, making it appear as though each letter was personally typed.

- The merge function combines a **primary file** which contains text and merge codes, with the **secondary file**, which contains names and addresses and/or other variable information.

- The **primary file** contains information that does not change. Codes are inserted where the variable information will be placed. (Variable information contains text that will change from letter to letter.) In a typical letter, the variable information would include the inside address and the salutation.

- Each variable must be identified. This identifier is called a **field**. Each field is referenced either by number or name. In this exercise, the fields will be referenced by number.

- In the example below, the inside address and salutation are divided into fields, with each one given a number. The illustration below left indicates how fields display on the screen after the codes are entered in WordPerfect 5.0, while the illustration below right shows the screen display in WordPerfect 5.1. The first field will contain the "title," the second field will contain the "first name," the third field will contain the "last name," the fourth field will contain the "address," the fifth field will contain the "city," the sixth field will contain the "state," and the seventh field will contain the "zip."

WP50:	WP51:
Today's Date	Today's Date
^F1^ ^F2^ ^F3^	{FIELD}1~ {FIELD}2~ {FIELD}3~
^F4^	{FIELD}4~
^F5^ ^F6^ ^F7^	FIELD}5~, {FIELD}6~ {FIELD}7~
Dear ^F1^ ^F3^:	Dear {FIELD}1~ {FIELD}3~:

- As you enter each field, space between the fields as you would want the spacing to appear when text is inserted in the letter.

- The same field number can be inserted in the letter as many times as desired. Note that ^F1^ and ^F3^ are used twice since the letter contains two occurrences of someone's title and last name.

Exercise Directions:

1. Start with a clear screen.

2. Create a primary file from the letter on the right, inserting a code for each field. Begin on Ln. 2.5".

3. Unjustify the document **(for WP5.0)**; (Left justify for **WP5.1**).

4. Spell check the exercise.

5. Print one copy. (On your printout, hand write a label for each field code with the actual field name.)

6. Save the exercise; name it **INVITE.PF**.

```
Today's date


^F1^ ^F2^ ^F3^
^F4^
^F5^, ^F6^  ^F7^

Dear ^F1^ ^F3^:

You are cordially invited to attend our annual spring fashion
show.  The show will take place at the Plaza Hotel in New York
City on Friday evening, June 22 at 7:30 p.m.  Refreshments will
be served.

We appreciate your contributions and continued support of the
Fashion Institute.  We know you will see several outstanding
collections at the showing.  Please let me know if you plan to
attend by calling my office any day between 9 a.m. and 5 p.m.

We are looking forward to your attending this special event.

Sincerely,


Thomas Mann
President
Fashion Institute

tm/yo
```

TO CREATE A PRIMARY FILE AND SAVE

1. Place cursor where field is to be placed.
2. Press **Shift + F9**..... **Shift** + **F9**
3. Select **F**..................................... **F**
4. Type field number.
5. **ENTER**.................................... ↵
6. Repeat steps 1-5 for each field.
7. Type remainder of document.
8. Press **F7**.................................. **F7**
9. Type **Y**..................................... **Y**
10. Type document name.
11. **ENTER**.................................. ↵
12. **ENTER**.................................. ↵

MERGING TEXT - Preparing the <u>Secondary</u> File

Notes:

• In this exercise, you will create a secondary file. The secondary file will contain the inside addresses and salutations of those people who will be receiving the letter created in the primary file. A secondary file may contain many **records.** A record is a collection of related information. In this exercise, a record would be the inside address and salutation of one person. The information in each record is divided into "fields." **The fields used in the primary file MUST match the information used in the secondary file.** An example of one record in a secondary file appears below. The illustration on the left shows how field information is displayed on the screen in WordPerfect 5.0, while the illustration on the right shows the screen display in WordPerfect 5.1. Note that the information for each field matches the fields used in the primary file. Notice, too, that the comma used after the city was inserted in the primary file. It should not be entered again in the secondary file. Otherwise, two commas will result when the documents are merged. After the secondary file is created, it must be saved.

	WP5.0	WP5.1
Field Names		
TITLE -	Mr.^R	Mr. {END FIELD}
FIRST -	John ^R	John {END FIELD}
LAST -	Smith^R	Smith {END FIELD}
ADDRESS -	405 West End Avenue^R	405 West End Avenue {END FIELD}
CITY -	New York^R	New York {END FIELD}
STATE -	NY^R	NY {END FIELD}
ZIP -	10087^R	10087 {END FIELD}
END OF RECORD -	^E	{END RECORD}

• In the next exercise, you will merge the secondary file with the primary file.

Exercise Directions:

1. Start with a clear screen.
2. Create a secondary file from the records on the right. Begin on Ln. 1".
3. Check to see that the fields used in the primary file are the same as those used in the secondary file.
4. Save the exercise; name it **INVITE.SF** .

```
Mr.^R
Peter^R
Ringler^R
23 Preston Avenue^R
Bellemore^R
NY^R
11010^R
^E
===============================================================
Mr.^R
Fred^R
LeBost^R
98-67 Kew Gardens Road^R
Forest Hills^R
NY^R
11432^R
^E
===============================================================
Ms.^R
Mary^R
McClean^R
765 Belmill Road^R
Roslyn^R
NY^R
11577^R
^E
===============================================================
Ms.^R
Lorraine^R
Oelser^R
1275 Broadway^R
New York^R
NY^R
10028^R
^E
```

TO CREATE A SECONDARY FILE AND SAVE

1. Type data for first merge field.
2. Press **F9** (End Field)................ `F9`
3. Repeat Steps 1 and 2 for each field.
4. After all fields are entered:
   Press **Shift + F9**..... `Shift` + `F9`
5. Select **E**.................................... `E`
   to end record.
   NOTE: This will insert a page break.

6. Repeat steps 1-5 for each record.
7. Press **F7**.................................... `F7`
8. Type **Y**...................................... `Y`
9. Type document name.
10. **ENTER**.................................... `↵`
11. **ENTER**.................................... `↵`

MERGING TEXT - Merging the Primary and Secondary Files

Notes:

- If the primary and secondary files do not merge properly, then compare the primary and secondary files to see that the fields used in the primary file have information that matches the fields used in the secondary file.

- The final merged document will appear as separate pages, each page representing each record. This document may be saved under its own file name. This is particularly helpful if you wish to edit individual documents. For example, a P.S. notation might be added to selected letters through this process.

- It is also possible to print selected records rather than all the records contained in the secondary file. This feature will not be covered in these exercises.

WP5.0:	**Example:** Primary File ^F1^ ^F2^ ^F3^ ^F4^ ^F5^ ^F6^ ^F7^, ^F8^ ^F9^ Dear ^F1^ ^F3^: Thank you, ^F1^ ^F3^, for	**Example:** Secondary File Mr.^R Anthony^R Salazar^R Marketing Dept^R DDC^R 14 East 38th St.^R New York^R NY^R 10016^R ^E	**Merged Record** Mr. Anthony Salazar Marketing Dept. Dictation Disc Co. 14 East 38th Street New York, NY 10016 Dear Mr. Salazar: Thank you, Mr. Salazar, for ...
WP5.1:	**Example:** Primary File {FIELD}1˜ {FIELD}2˜ {FIELD}3˜ {FIELD}4˜ {FIELD}5˜ {FIELD}6˜ {FIELD}7˜ {FIELD}8˜ {FIELD}9˜ Dear {FIELD}1˜ {FIELD}3˜: Thank you,{FIELD}1˜{FIELD}3˜, for ...	**Example:** Secondary File Mr.{END FIELD} Anthony{END FIELD} Salazar{END FIELD} Marketing Dept.{END FIELD} Tri-Star Music Inc.{END FIELD} 2121 Cypress Lane{END FIELD} Yonkers{END FIELD} NY{END FIELD} 10312{END FIELD} {END RECORD}	**Merged Record** Mr. Anthony Salazar Marketing Dept. Tri-Star Music Inc. 2121 Cypress Lane Yonkers, NY 10312 Dear Mr. Salazar: Thank you, Mr. Salazar, for ...

Exercise Directions:

1. Start with a clear screen.

2. Merge the primary file **INVITE.PF** with the secondary file, **INVITE.SF**.

3. Print the full document (one copy of each merged letter.)

4. Save the merged letters under a new document name: **INVITE.FI**

TO MERGE A PRIMARY AND SECONDARY FILE

1. Press **Ctrl + F9**............ `Ctrl` + `F9`
2. Select **M**.. `M`
3. Type name of primary file.
4. **ENTER**.. `↵`
5. Type name of secondary file.
6. **ENTER**.. `↵`

   NOTE: The merged document will appear on the screen.

MERGING TEXT - Creating a <u>Primary</u> File

Notes:

• In this exercise, you will create a primary file containing more variables than in the previous exercise. Note that the same field number is assigned to variables that will contain the same information.

Exercise Directions:

1. Start with a clear screen.

2. Create a primary file from the letter on the right, inserting a code for each field. Begin on Ln. 2.5".

3. Unjustify the document (for WP5.0); (left justify for WP5.1)

4. Spell check the exercise.

5. Print one copy. (On your printout, hand write a label for each field code with the actual field name.)

6. Save the exercise; name it **DUE.PF.**

                              Today's Date

^F1^ ^F2^ ^F3^
^F4^
^F5^, ^F6^ ^F7^

Dear ^F1^ ^F3^:

Just a brief reminder, ^F1^ ^F3^, that your account is now past
due. As you can see from the enclosed statement, you still have
an outstanding balance of $^F8^ which was due on ^F9^.

We need your cooperation so that we can continue to give you the
service we have provided you for many years.

Please mail your remittance for $^F8^ today, so we are not forced
to send your account to our collection agency.

                              Cordially,

                              Brenda Nadia
                              Collection Manager

bn/yo
Enclosure

MERGING TEXT - Creating a <u>Secondary</u> File

Notes:

- When creating a secondary file where fields are used more than once, it is not necessary to repeat the variable information. In this exercise, for example, WordPerfect will insert the information that relates to ^F1^,^F3^ and ^F8^ in the appropriate place during the merge process.

Exercise Directions:

1. Start with a clear screen.

2. Create a secondary file from the records on the right. Begin on Ln. 1."

3. Check to see that the fields used in the primary file are the same as those used in the secondary file.

4. Save the exercise; name it **DUE.SF**.

```
Ms.^R
Vanessa^R
Jackson^R
48 Endor Avenue^R
Brooklyn^R
NY^R
11221^R
256.98^R
March 1^R
^E
==================================================================
Mr.^R
Kenneth^R
Hall^R
5 Windsor Drive^R
West Long Branch^R
NJ^R
07764^R
450.50^R
March 15^R
^E
==================================================================
Mr.^R
Glenn^R
Babbin^R
187 Beach 147 Street^R
Queens^R
NY^R
11694^R
128.86^R
February 28^R
^E
==================================================================
Ms.^R
Stefanie^R
Eaton^R
137 Brighton Avenue^R
Perth Amboy^R
NJ^R
08861^R
612.75^R
February 15^R
```

MERGING TEXT - Merging the Primary and Secondary Files

Notes:

• After merging the primary and secondary files, insert a P. S. notation in the letter indicated, two lines below the initials. "P. S." stands for "post script" -- a thought that occurs after the letter has been written. If the P. S. notation is longer than two lines, the second line should not be typed under the "P." or the "S," but directly under the previous typed line of copy. (See format below.) After typing the "S," press the indent key. Space once between the P. and the S. An example of the format appears below:

```
                                       Sincerely,


                                       Robert Linden
                                       Vice President



  rl/yo

  P. S.    Please don't forget that we have a luncheon appointment next
           Wednesday at 12:30 p.m.  I look forward to seeing you then.
```

Exercise Directions:

1. Start with a clear screen.

2. Merge the primary file **DUE.PF** with the secondary file, **DUE.SF.**

3. Add a P. S. notation to Glenn Babbin's letter that reads:

   ```
   P. S. Since this is your first late
         payment, we are not charging
         you our usual late fee.
   ```

4. Print the full document (one copy of each merged letter).

5. Save the merged letters under a new document name: **DUE.FI**

Exercise Directions:

1. Start with a clear screen.

2. Merge the primary file **DUE.PF** with the secondary file, **DUE.SF.**

3. Add a P. S. notation to Glenn Babbin's letter that reads:

   ```
   P. S. Since this is your first late
         payment, we are not charging
         you our usual late fee.
   ```

4. Print the full document (one copy of each merged letter).

5. Save the merged letters under a new document name: **DUE.FI**

MERGING TEXT - Preparing a Primary File with a Blank Line

Notes:

- In the two previous exercises, the records in the secondary file contained the same number of lines. However, this is not always the case. For example, not all inside addresses are three lines. Some inside addresses may contain a company name. Assume you created a **primary** file that contained the following fields...

      ^F1^ ^F 2^ ^F3^
      ^F4^
      ^F5^
      ^F6^,^F7^ ^F8^

  ...then all your records in the secondary file would have to contain the same amount of fields. BUT...

- Suppose some of the records in the secondary file do not contain a company name (the ^F4^ location.) You must then indicate to WordPerfect that there might <u>not</u> be information to merge in this field. To do this, it is necessary to insert a question mark in the field where there might not be information in the record.

- The fields for the primary file would look like the following: (The illustrations below were created in WordPerfect 5.0. However, the concepts are the same for WordPerfect 5.1.)

      ^F1^ ^F2^ ^F3^
      ^F4?^
      ^F5^
      ^F6^,^F7^ ^F8^

- When preparing the secondary file, a merge code must be entered even though there is no information for that field. Remember, there must be the same number of lines in the secondary file to match the fields in the primary file. The record illustrated below on the left does not have a company name. The record illustrated on the right has a company name. In both cases, there are eight lines per record in the secondary file to match the eight fields in the primary file.

      Ms.^R   Mr.^R
      Roberta^R   Anton^R
      Tanner^R   Johnson^R
      ^R   ABC Manufacturing Co.^R
      45 West Street   One Gracie Terrace^R
      Los Angeles^R   New York^R
      CA^R   NY^R
      90026^R   10087^R

Exercise Directions:

1. Start with a clear screen.

2. Create a primary file from the letter on the right, inserting a code for each field and a question mark in the indicated fields. Begin on Ln. 2.5".

3. Unjustify the document (for WP5.0); (Left justify for WP5.1).

4. Spell check the document.

5. Print one copy. (On your printout, hand write a label for each field code with the actual field name.)

6. Save the exercise; name it **BUY.PF**.

```
                           Today's date


^F1^ ^F2^ ^F3^
^F4?^
^F5^
^F6^, ^F7^   ^F8^

Dear ^F1^ ^F3^:

We received your order for ^F9^ ^F10^ software packages.  We will
process it immediately.  To expedite the order, we are arranging
to have the software shipped directly from our warehouse in your
city, ^F6^.

The cost for the software packages totals $^F11^.  We would
appreciate payment as soon as you receive your order.

Thank you, ^F1^ ^F3^, for your confidence in our company.  I know
you will be satisfied with our customer support service.

                              Sincerely,


                              Yolanda Reeves
                              Sales Manager


yr/yo
```

TO INSERT MERGE CODES FOR BLANK LINES IN PRIMARY FILE

1. Place cursor where field is to be placed.
2. Press **Shift + F9**....... `Shift` + `F9`
3. Select **F**..................................... `F`
4. Type field number
5. Type a question mark.
6. **ENTER**.................................... `↵`

MERGING TEXT - Preparing a <u>Secondary</u> File with a Blank Line; Merging the Primary and Secondary Files

Notes:

- As explained in Exercise 55, a merge code must be entered in the secondary document even though information may not be available for that field.

- In this exercise, the variable information is given to you in unarranged format. Therefore, it will be necessary for you to create a secondary file and insert the proper codes.

- When you complete the secondary file, you will merge it with the primary file.

Exercise Directions:

1. Start with a clear screen.

2. Create a secondary file from the appropriate information on the right. Begin on Ln. 1."

3. Check to see that you have the same number of lines in the secondary file as fields in the primary file.

4. Save the exercise; name it **BUY.SF**.

5. Merge the primary file, **BUY.PF**, with the secondary file, **BUY.SF**.

6. Print the full document (one copy of each merged letter.)

7. Save the merged letters under a new document name: **BUY.FI**.

```
Mr. Jason Lochner
Computerland Associates
65 Linden Boulevard
Houston, TX  77069

Quantity ordered:  two

Software ordered:  Lotus 1-2-3

Total cost:        810.76
============================================================

Ms. Rose Zaffarano
Richmond Tile Company
654 Hammond Drive
Oklahoma City, OK  73212

Quantity ordered:  three

Software ordered:  Professional File

Total cost:        618.75
============================================================
Ms. Mia Sheffler
70 Klondike Avenue
Cleveland, OH  44102

Quantity ordered:  four

Software ordered:  PrintShop

Total cost:        245.85
============================================================
Ms. Marie Lubalin
29 Hazelnut Lane
Des Moines, IA  50356

Quantity ordered:  two

Software ordered:  WordPerfect 5.1

Total cost:         512.45
============================================================
```

TO INSERT MERGE CODES FOR BLANK LINES IN SECONDARY FILE

1. Type the data for the first merge field.
2. Press **F9**.................................. **F9**
   (even if the field is blank)
3. Repeat steps 1-2 for each field in the record.
4. After all fields are entered:
   Press **Shift + F9**...... **Shift** + **F9**
5. Select **E**...................................... **E**
   to end record.

MERGING TEXT - PREPARING ENVELOPES

Notes:

- After printing the merged final document containing all the records, you will need to address envelopes to mail them. Rather than type each inside address on an envelope (or a label), WordPerfect makes it possible for you to create an **envelope primary file** and merge it with the secondary file you just created.

- Since envelopes and mailing labels come in various sizes, your envelope primary file must be adjusted to the size of the envelope or mailing label you intend to use.

- On a standard legal-size envelope, the address is usually printed 14 lines or 2.33" down from the top and 4" in from the left margin. Therefore, the first procedure is to change the margins and line format of your page.

- The second procedure is to enter the fields you will need for the envelope...that is, only the fields used in the inside address.

- If you wanted to prepare envelopes for the records in Exercise 55, you would enter the same fields you used in the inside address in that exercise -- <u>after</u> you formatted your page for a legal-size envelope.

  ^F1^ ^F2^ ^F3^
  ^F4?^
  ^F5
  ^F6^,^F7^ ^F8^

- After the envelope primary file is created, it is saved. It is then merged with the secondary file you created containing records (the name and address list). The result will be an address record file; each name and address will appear on a separate page. You should save this merged file under a new filename. The last procedure is to print the full document of the new merged envelope file.

- To print mailing labels, check the software documentation for printing information.

Exercise Directions:

1. Start with a clear screen.

2. Set the appropriate page and margin options (see procedures to the right).

3. Create a primary envelope file as indicated on the right.

   (The inside address fields are those used in the document, **BUY.PF**, in the previous exercise.)

4. Save the exercise; name it **ENV.PF**.

5. Merge the primary file, **ENV.PF**, with the secondary file, **BUY.SF**.

6. Print all the envelopes for the merged document.

```
^F1^  ^F2^  ^F3^
^F4?^
^F5^
^F6^,  ^F7^   ^F8^
```

TO CREATE AN ENVELOPE PRIMARY FILE

NOTE: This procedure is for hand feeding legal-size envelopes 9.5" x 4".

WP5.0 USERS:

1. Press **Shift + F8**............... `Shift` + `F8`
2. Select **P** (page)................................. `P`
3. Select **S** (size).................................. `S`
4. Select **E** (envelope)........................... `E`
5. Select **E** (envelope)........................... `E`
6. Press **F7**... `F7`
7. Press **Shift + F8**............... `Shift` + `F8`
8. **Select L** (line)................................... `L`
9. Select **M** (margins)............................. `M`
10. Type **4.0** (left margin)......................... `4`
11. **ENTER**... `↵`
12. Type **0** (right margin).......................... `0`
13. **ENTER**... `↵`
14. **ENTER**... `↵`
15. Select **P** (page)................................. `P`
16. Select **C**(center page-top to bottom)... `C`
17. Press **F7** (return to document)........... `F7`

WP5.1 USERS:

1. Press **Shift + F8**................. `Shift` + `F8`
2. Select **P** (page)................................. `P`
3. Select **S** (size).................................. `S`
4. Select **A** (add).................................. `A`
5. Select **E** (envelope)........................... `E`
6. Select **S** (size).................................. `S`
7. **Select E** (Envelope 9.5" x 4")................ `E`
8. **ENTER**... `↵`
9. Select **S** (select)............................... `S`
10. **ENTER**... `↵`
11. Select **L** (line).................................. `L`
12. Select **M** (margins)............................. `M`
13. Type **4.0** (left margin)......................... `4`
14. **ENTER**... `↵`
15. Type **O** (right margin)......................... `0`
16. **ENTER**... `↵`
17. **ENTER**... `↵`
18. Select **P** (page)................................. `P`
19. Select **C** (center page - top to bottom).......... `C`
20. Type **Y** (yes)................................... `Y`
21. Press **F7** (return to document)............. `F7`

MERGING TEXT - Preparing Primary, Secondary and Envelope Files; Merging

Notes:

- In this exercise, you will create a primary file for the letter illustrated, a secondary file for the variable information and a primary envelope file for the envelopes.

- To make it easier to identify the type of document you are creating, a primary file may be given a file name extension of ".pf," while a secondary file may be given a file name extension of ".sf."

Exercise Directions:

1. Start with a clear screen.

2. Begin the document on Ln. 2.5".

3. Unjustify the document (for WP5.0); (left justify for WP5.1).

4. Create a primary file from the letter to the right, inserting the proper merge codes where necessary.

5. Spell check the document.

6. Save the file; name it **ERROR.PF**.

7. Create a secondary file from the variable information indicated on the bottom right.

8. Save the exercise; name it **ERROR.SF**.

9. Merge the primary file, **ERROR.PF**, with the secondary file, **ERROR.SF**.

10. Print the full document (all records in the file).

11. Save the merged letters under a new document name: **ERROR.FI**

12. Create and save a primary envelope file; name it **ERRENV.PF**

13. Merge the primary envelope file, **ERRENV.PF**, with the secondary file, **ERROR.SF**.

14. Print all the envelopes for the merged document.

Today's date

--- --- --- ---

-----, -- -----

Dear --. ----:

Thank you for your check No. ---, in the amount of $---.--. We
notice that you erroneously deducted a discount, even though the
discount period has expired.

We know this is an oversight. We are returning your check
No. ---, and we would appreciate your sending us another check
for $---.-- to cover the correct amount.

Thank you for your attention to this matter.

Sincerely,

Arnold Zahn
Credit Manager

az/yo

Mr. Harold Dembo Holistic, Inc. 654 Sanborn Street Denver, CO 80202	Ms. Jennifer Downing 7659 Utica Avenue San Antonio, TX 78202	Mr. Daniel Davis Acme Plumbing Supply 90 Plaza Z Milwaukee, WI 53212
Check No: 8768	6543	7888
Amount: 654.86	76.99	333.33
New Amount: 682.75	109.10	386.86

DOCUMENT ASSEMBLY - Preparing Standardized Paragraphs

Notes:

- Some companies, when preparing specific documents, use the same wording for many of the paragraphs in those documents. For example, many companies must write letters to customers who do not pay their bills on time. "Collection" letters are commonplace to a business. Another example: When a lawyer prepares a Last Will and Testament, many of the paragraphs are standard and are used for all clients. Only those paragraphs that relate to specific items or names are changed, and sometimes relevant information is inserted after the paragraph Is retrIeved. It Is commonplace for real estate and insurance companies to use standardized text in preparing many of their documents; and since the closing of a letter is standard in a company, a paragraph library may be created for that as well.

- Standardized text is also called "boilerplate," "repetitive text" or "paragraph libraries."

- **Document assembly** is the process of combining standardized text with new text to form a new document.

- Text that is considered "standardized," may be saved under its own filename and may be retrieved to place into a document when needed.

- As you create a document, you might determine that a paragraph or a portion of the document can be used sometime in the future. It is possible for you to highlight the paragraph, save the blocked paragraph for future use, and continue with the document you are creating.

- In this exercise, you will create a "library" of collection letter paragraphs, paragraphs that are standard for a Last Will and Testament, and a closing. You will create a separate document for each of the paragraphs listed. These paragraphs will be retrieved in future exercises to assemble various documents.

Exercise Directions:

1. Start with a clear screen.

2. Create a separate document, exactly as shown, for each of the standardized paragraphs indicated on the next page.

3. Begin each paragraph at the top of your screen.

4. Save each paragraph under the indicated filename.

5. Print one copy of each document.

Paragraph Name: COL1

I know this is just an oversight, but your account is now past due. We would appreciate a remittance from you as soon as possible. ↓2x

Paragraph Name: COL2

Unless we receive your full payment within five days, we will be forced to turn your account over to our collection department. ↓2x

Paragraph Name: COL3

Thank you for your attention to this matter. ↓2x

Paragraph Name: CLOSING

Cordially,

↓4x

Carole V. Russo
Manager
↓2x
cvr/

Paragraph Name: WILL1

I, *, of *, do make, publish and declare this to be my Last Will and Testament, hereby revoking all wills and codicils heretofore made by me. ↓2x

Paragraph Name: WILL4

IN TESTIMONY WHEREOF, I have to this my Last Will and Testament, subscribed my name and affixed my seal, this * day of *, 199*. ↓2x

_____   * ◄ (Pos 4.1")

Signed, sealed, published and declared by the above-named testator, as and for his Last Will and Testament, in our presence, and we at his request, in his presence and in the presence of each other, do hereunto, sign our names and set down our addresses as attesting witnesses, all on this * day of * 199*. ↓2x

_____ residing at _____

_____ residing at _____

_____ residing at _____

(Pos 3.8")   (Pos 5.1")   (Pos 7.4")

141

DOCUMENT ASSEMBLY - Assembling Documents from Standardized Paragraphs; Saving a Blocked Paragraph

Notes:

- When paragraphs are retrieved to create a new document, the retrieved paragraphs retain their formats.

- In this exercise, you will create a document from the standardized paragraphs you saved in the previous exercise. Be sure to double space between paragraphs. You will also save the subject line so that you can retrieve it for use in future collection letters.

Exercise Directions:

1. Start with a clear screen.

2. Begin the exercise on Ln. 2.5".

3. Unjustify the text (for WP5.0); (Left justify for WP5.1).

4. Retrieve the paragraphs indicated to assemble the letter on the right.

5. Block highlight and save the subject line; name it **SUBJECT.**

6. Save the assembled document; name it **COLLECT.**

7. Print one copy of the assembled document.

Today's date

Ms. Anita Kane
Haneswear Sports, Inc.
65 Mountain Lane
Wichita, KS   72087

Dear Ms. Kane:

Save as a new document

(Retrieve COL1) →   SUBJECT: YOUR OVERDUE ACCOUNT

¶You are a valued customer. We would not like to see your credit
standing jeopardized.

(Retrieve COL2) → ¶

(Retrieve COL3) → ¶

(Retrieve CLOSING) →

TO SAVE STANDARDIZED
TEXT USING BLOCK

1. Type text.
2. Press **Alt + F4**............ **Alt** + **F4**
   or
   or F12 (enhanced keyboard)............ **F12**
3. Highlight text to be saved.
4. Press **F10**.................................. **F10**
   ("Block name:" will appear)
5. Type name of document.
6. **ENTER**....................................... ↵

DOCUMENT ASSEMBLY - Assembling Documents from Standardized Paragraphs; Inserting Variable Text

Notes:

• In this exercise, you will create a Last Will and Testament by retrieving previously-saved standardized paragraphs. When you created the standardized paragraphs for the Will, you inserted an asterisk (*) in locations where variable information will be inserted. In order to insert the appropriate text at the proper locations of the asterisks, it is recommended that you use the search feature to locate the asterisk quickly, backspace to delete the asterisk, and then insert the appropriate information.You may also use the "GO TO" feature which will direct the cursor to "go to" a specified location.

• A review of the search and "GO TO" procedures is outlined in this lesson.

Exercise Directions:

1. Start with a clear screen.

2. Begin the centered heading on Ln. 2.0".

3. Unjustify the document (for WP5.0); (left justify for WP5.1).

4. Retrieve the paragraphs indicated to assemble the Last Will and Testament on the next page.

5. Using the search or "GO TO" features, locate each asterisk and insert the <u>appropriate</u> information indicated.

6. Save the assembled Last Will and Testament; name it **LASTWILL.**

LAST WILL AND TESTAMENT
OF
JOHN RICHARD ADAMS

(Retrieve WILL1)⟶ *¶*   * = John Richard Adams   * 105 Oakwood Lane, Goshen, New York   ↓3x

FIRST: ⟶ *Indent* I direct that all my just debts, the expenses of my last illness and funeral and the expenses of administering my estate be paid as soon as convenient.

SECOND: ⟶ *Indent* I give all my articles of personal, household or domestic use or adornment, including automobile and boats, to my wife, Mary Adams, or, if she does not survive me, to my children, Thomas Adams and Betsy Adams, as shall survive me, in shares substantially equal as to value.

THIRD: ⟶ *Indent* I give and devise all my residential real property, and all my interest in any policies of insurance thereon, to my wife, Mary Adams, if she survives me or if she does not survive me, to my surviving children, to be held by them jointly.

(Retrieve WILL4)⟶ *¶*   * = third   * = January   * 1992
* = John Richard Adams

TO RETRIEVE TEXT INTO A DOCUMENT

1. Place cursor in location where text is to be retrieved.
2. Press **Shift + F10**..... `Shift` + `F10`
3. Type name of document to be retrieved.
4. **ENTER**.. `↵`

TO SEARCH

1. Place cursor BEFORE text to be searched.
2. Press **F2**.................................... `F2`
3. Type search text or codes.
4. Press **F2**.................................... `F2`
   to begin search.
5. When cursor stops at first match, type replacement.
6. Press **F2 twice**............. `F2` `F2`
   to repeat search.

TO "GO TO"

1. Place cursor before text to be searched.
2. Press **Ctrl + HOME**... `Ctrl` + `Home`
3. Type character to "go to."
4. Repeat steps 2-3 for each desired "go to."

APPENDING TEXT

Notes:

- The append feature allows you to add a block of text to the end of a file which has been saved on a disk.

- The append feature is helpful when you are creating a document and decide that a portion of it may be used in another document.

- When you direct WordPerfect to append text to a file, but the file cannot be found, a file is automatically created for you. Therefore, if you decide you would like to "move" text to another file for later use, you can use the append feature. This new file may then be retrieved at a later time into an existing document or may be retrieved to create a new document.

- In this exercise, you will create another collection letter by retrieving previously-saved standardized paragraphs. After you retrieve the closing, it will be necessary for you to tab the text to 4.5" to maintain the block-style letter format. You will also add a P. S. notation (indicated in the directions) which you will then append to another document which has already been saved.

- After appending text to another file, it is recommended that you retrieve that file and adjust spacing as needed before you print.

Exercise Directions:

1. Start with a clear screen.

2. Retrieve the paragraphs indicated to assemble the letter on the right.

3. Unjustify the document (for WP5.0); (Left justify for WP5.1).

4. Begin the exercise on Ln. 2.5".

5. Send this letter CERTIFIED MAIL; (See Ex. 40 for review) include a P. S. notation that reads:
P. S. Please forward your check to our new offices, 50 Harbor Street, Philadelphia, PA 19103.

6. Append the P. S. notation to the document, COLLECT.

7. Save the assembled document; name it **PASTDUE.**

8. Print one copy of PASTDUE and one copy of COLLECT.

146

Today's date

Mr. Judd Yakov, President
Accessories, Inc.
56 Waverly Place
Rochester, NY 14602

Dear Mr. Yakov:

(Retrieve SUBJECT) →

We are disappointed that you have not responded to our previous letters in which we reminded you that your account is now more than three months past due.

(Retrieve COL2) → ¶

(Retrieve COL3) → ¶

(Retrieve CLOSING) → ¶

TO APPEND TEXT

1. Place cursor on first character of text to be appended.
2. Press **Alt + F4**............ **Alt** + **F4**
   or
   F12 (enhanced keyboard)....... **F12**
3. Highlight text.
4. Press **Ctrl + F4**........... **Ctrl** + **F4**
5. Select **B**....................................... **B**
6. Select **A**....................................... **A**
7. Type name of document to which block will be appended.
8. **ENTER**....................................... ↵

APPENDING TEXT

Notes:

- In this exercise, you will create a single-spaced report. After completing it, you will append the last paragraph, as indicated, to a new file and name it WARRANTY. In a later exercise, you will retrieve the WARRANTY file.

Exercise Directions:

1. Start with a clear screen.
2. Create the document on the right as indicated. Begin the exercise on Ln. 2".
3. Unjustify the document (for WP5.0); (Left justify for WP5.1).
4. Append the warranty paragraph as indicated to a new file; name it WARRANTY.
5. Spell check the exercise.
6. Print one copy.
7. Save the exercise; name it **LASER.**

FACTS ABOUT LASER POINTER HIGHLIGHTER

The Trinitron Laser Pointer Highlighter is a unique device which allows you to point to relevant drawings, illustrations, or other references when you are conducting a lecture. All you need to do is aim the red laser beam at whatever it is you are referring to. Your audience will be immediately focused. Using the Trinitron Laser Pointer is a professional way to conduct a presentation, especially when there is a need to make reference to charts, etc. Here are some facts and safety tips:

TAB ⟶   INDENT

1. ⟶ **POWER.** Use two 9-volt alkaline batteries which are supplied. An AC Adaptor/Charger and a three-hour rechargeable Ni-cad power pack are optional.

2. **SAFETY.** The Trinitron Highlighter laser pointer complies with all electrical and safety regulations covering class II laser products. Staring into the beam should be avoided. **Do not direct the beam toward a person's eye.**

3. **BATTERIES.** The Trinitron Highlighter laser pointer uses two 9-volt alkaline batteries which are installed.

4. **OPERATION.** Slide the on/off safety switch up to turn on the laser pointer. Turn it off after use to prevent accidental use and drainage of batteries. To use the pointer, aim it at the object or area to be highlighted. Turn on the laser by pressing the on/off red bar-switch. Releasing the switch turns off the laser.

5. **WARRANTY.** Trinitron warrants this unit will be free of defects in workmanship and materials for a period of one year from the date of purchase. This warranty does not cover damages resulting from accident, misuse or neglect. If your laser pointer fails to operate properly under normal use during the warranty period because of a defect in workmanship or material, Trinitron will repair or replace (at our option) the laser pointer with no cost to you except for shipping.

append to new file

CREATING MACROS

Notes:

- A **macro** is a saved series of keystrokes which may be recalled at a later time.

- If a document contains repetitive phrases or clauses, the phrase or clause may be recorded as a macro and whenever the phrase or clause is needed, it is played back with a single keystroke.

- Macros may be used for saving phrases, formats or commands necessary to accomplish a particular task like printing or spell checking a document. Rather than depress many keys to access a task, it is possible to "record" the process and play it back with one key.

- Once a macro is created, it must be named for future recall.

- A saved macro file is given a .WPM extension by WordPerfect.

- The macro may be retrieved anywhere in the document.

- In this exercise, you will create and save several macros which will be retrieved in the next several exercises. One of the macros you will create is a closing. A closing was saved as standardized text in an earlier exercise. You have the option of either creating a separate file or a macro for repetitive text. When you assemble documents, you may retrieve a file containing the standardized text or a macro.

- Create a macro carefully. When the "macro def" is flashing on the screen, any key that you depress will be captured into the macro.

Exercise Directions:

1. Start with a clear screen.

2. Create and save each of the macros <u>exactly</u> as indicated on the right under the macro filename shown. Use a hard space (Home + Spacebar) between words in the P & G macros.

3. Clear the screen after completing each macro and before starting the next macro.

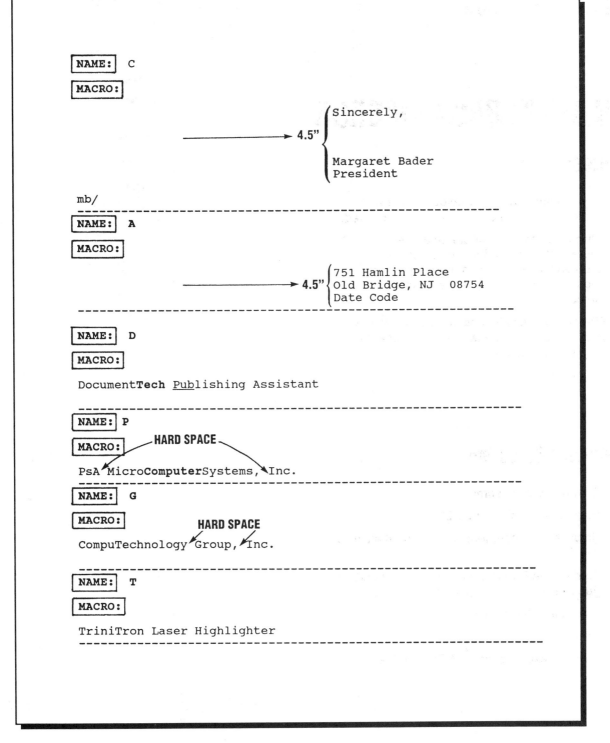

NAME:	C
MACRO:	

```
                               ⎧ Sincerely,
              ─────────▶ 4.5" ⎨
                               ⎪ Margaret Bader
                               ⎩ President
```

mb/

NAME:	A
MACRO:	

```
                               ⎧ 751 Hamlin Place
              ─────────▶ 4.5" ⎨ Old Bridge, NJ   08754
                               ⎩ Date Code
```

NAME:	D
MACRO:	

Document**Tech** Pu̲blishing Assistant

NAME:	P
MACRO:	

HARD SPACE

PsA Micro**Computer**Systems, Inc.

NAME:	G
MACRO:	

HARD SPACE

CompuTechnology Group, Inc.

NAME:	T
MACRO:	

TriniTron Laser Highlighter

TO CREATE A MACRO

1. Press **Ctrl + F10**........ **Ctrl** + **F10**
2. Press **Alt + (one letter)**.....

    ....**Alt** + **(one letter)**

3. Type a one-word description of macro.   (Optional)
4. **ENTER**...................................... **↵**
   to begin macro capture.
   ("Macro Def" starts blinking).
5. Type keystrokes to be recorded.
6. Press **Ctrl + F10**........ **Ctrl** + **F10**
   to end macro capture.

PLAYING BACK MACROS

Notes:

* Once a macro has been saved, it can be recalled and "played back" whenever desired.

* In this exercise, you will create a "News Release" which is a document that is prepared and sent to various newspapers and magazines announcing a new product of a company.

* Each time the product name appears, you will play back one of the macros you created in the previous exercise.

Exercise Directions:

1. Start with a clear screen.

2. Begin the exercise on Ln. 2".

3. Unjustify the document (for WP5.0); (Left justify for WP5.1).

3. Retrieve the **D** macro wherever Document**Tech** Publishing Assistant appears in the text.

4. Spell check the exercise.

5. Print one copy.

6. Save the exercise; name it **DOCUMENT**.

```
                    PRESS RELEASE
                 For Immediate Release

For more information contact:   Corine Cardoza


       INTRODUCING THE DocumentTech Publishing Assistant

Cambridge, Massachusetts, March 7, 199-

The DocumentTech Publishing Assistant is the first in a series of
publishing products that put together three distinct technologies
--digital scanning, laser imaging and xerograph--into one
simplified publishing solution.  The DocumentTech Publishing
Assistant provides high quality, low cost and quick turnaround.
DocumentTech Publishing Assistant eliminates complicated pre-
press operations.  It has a built-in scanner and quickly captures
text, line art and photos, and converts them to digital masters.

Even booklet marking becomes easier.  DocumentTech Publishing
Assistant has a signature booklet feature which will
automatically turn out 11 x 17 or digest size (8.5 x 11) collated
sets ready to be stitched, folded and trimmed.  DocumentTech
Publishing Assistant prints an amazing 135 pages per minute and
has a concurrent input/output capability.  This means that while
you are publishing one job, you'll be scanning, revising and
readying others.  Furthermore, DocumentTech Publishing Assistant
comes in a networked version.
```

TO PLAY BACK A MACRO

1. Place cursor where macro is to be played back.
2. Press **Alt** + **letter** (used when creating)...........**Alt** + (letter)

PLAYING BACK MACROS; CREATING A PERSONAL BUSINESS LETTER

Notes:

- In this exercise, you will create a personal business letter by recalling and playing back two macros that you saved in a previous exercise.

- A **personal business letter** is written by individuals for personal-business purposes, not company-related business purposes. In other words, a personal business letter represents you -- it does not represent a company.

- The personal business letter contains the writer's address (sometimes referred to as a "return address"). The placement of the "return address" depends on the letter style used.

- A personal business letter may be formatted in either block or modified-block style. The example shown on the right is formatted in modified-block style. The return address should begin on Ln 2.17".

- A block-style format appears below. Note that in a block-style format the "return address" is typed below the writer's name. Using this format, the date line should begin on Ln. 2.5" --the same starting line used for any business letter.

BLOCK STYLE FORMAT

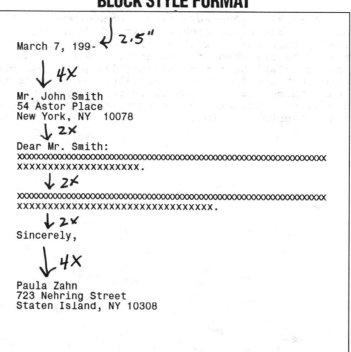

Exercise Directions:

1. Start with a clear screen.

2. Begin the exercise on Ln 2.17".

3. Unjustify the document (for WP5.0); (Left justify for WP5.1).

4. With your cursor at the left margin, retrieve the **A** macro on Ln 2.17"; retrieve the **T** macro wherever TriniTron Laser Highlighter appears in the text.

5. Spell check the exercise.

6. Print one copy.

7. Save the exercise; name it **INQUIRE**.

MODIFIED BLOCK STYLE FORMAT

2.17" ←— Play back MACRO A ———→ RETURN ADDRESS

↓ 3 or 4x

Ms. Wendy Simms, Manager
Trinitron, Inc.
520 Boxtree Lane
Floral Park, NY   11010

Dear Ms. Simms:

Three weeks ago, I purchased a TriniTron Laser Highlighter from a
local store in my neighborhood. The TriniTron Laser Highlighter
is an outstanding product, and I have enjoyed using it.

I am an assistant director of an advertising agency, and I have
to make frequent presentations. Last week, I used the TriniTron
Laser Highlighter during a presentation to a group of executives.
As I was "pointing" to a chart, the laser beam began to flash,
made a funny noise and then the ray of light went out. I am sure
that I followed the directions for use very carefully, since I
used the TriniTron Laser Highlighter on two other occasions
without a problem.

My local dealer indicated that the TriniTron Laser Highlighter
came with a one-year warranty and that I needed to send in the
warranty card to you in order to have it repaired. I never
received the warranty card. I would appreciate your sending me
this card so that I can have my TriniTron Laser Highlighter
repaired. My bill of sale is enclosed.

Your prompt attention to this matter would be greatly
appreciated.

                              Sincerely,

                              Rosetta Stone

enclosure

PLAYING BACK MACROS

Notes:

- In this exercise, you will create a legal letter, and where indicated, recall and play back two macros created in a previous exercise. You will note that this document contains a "re" line, which is commonly used in legal letters. "Re" means "in reference to" or "subject." Two returns are inserted before and after typing the "re" line.

Exercise Directions:

1. Start with a clear screen.
2. Create the letter on the right. Begin the exercise on Ln. 2.5".
3. Justify the document (for WP5.0); (Full justify for WP5.1).
4. Retrieve the **P** and **G** macros wherever they appear in the text.
5. Spell check the exercise.
6. Print one copy.
7. Save the exercise; name it **SETTLE.**

Today's date

Thomas Wolfe, Esq.
Wolfe, Escada & Yates
803 Park Avenue
New York, NY 10023

Dear Mr. Wolfe:

Re: [macro P] vs.
     ABC Manufacturing Company

I am enclosing a copy of the Bill of Sale that transfers all
Gordon's assets to [macro P].

In addition, you asked us to represent [macro G] in their $200,000
payment to [macro P]. Because of this payment, [macro G] became
subrogated to the claim made by [macro P], and [macro P] cannot
settle this matter without the approval of [macro G].

[macro G] would also be entitled to recover some portion of any
judgment recovered by [macro P] in the above action. In order to
get a settlement in this matter, we will need to obtain a release
of ABC Manufacturing Company by [macro G].

Let's discuss this so that we can quickly settle this matter.

Very truly yours,

David Altmann, Esq.

da/yo
enclosure

CREATING A MACRO WITH A PAUSE; PLAYING BACK A MACRO WITH A PAUSE

Notes:

- It is possible to create a macro that contains variable information. When the macro is being created, a "pause" code is entered at the point where the variable information will be inserted. When the macro is then played back, it will pause for you to type in the variable text.

- In this exercise, you will create two macros that contain pauses. You will then create a letter and play back the macros, inserting the variable text indicated. In addition, you will retrieve a closing and the standardized paragraph you created in a previous exercise.

Exercise Directions:

1. Start with a clear screen.

2. Create each of the macros on the right, inserting a "pause" code where indicated. Save each macro under the filename shown.

3. Clear your screen after each macro.

4. Create the letter shown below the macros. Begin on Ln. 2.5".

5. Play back each macro indicated. When a pause occurs, insert the variable shown.

6. Justify the document (for WP 5.0); (Full justify for WP5.1).

7. Spell check the exercise.

8. Print one copy.

9. Save the exercise; name it **PAUSE**.

```
  ┌───────┐
  │ NAME: │    S
  └───────┘
  ┌────────┐
  │ MACRO: │
  └────────┘
  We shall expect your remittance in the amount of -pause- within the
  next ten days.
  ----------------------------------------------------------------
  ┌───────┐
  │ NAME: │    R
  └───────┘
  ┌────────┐
  │ MACRO: │
  └────────┘
  Our last reminder to you that your account was past due was mailed
  to you on -pause-.
  ----------------------------------------------------------------


  Today's date


  Mr. Andrew S. Stone
  321 Saxony Place
  Indianapolis, IN  46204

  Dear Mr. Stone:

  Your account is now more than thirty days past due.  [macro R -
  January 5-]

  [macro S -$288.94-]

  We do value your patronage.  The best way to maintain a good
  working relationship is to have a good credit record.  If you have
  any questions, please feel free to phone me.
```

Retrieve CLOSING →

TO CREATE A MACRO WITH A PAUSE

1. Press **Ctrl + F10**....... `Ctrl` + `F10`
2. Type macro name.
   NOTE: A one-letter name is desirable.
3. **ENTER**..................................... `↵`
4. Type a one-word description of macro. (Optional)
5. **ENTER**..................................... `↵`
   to begin macro capture.
   ("Macro Def" starts blinking.)

6. Type keystrokes to be recorded.
7. Press **Ctrl + PgUp**. `Ctrl` + `Pg Up`
8. Select **P** (pause)........................ `P`
9. **ENTER**.................................... `↵`
10. Continue defining macro.
11. Press **Ctrl + F10**........ `Ctrl` + `F10`
    to end macro capture.

TO PLAY BACK MACRO WITH A PAUSE

1. Place cursor where macro is to be played back.
2. Press **Alt + F10**.......... `Alt` + `F10`
3. Type macro name.
4. **ENTER**..................................... `↵`
5. Type desired text when macro pauses.
6. **ENTER**..................................... `↵`
   to continue playback.

Exercise Directions:

1. Create a primary and a secondary file from the information below.

2. Format the primary file in any letter style.

3. Name the primary file: TRAVEL.PF; name the secondary file: TRAVEL.SF.

4. Merge the primary and secondary files.

5. Save the merged letters under a new document name: TRAVEL.FI.

6. Print a copy of the merged file.

7. Prepare an envelope for each person listed by creating a primary envelope file and properly merging it; name the envelope file: TRAENV.PF.

8. Print an envelope for each person on the list.

```
Today's Date//Thank you for your inquiry about a cruise
to ------.  We are enclosing a brochure on ------ which might be
of interest to you if you should decide to sail to ----.//
There are two sailings scheduled during the ---- months:  ------
and ------.  The cost varies depending upon your
accommodations.//If you would like more information about a
vacation of a lifetime, call -----, who is one of the
representatives in our office who will be delighted to help
you.//Sincerely,//Susan Crawford/Travel Agent/sc:yo
```

Ms. Beverly Oberlin 65 Court Street Portland, ME 04141	Mr. Wayne Viscosa ABC, Incorporated 690 Eldridge Drive Petersburgh, VA 23808	Ms. Edna T. Hamilton 76 Rider Avenue Baltimore, MD 21201
Cruise To: Spain	 Bahamas	 Trinidad
Brochure on: <u>Hidden Treasures</u>	 <u>Carribbean Coral</u>	 <u>Breathtaking Voyages</u>
Sailings: winter December 15 February 12	 summer June 29 August 1	 winter December 15 February 12
Representative: Sarah	 Patricia	 Michael

Lesson 7
Summary Exercise B

Exercise Directions:

1. Create the letter below in modified-block style.

2. Unjustify the document (for WP5.0); (Left justify for WP5.1).

3. Play back the macros indicated.

4. Retrieve the document, WARRANTY, where indicated. Indent the pargraph .5" on the left and right.

5. Spell check your document.

6. Print one copy.

7. Save the file; name it **CLIENT.**

Today's Date//Ms. Rosetta Stone/751
Hamlin Place/Old Bridge, NJ 08754/
Dear Ms. Stone://I am delighted to
learn that you have purchased a [macro
T] and that you are enjoying the use
of it. I am sorry that you did not
receive the warranty card which should
have been enclosed with your [macro
T].//I do not have any loose warranty
cards that I can send you. However, I
will state the warranty policy in the
paragraph below.//[Retrieve WARRANTY.]
//Show this letter with the indicated
warranty policy, along with your bill
of cale, to your local dealer. He
will then repair your [macro T].//If
you should have any problems, let me
know. I know you will get many years
of enjoyment from your [macro T.]//
[macro C].

> **LESSON 8:**
> CREATING TEXT COLUMNS, TABULATED COLUMNS; USING MATH

CREATING NEWSPAPER-STYLE COLUMNS

Notes:

- WordPerfect's newspaper-style column feature allows text to flow from one column to another. When the first column is filled with text, additional text will automatically continue to flow into the next column.

- Newspaper-style columns are particularly helpful when creating newsletters, pamphlets, brochures, lists or articles.

- WordPerfect gives you the option of selecting the number of columns you desire for a particular document. You can also select the distance between columns, sometimes called the **gutter** space. If you do not specify the distance between columns, WordPerfect will do so. WordPerfect will automatically calculate columns of equal width; however, the column margins can be set individually to create unequal columns.

- When the column feature is turned on, the word "Col" will appear in the status line. It is important to turn the column feature off when you have completed your columnar document if you plan to continue the document without columns.

- It is possible to retrieve text from a file into newspaper-style columns. When retrieving text from a file into columns, be sure your cursor is within the column mode. You can do this by checking to see that the status area contains the word "Col".

- The cursor can be moved from column to column quickly. (See keystrokes on next page.)

Exercise Directions:

1. Start with a clear screen.

2. Begin columns on Ln 2".

3. Create the article on the next page using a two-column newspaper-style format. Use the preset distance between columns.

4. Justify your document (for WP5.0); (Full-justify for WP5.1).

5. Double space the document.

6. Spell check the exercise.

7. View your document.

8. Print one copy.

9. Save the exercise; name it **PROCESS**.

continued...

The computer is an electronic device that can process vast amounts of facts and numbers and perform calculations at very high rates of speed. While a computer can accomplish many things, IT CANNOT THINK. A computer has to be "told" what to do with the information it receives. **Programs** are machine-language instructions which tell a computer what to do with information. Programs are developed by computer programmers.

Computers come in various sizes. Some computers are so large they fill an entire room, while others are so small, they can be held in your hand. No matter what their size, computers contain the same basic parts. Every computer has a way through which the operator can enter instructions and information. A keyboard is an "input" device which is common to all computers. The "storage" device (sometimes called memory) receives the information from the input device and holds it until it is needed. A "processing" device selects the instructions from the storage unit and processes the information as it has been directed. The "output" device translates the processed information into readable form. A typical output device would be a printer or a visual display.

TO CREATE COLUMNS

WP5.0:
1. Place cursor where column is to begin.
2. Press **Alt + F7**.......... `Alt` + `F7`
3. Select **D** (define)......................... `D`
   NOTE: A two-column newspaper type column is the default.
4. Change <u>none</u>, <u>any</u>, or <u>all</u> of the following options as desired:

T (type)................................. `T`
   Select a column type:
   N (Newspaper) or................ `N`
                                              or
   P (Parallel) or........................ `P`
                                              or
   B (Parallel with block protect)..... `B`

N (number of columns)................. `N`
   • Type desired number of columns.
   • Enter

D (distance between columns)..... `D`
   • Type desired distance between columns.
   • Enter

M (margins)...................................... `M`
   • Type left margin.
   • Enter
   • Type right margin
   • Enter
   • Repeat margin steps above until all margins are set.
5. Press **F7** (to accept column settings). `F7`
6. Select **C** (column on/off)............. `C`
   NOTE: "Col 1" is added to the status line.
7. Type text.

WP5.1:
1. Follow steps 1-2 above.
2. Select **C** (columns)...................... `C`
3. Follow steps 3-5 above.
4. Select **O** (on)............................... `O`
5. Type text.

TURN COLUMNS OFF

WP5.0:
1. Press **Alt + F7**............. `Alt` + `F7`

2. Select **C**.................................. `C`
   NOTE: "Col" disappears from status line.

WP5.1:
1. Press **Alt + F7**............ `Alt` + `F7`
2. Select **C**.................................. `C`
3. Select **F** (off).............................. `F`
   NOTE: "Col" disappears from status line.

TO MOVE CURSOR FROM COLUMN TO COLUMN:

To Previous Column:
Ctrl + Home, ← .... `Ctrl` + `Home` `←`
To Next Column:
Ctrl + Home, → ..... `Ctrl` + `Home` `→`
To First Column:
Ctrl + Home, Home, ← ....
   ...... `Ctrl` + `Home` `Home` `←`
To Last Column:
Ctrl + Home, Home, → ....
   ...... `Ctrl` + `Home` `Home` `→`

CREATING NEWSPAPER-STYLE COLUMNS

Notes:

• In this exercise, you will create an article using a three-column newspaper format. The heading should be centered before the column mode is turned on. If you turn the column mode on before you type the heading, the heading will be centered in the first column.

Exercise Directions:

1. Start with a clear screen.

2. Begin the exercise on Ln 2"; center the heading.

3. Create the article on the right using a three-column newspaper-style format. Use the preset distance between columns.

4. Unjustify your document (for WP5.0); (Left-justify for WP5.1).

5. Spell check the exercise.

6. View your document.

7. Print one copy.

8. Save the exercise; name it **COOK.**

THE ART OF COOKING

↓ 3x

Preparing a meal requires skill and patience. The results may mean the difference between eating just to exist and the satisfaction that comes from one of the major pleasures of life.

Cooking is an art. Every recipe should be prepared with tender, loving care and should be one of the primary ingredients. A cook must develop a feeling for what each ingredient will do in a recipe.

An outstanding meal must be prepared with high-quality raw materials, cooked simply but perfectly to enhance their natural flavor. It is important to plan your meal carefully. The menu should contain a contrast in textures, flavor and color. Salad should be served as a separate course. Use the best natural foods of the season and plan menus around them. Try not to use packaged frozen items if you can get them fresh. If you have a garden, use the fresh garden vegetables and fruit whenever you can. It's a challenge to try to fit all the fruit -- strawberries, raspberries, cantaloupes, watermelons, blueberries, blackberries, peaches, nectarines, cherries, and plums into the menu. You might want to try to use fresh herbs like dill, parsley, basil, or tarragon. Or you might want to try a variety of garden lettuces and home-grown tomatoes like beefsteaks, plum and cherry-size.

In the fall and winter, there are a variety of foods that are available for your menu and will add zest to your meal. The apples, eggplant, cauliflower, pears, and chestnuts are wonderful ingredients for a meal.

When you are preparing a meal for guests, never serve a dish which you have not prepared at least once or twice before.

To make your meal presentable, do not serve too much on the plate. Servings should be small. This way, your guests will ask for second helpings.

Are you getting hungry?

167

CREATING UNEQUAL NEWSPAPER-STYLE COLUMNS

Notes:

- In this exercise, you will create an article using a two-column newspaper-style format in which the second column is narrower than the first. The text does not fill up the first column and will require that you force the cursor to the top of the second column. This is done by depressing **Ctrl + ENTER** when you are ready to move to the top of the second column. You will also change your line spacing back to single space when you begin the second column. Remember to type the centered heading before you turn the columns feature on.

Exercise Directions:

1. Start with a clear screen.
2. Begin the exercise on Ln 2"; center the heading.
3. Create the exercise on the right using a two-column newspaper-style format. Set column one left margin at 1"; right margin at 6". Set column two left margin at 6.5"; right margin at 7.5". (Use the preset distance between columns.)
4. Double space the first column; single space the second column.
5. Unjustify your document (for WP5.0); (Left-justify for WP5.1).
6. Spell check the exercise.
7. View your document.
8. Print one copy.
9. Save the exercise; name it **GOODBYE.**

VACATION PLANNING

It can be very exciting to plan a vacation. There are a number of ways to go about it. Of course, you could have a travel agent make all the arrangements. But it is more exciting to investigate all the possibilities of travel.

First, you can check the hundreds of guidebooks which can be purchased at bookstores. Then, you can send away to the government tourist offices in the country you are planning to visit. They will send you lots of free literature about the country -- places to visit and a list of accommodations. The travel advertisements in your newspaper will tell you where the bargains are.

After you have planned your trip by looking through the guidebooks listed to the right, ask your travel agent to do the actual booking. Enjoy!

OFFICIAL AIRLINE GUIDE

RUSSELL'S NATIONAL MOTOR COACH GUIDE

STEAMSHIP GUIDE

HOTEL AND RESORT GUIDE

AUTO RENTAL GUIDE

RES-TAURANTS, INNS AND MUSEUMS GUIDE

SIGHT-SEEING GUIDE

CAMP-GROUND, FARM VACATIONS AND ADVENTURE TRAVEL GUIDE

TO CREATE COLUMNS OF UNEQUAL MARGINS

WP5.0:

1. Place cursor where column is to begin.
2. Press **Alt + F7** .... `Alt` + `F7`
3. Select **D** .... `D`
   NOTE: A two-column newspaper-type column is the default.
4. Select **T** .... `T`
5. Select a column type:
   N (Newspaper) .... `N`
   or

   or **P**(Parallel) .... `P`
   or
   or **B** (Parallel with block protect)...... `B`
6. Select **N** (number of columns) .... `N`
7. Type desired number of columns.
8. **ENTER** .... `↵`
9. Select **M** (margins) .... `M`
10. Type left margin.
11. **ENTER** .... `↵`
12. Type right margin.
13. **ENTER** .... `↵`

NOTE: Repeat steps 10-13 for each margin in each column.
14. Press **F7** (to accept column settings).. `F7`
15. Select **C** (column on/off)............. `C`
16. Type text.

WP5.1:

1. Follow steps 1-2 above.
2. Select **C** (columns)..................... `C`
3. Follow steps 3-14 above.
4. Select **O** (on)............................... `O`
5. Type text.

169

CREATING PARALLEL COLUMNS

Notes:

- WordPerfect's parallel column feature allows text to move across the columns.

- Parallel columns are particularly helpful when creating a list, a script, an itinerary, minutes of a meeting or any other document in which text is read horizontally.

- The procedure for creating parallel columns is the same as creating newspaper-style columns, except the "Column Type" must be changed to "Parallel."

- After text is entered in the first column, you must enter a hard page break (**Ctrl + Enter**) to force the cursor to move to the next column. After text is entered in the second column, a hard page break must be entered to force the cursor to the third column. A hard page break is needed to move the cursor back to the first column.

- Text cannot be retrieved into parallel columns.

- In this exercise, you will create minutes of a meeting. The columns will be unequal -- the first column will be narrower than the second. Be sure to type the centered heading before you turn on the column feature.

Exercise Directions:

1. Start with a clear screen.

2. Begin the exercise on Ln 2"; center the headings.

3. To create the horizontal line, set the repeat value to 65 and use the "greater than" symbol.

4. Create the exercise on the right using a two-column parallel-style format. Set the right margin in the first column to 3"; set the left margin in the second column to 3.5".

5. Justify your document (for WP5.0); (Full-justify for WP5.1).

6. Spell check the exercise.

7. Print one copy.

8. Save the exercise; name it **AGELESS**.

```
                   PERFECTION PLUS, INCORPORATED
                   MINUTES OF MEETING

                        March 29, 199-

>>>>>>>>>>>>>>>>>>>>>>>>>>>>>>>>>>>>>>>>>>>>>>>>>>>>>>>>>>>>>>>>
```

Present   Robin Jones, Quincy Garin, Zachary
                      Malavo, Wendy Carley, Bill McKinley,
                      Andrew Yang, Shirley DeChan.

Research   Mr. Malavo announced the development of
                      a new product line. Several new
                      chemical formulas were developed for a
                      cream which will reduce skin wrinkling.
                      The cream will be called **AgeLess**.

Publicity   To launch this new product, Ms. Carley
                      announced that promotions would be made
                      at all the high-end New York department
                      stores. Samples of the product will be
                      given away at demonstration counters.
                      Press releases will be sent to members
                      of the press.

Advertising   The advertising budget was estimated at
                      $5,223,000. Several advertising
                      agencies were asked to submit
                      presentations, and a decision will be
                      made by the Advertising Committee as to
                      which agency will represent this new
                      line.

Sales   Mr. Garin, National Sales Manager,
                      projected that sales could reach
                      $10,000,000 the first year.

Adjournment   The meeting was adjourned at 4:00 p.m.
                      Another meeting has been scheduled for
                      Tuesday of next week to discuss future
                      research and marketing of this new
                      product.

CREATING PARALLEL COLUMNS

Notes:

- In this exercise, you will create a name and address list using an equal parallel-column format.

Exercise Directions:

1. Start with a clear screen.

2. Begin the exercise on Ln 2"; center the heading, BUSINESS ASSOCIATION DIRECTORY.

3. Create the list using an <u>equal</u> three-column parallel-style format.

4. After the column feature is turned on, center NAME (**Shift + F6**); then move cursor to the second column (**Ctrl + Enter**) and center ADDRESS; move the cursor to the third column and center RESPONSIBILITY.

5. Print one copy.

6. Save the exercise; name it **LIST.**

BUSINESS ASSOCIATION DIRECTORY

NAME	ADDRESS	RESPONSIBILITY
Adams, Brenda	765 West Avenue New York, NY 10098 212-876-9876	Convention
Appel, Peter	319 East 96 Street Brooklyn, NY 11234 718-345-4442	Publicity
Barnes, Desmond	10 West 66 Street New York, NY 10054 212-654-4692	Newsletter
Brady, Edward	21 Dolin Road Bronx, NY 10456 212-323-0087	Membership
Brown, Donna	2109 Broadway New York, NY 10192 212-654-3321	Political Action
Chou, David	76 River End Road Queens, NY 11312 718-457-9934	Convention Registration
Hausman, Gregory	225 Racliff Street Bronx, NY 10456 212-555-4455	Membership
LeChamp, Renee	200 East 77 Street New York, NY 10023 212-675-9090	Newsletter
Scoville, Cynthia	76 Kings Highway Brooklyn, NY 11223 718-455-4729	Publicity

CREATING PARALLEL COLUMNS

Notes:

- In this exercise, you will create an itinerary using an unequal parallel-column format.

- An itinerary is a travel schedule which includes departure and arrival dates and times, hotel/motel accommodations, and means of travel used. There are several acceptable formats for an itinerary.

Exercise Directions:

1. Start with a clear screen.

2. Begin the exercise on Ln 2"; center the heading.

3. Create the itinerary using an <u>unequal</u> three-column parallel-style format. Set the right margin in the first column to 2"; set the left margin in the second column to 2.5"; set the right margin in the second column to 3.5"; set the left margin in the third column to 4".

4. Unjustify your document (for WP5.0); (Left justify for WP5.1).

5. Insert a hard space (HOME + Spacebar) between words that should be kept together.

6. Print one copy.

7. Save the exercise; name it **ITINER**.

                    ITINERARY OF ANGELA BATTAGLIA
                         April 6-7, 199-

Monday,   8:00 a.m.   Leave Newark International Airport,
April 6   American Airlines, Flight 444.

                 10:30 a.m.   Arrive Miami International Airport.
                                Reservation at Marriott
                                Airport Hotel. Confirmation No.
                                4455117778-0.

                 12:30 p.m.   Lunch with Dr. Andrew Zarou at Palm
                                Restaurant in Marriott Hotel.
                                Dr. Zarou will meet you in
                                restaurant.

                 3:30 p.m.   Tour of computer facility at
                                University of Miami.

                 7:00 p.m.   Dinner with Dr. Lauren Namin,
                                Director of Admissions. Dr. Namin
                                will pick you up at your hotel.

Tuesday,   10:00 a.m.   Conference at Seaview Hotel.
April 7   Courtesy bus will pick you up
                                outside your hotel at 9:15 a.m.

                 12:30 p.m.   Lunch with Ms. Jackie Smith and
                                Mr. Raymond Weill at Palm Court
                                Restaurant at Seaview Hotel to
                                discuss curriculum issues.

                 3:00 p.m.   Presentation on "Using the Computer
                                Across the Curriculum."

                 7:00 p.m.   Leave Miami International Airport,
                                American Airlines, Flight 52.

                 9:45 p.m.   Arrive Newark International
                                Airport. Limousine service home.

CREATING TABULATED COLUMNS (Without Column Headings)

Notes:

- WordPerfect does not have an automatic column layout feature. In order to horizontally and vertically center tabulated material, it is important to note how the text will be formatted in the columns. For example, when you look at the text in a column, you must determine if the text is **Left Aligned, Right Aligned, Centered** (within the column), or **Aligned at the Decimal.** Note these examples of the types of tabs that can be set:

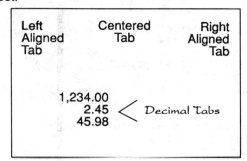

- Columns of text are generally horizontally centered between the existing margins.

- Before you can actually set your tabs, you must calculate where tab settings should be made. The procedure for calculating tab settings is as follows:

  1. Depress Shift + F6 (center) and type the longest line of each column and the intercolumn space. The recommended intercolumn space is as follows:

     2-column table = 10 spaces between columns

     3-column table = 8 spaces between columns

     4-column table = 6 spaces between columns

     5-column table = 4 spaces between columns

  2. Use this "centered" line as your "reference line" to set the tab stops.

  3. Move the cursor to the first character in column one of the "centered" line and note the POS indicator. (You will set your first tab at the number shown at the POS indicator for WP5.0, 1" less for WP5.1.) Repeat this procedure for each column.

Exercise Directions:

1. Start with a clear screen.

2. Use the preset margins.

3. Calculate tab settings to horizontally center the table on the right.

4. Clear the preset tabs.

4. When you have noted where each tab set will be made, delete the reference line.

- To set new tabs, you must access the "tab ruler" (**Shift + F8, L, T**). The tab ruler displays preset tabs, 1/2" apart, which are indicated by an "L".

WP5.0 Tab Ruler

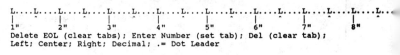

WP5.1 Tab Ruler

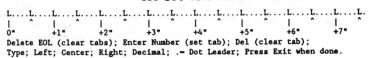

- Before you can set new tab stops, you must first delete the preset tabs. After deleting the preset tabs, set your new tabs according to how you want the text in the column to be formatted. (Left Aligned, Right Aligned, Centered, Decimal Aligned.) (See procedure on next page.)

- NOTE: WordPerfect 5.0 measures tabs from the left edge of the paper, (referred to as an "Absolute" setting) while WordPerfect 5.1 measures tabs from the left margin (referred to as a "Relative" setting).

- These exercises were created using WP5.0 which contain absolute tab settings. If you are using WP5.1, you must change the type of tab setting to "Absolute" to insure that tabbed columns align correctly according to the exercise directions. To do this, press Shift + F8, 1, 8, T, A.

- In this exercise, you will format a two-column table. The first and second columns are "Left Aligned."

- There are two methods of setting a "Left-Aligned" tab. You may type the desired inches where you want tabs inserted. For example, If you desire tabs at 1", 2 1/2", and 4", you would delete all current tab settings, then type 1.0, Enter, 2.5, Enter and 4.0, Enter. Or, you may move the cursor to your desired tab setting and press "L".

- Text is affected below the tab change. Tabs may be changed throughout a document.

5. Set left-aligned tabs for both columns.

6. Vertically center the exercise.

7. Print one copy.

8. Save the exercise; name it **PRES.**

```
          Presidents of the United States
                    1901-1992

     Theodore Roosevelt          1901-1909
     William H. Taft             1909-1913
     Woodrow Wilson              1913-1921
     Warren G. Harding           1921-1923
     Calvin Coolidge             1923-1929
     Herbert C. Hoover           1929-1933
     Franklin D. Roosevelt       1933-1945
     Harry S. Truman             1945-1953
     Dwight D. Eisenhower        1953-1961
     John F. Kennedy             1961-1963
     Lyndon B. Johnson           1963-1969
     Richard M. Nixon            1969-1974
     Gerald R. Ford              1974-1977
     James E. Carter, Jr.        1977-1981
     Ronald W. Regan             1981-1989
     George H. W. Bush           1989-199-
```

TO SET TAB STYLES

1. Place cursor at location in document for tab change.
2. Press **Shift + F8**...... `Shift` + `F8`
3. Select **L** (line)............................ `L`
4. Select **T** (tab set)...................... `T`
5. Press **Home, Home, ¬** ....
   .... `Home`, `Home`, `←`
6. Press **Ctrl + End** (to clear all tabs)
   .... `Ctrl` + `End`
7. Using cursor directional keys, move cursor to desired location for tab set.
   or
   • Type the desired tab setting (in inches)
   • Enter.................................... `↵`

8. Select one of the following tab styles:
   L (left align [default])................... `L`
   R (right align)............................... `R`
   D (decimal align)......................... `D`
   C (center text)............................. `C`
   L. (left align, preceded by dot leader)........................ `L`,`.`
   R. (right align, preceded by dot leader)........................ `R`,`.`
   D. (decimal align, preceded by dot leader)........................ `D`,`.`
   C. (center text, preceded by dot leader)........................ `C`,`.`

NOTE: Those tabs that require a dot leader will be displayed on the tab ruler in reverse video

9. Repeat steps 7 & 8 for each desired tab.
10. Press **F7**.................................. `F7`
    to return to line format menu.
11. Press **F7**.................................. `F7`
    to return to document.
    NOTE: An individual tab can be deleted by moving cursor under the tab set and pressing the delete key.

177

CREATING TABULATED COLUMNS (With Dot Leaders)

Notes:

- In this exercise you will create a two-column table in which the first column has a left-aligned tab set and the second column has a right-aligned tab set with a preceding dot leader.

- A dot leader is a series of dots that connect one column to another to keep the reader's eye focused from the beginning to the end of the line. The dot leader feature will make your document more attractive.

- To calculate a right-aligned tab, move your cursor just past the last character in the right-aligned column, and check the POS indicator for the tab setting. Press "R" to set the right-aligned tab; then press period (.) to set a preceding dot leader.

- After your settings are made, use the tab key to advance to each column. The dot leaders will automatically appear.

Exercise Directions:

1. Start with a clear screen.

2. Use the preset margins.

3. Horizontally center the table on the right. Set the first column with a left-aligned tab; set the second column with a right-aligned tab preceded by a dot leader.

4. Vertically center the exercise.

5. Print one copy.

6. Save the exercise; name it **PLANET.**

```
            PLANETS AND THEIR DISTANCE FROM THE SUN
                         (In Miles)


        Mercury  .  .  .  .  .    36,000,000
        Venus  .  .  .  .  .  .    67,230,000
        Earth  .  .  .  .  .  .    92,960,000
        Mars .  .  .  .  .  .  .  141,700,000
        Jupiter  .  .  .  .  .   483,700,000
        Saturn .  .  .  .  .  .   885,200,000
        Uranus .  .  .  .  .   1,781,000,000
        Neptune  .  .  .  .   2,788,000,000
        Pluto  .  .  .  .  .   3,660,000,000
```

CREATING TABULATED COLUMNS

Notes:

• In this exercise, you will create a two-column table in which the first column has a left-aligned tab set and the second column has a decimal-aligned tab set.

• When you set a decimal-aligned tab, move your cursor to the location of the decimal (in the reference line); then press "D."

Exercise Directions:

1. Start with a clear screen.

2. Use the preset margins.

3. Horizontally center the table on the right. Set the first column with a left-aligned tab; set the second column with a decimal-aligned tab.

4. Vertically center the exercise.

5. Print one copy.

6. Save the exercise; name it **INCOME.**

```
                    ACME COMPUTER SUPPLY
         SALES INCOME - 1991 - ON SELECTED PRODUCTS


              Keyboards           $ 45,345.67
              Modems                65,655.22
              Computers            211,888.75
              Disk Drives           76,558.88
              Scanners              23,446.99
              Printers              77,854.00
              Monitors               9,900.90
```

CREATING TABULATED COLUMNS

Notes:

- In this exercise, you will determine what column type is needed and create the two-column Table of Contents indicated.

Exercise Directions:

1. Start with a clear screen.
2. Use the preset margins.
3. Horizontally center the table on the right, setting the proper column type.
5. Vertically center the exercise.
6. Print one copy.
7. Save the exercise; name it **CONTENTS.**

BIOLOGY CONCEPTS
TABLE OF CONTENTS

CREATING TABULATED COLUMNS

Notes:

- In this exercise, you will determine what column type is needed and create the three-column table indicated.

Exercise Directions:

1. Start with a clear screen.
2. Use the preset margins.
3. Horizontally center the table on the right, setting the proper column type.
5. Vertically center the exercise.
6. Print one copy.
7. Save the exercise; name it **WAGES.**

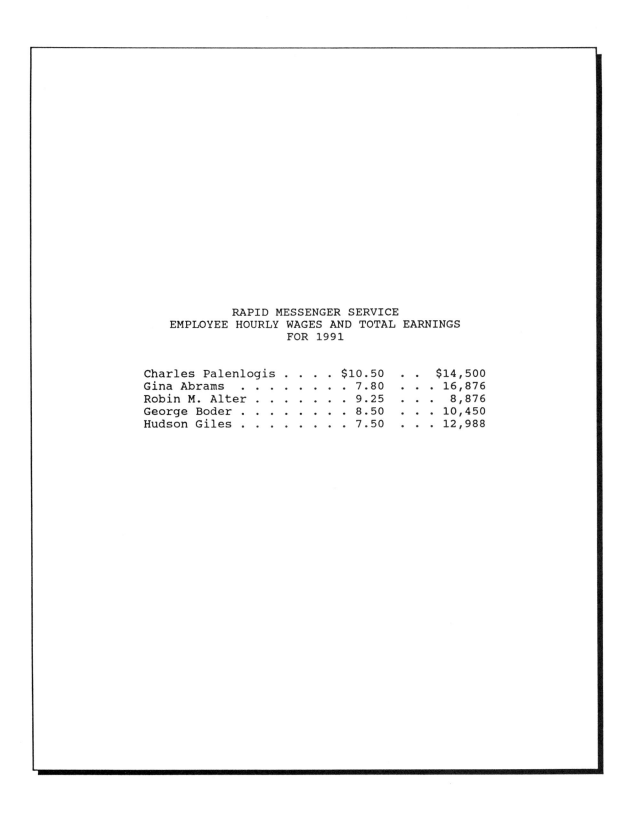

```
               RAPID MESSENGER SERVICE
        EMPLOYEE HOURLY WAGES AND TOTAL EARNINGS
                      FOR 1991


Charles Palenlogis . . . . $10.50  . .  $14,500
Gina Abrams  . . . . . . . . 7.80  . . . 16,876
Robin M. Alter . . . . . . . 9.25  . . .  8,876
George Boder . . . . . . . . 8.50  . . . 10,450
Hudson Giles . . . . . . . . 7.50  . . . 12,988
```

CREATING TABULATED COLUMNS

Notes:

- In this exericse, you will create a three-column income statement and determine what column type is needed to create it.

- An income statement shows the net income or loss earned by a business during a particular period.

Exercise Directions:

1. Start with a clear screen.

2. Use the preset margins.

3. Horizontally center the income statement on the right, setting the proper tabs and column types.

4. Leave four spaces between the columns.

5. Vertically center the exercise.

6. Print one copy.

7. Save the exercise; name it **IS.**

```
                    PAUL B'S CARD SHOP
                     INCOME STATEMENT
             For the Month Ended April 30, 199-


Revenue:
     Sales . . . . . . . . . . . . . . . 25,700
     Less Sales Returns and Allowances . . . .  700
     Net Sales . . . . . . . . . . . . . . . . .          25,000
Cost of Merchandise Sold:
     Merchandise Inventory, April 1 . . . . . 50,250
     Purchases . . . . . . . . . . . . . .  9,250
     Merchandise Available for Sale. . . . . 59,500
     Less Merchandise Inventory, April 30 . . 40,000
          Cost of Merchandise Sold . . . . . . . .       19,500
Gross Profit on Sales . . . . . . . . . . . . . .         9,000
Operating Expenses:
     Salaries  . . . . . . . . . . . . . .  4,000
     Rent . . . . . . . . . . . . . . . .  1,666
     Taxes . . . . . . . . . . . . . . . .   400
     Utilities . . . . . . . . . . . . . .   345
     Advertising . . . . . . . . . . . . .   500
     Depreciation on Equipment . . . . . . .   210
     Insurance . . . . . . . . . . . . . .    65
          Total Operating Expenses . . . . . . . .       7,186
Net Income: . . . . . . . . . . . . . . . . . . .        1,814
```

CREATING TABULATED COLUMNS (With Left-Aligned Column Headings); CHANGING THE ALIGNMENT CHARACTER

Notes:

- In this exercise you will create a table containing column headings which are left aligned with the column. This style of column heading is becoming more popular because it requires less calculation.

- WordPerfect allows you to align text on a character other than a decimal point. In this exercise, you will align the second and third column data on the comma. This will require that you change the alignment character. (See procedures on next page.) Changing the alignment character should be done before you begin the exercise.

- To determine tab settings for this exercise, create two "reference lines": 1. Center the longest line in each column including the intercolumn space. 2. Type one item in the second and third columns under the column headings. (See illustration below.) Then, access the tab ruler and set a left-alignment tab for each of the three columns and set a decimal alignment tab where the <u>comma</u> appears.

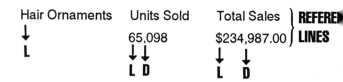

Exercise Directions:

1. Start with a clear screen.

2. Use the preset margins.

3. Change the alignment character to a comma.

4. Horizontally center the table on the right, setting left alignment and decimal tabs where appropriate.

5. Vertically center the exercise.

6. Print one copy.

7. Save the exercise; name it **UNITS.**

```
                    ACCESSORIES, LTD.
                UNITS SOLD/TOTAL SALES
        WOODBRIDGE, NJ and STATEN ISLAND MALLS
                        199-


    Item                Units Sold        Total Sales

    Earrings              65,098          $234,987.00
    Bracelets             32,812           14,198.88
    Hair Ornaments        99,100          623,543.58
    Handbags              56,987          100,187.76
    Necklaces             14,111           99,123.23
    Pins                   2,198           14,678.32
    Belts                  8,120           27,984.00
    Scarves                5,100           25,344.44
```

TO CHANGE ALIGNMENT CHARACTER

1. Move cursor to where alignment character will be changed.
2. Press **Shift + F8**........ **Shift** + **F8**
3. Select **O** (other)............................ **O**
4. Select **D** (decimal / align character)

   .... **D**
5. Type new alignment character.
6. **ENTER**.. **↵**
7. Press **F7**.................................... **F7**

   to return to document.

CREATING TABULATED COLUMNS (With Left-Aligned Column Headings); CHANGING THE ALIGNMENT CHARACTER

Notes:

- In this exercise, you will create a table containing column headings which are left aligned with the column.

- To align the first column items at the slash, you will need to change the alignment character to a slash (/).

Exercise Directions:

1. Start with a clear screen.

2. Use the preset margins.

3. Change the alignment character to a slash (/).

4. Using the repeat value key, create the horizontal line using any desired character.

5. Horizontally center the table on the right, setting the appropriate alignment tabs. Set a right alignment tab for the items in the last column.

6. Vertically center the exercise.

7. Print one copy.

8. Save the exercise; name it **PURCHASE.**

```
                    MIDDLETOWN HIGH SCHOOL

                      SPRING SUPPLY ORDER
                            199-

+++++++++++++++++++++++++++++++++++++++++++++++++++++++++++++++++

    Catalog Number        Quantity       Description      Unit Price

       23/2D4             10 boxes       Staplers          4.25
       D14/56             12 boxes       Paper Clips       1.25
        4/346             12 each        Blotters          5.00
       S3/1112            10 reams       Memo Pads         9.48
        DO/9              12 boxes       Disks             7.88
       T99/9-1            10 boxes       Markers           8.65
       CH/334             50 boxes       Chalk             1.10


+++++++++++++++++++++++++++++++++++++++++++++++++++++++++++++++++
```

CREATING TABULATED COLUMNS (With Left-Aligned Column Headings within a Document); CHANGING THE ALIGNMENT CHARACTER

Notes:

- In this exercise, you will create a letter which includes a centered table with left-aligned column headings.

- When a table is inserted within a document, it is suggested that the amount of intercolumn space usually recommended for a table be divided in half. If the material in the table is long, it is recommended that the margins be widened.

- To align the last column data at the % symbol, you will need to change the alignment character to %.

Exercise Directions:

1. Start with a clear screen.
2. Use the preset margins
3. Begin the exercise at Ln 2.5".
4. Create the letter on the right, centering the inserted table.
5. Set the appropriate alignment tabs; change the alignment character to the percentage symbol (%).
6. Print one copy.
7. Save the exercise; name it **EXEC.**

Today's date

Mr. Hugh Boland
23 Lark Avenue
New Orleans, LA 70112

Dear Mr. Boland:

As you requested, listed below is the information concerning
percentage of shares owned by the executive officers of the
SunDance Company for the fiscal year ended December 31, 1990.

NAME	POSITION	% OF SHARES
Richard D. Malverne	CEO	4.5%
Preston Richards	President	10.2%
Shirley Wong	VP-Operations	.8%
Ross Riley	VP-Sales	1.3%

If you desire any additional information about investing in
SunDance Company, please do not hesitate to call me.

Sincerely,

Thelma Wittier
Financial Services

tw/yo

CREATING TABULATED COLUMNS (With Centered Column Headings)

Notes:

- In this exercise, you will create a table containing column headings which are shorter than any of the items in the columns. To create an attractive table, the column headings are centered over the column.

- Since WordPerfect does not have an automatic column feature, it is necessary to calculate where tab settings should be made.

- The procedure for calculating tab settings with a centered column heading is as follows:

  1. Depress **Shift + F6** (center) and type the longest line of each column including the intercolumn space.

  2. Use this "reference line" to set the tab stops.

3. Access the tab ruler (**Shift + F8, L, T**) and set your tabs according to how you want the text in the column to be formatted. (Left-Aligned, Right-Aligned, Centered, Decimal-Aligned.)

4. Set a center tab at the center point of the longest line in each column.

5. Return to your document.

6. Tab to each center tab set to type the column heading.

7. Type the remainder of the table.

8. Delete the reference line.

9. Vertically center the exercise.

Exercise Directions:

1. Start with a clear screen.

2. Use the preset margins.

3. Horizontally center the table on the right, setting the proper column type and centering the column headings over the columns.

4. Vertically center the exercise.

5. Print one copy.

6. Save the exercise; name it **RATING.**

```
          NEC POWERMATE PERSONAL COMPUTER
               PERFORMANCE RATING


          Performance                     Score

     CPU-intensive applications      Satisfactory
     Disk-applications               Satisfactory
     Multitasking performance        Excellent
     File server performance         Satisfactory
     Software compatibility          Excellent
     Hardware compatibility          Excellent
     Expandability                   Good
```

CREATING TABULATED COLUMNS (With Centered Column Headings Within A Document)

Notes:

• In this exercise, you will create a memorandum with an inserted table. Note that the items in the memo heading are aligned at the colon. This will require you to change your alignment character for the memorandum heading. After the first paragraph is typed, you will create the table using the procedures outlined in Exercise 84. Remember to use half the amount of space between the columns.

Exercise Directions:

1. Start with a clear screen.

2. Use the preset margins.

3. Create the memo on the right, centering the inserted table.

4. Change the alignment character to a colon (:) and set the appropriate tab to align the colon in the memorandum side headings.

5. Unjustify your document for WP5.0; (left justify for WP5.1).

6. Reset the appropriate tab settings for the inserted table.

7. Print one copy.

8. Save the exercise; name it **OFFICER.**

```
TO:       Management Vice Presidents

FROM:     Carter Burlington

SUBJECT:  Executive Officers of Technology, Inc.

DATE:     Today's
```

The directors and executive officers of Technology, Inc. are listed in the table below and brief summaries of their business experience are outlined in a report that will be forwarded to you by the end of next week.

Name	Position
Stephen Richardson	President and CEO
Alan E. Ennis	Vice Chair, Bd. of Directors
Nicholas Stannis	Executive VP and CFO
Pricilla Carroll	VP--Director of Sales
Judy M. Blane	VP--Director of Marketing
Gladys R. Grafe	Director
Norman Miller	Director
Kenneth Newman, Ph.D.	Director, Consultant
Donna Brown	Director

Mr. Richardson and Ms. Brown are also members of the Executive Committee, while Mr. Miller and Ms. Blane are members of the Audit Committee.

yo

CREATING TABULATED COLUMNS (With Centered Column Headings)

Notes:

- In this exercise, you will create a table with centered column headings and dot leaders. Set the dot leader tab setting <u>after</u> you type the column headings. Otherwise, the dot leader will appear between the "WINNER" and "LEAGUE" columns.

Exercise Directions:

1. Start with a clear screen.

2. Use the preset margins.

3. Create the table on the right, setting the appropriate tabs to left align the columns on the left and center the headings.

4. Vertically center the exercise.

5. Print one copy.

6. Save the exercise; name it **ATBAT**.

THE WORLD SERIES

WINNERS/LOSERS
1955-1970

```
******************************************************************
     YEAR      WINNER        LEAGUE        LOSER        W-L
******************************************************************
     1955    Brooklyn   . .  National   New York       4-3
     1956    New York   . .  American   Brooklyn       4-3
     1957    Milwaukee  . .  National   New York       4-3
     1958    New York   . .  American   Milwaukee      4-3
     1959    Los Angeles .   National   Chicago        4-2
     1960    Pittsburgh  .   National   New York       4-3
     1961    New York   . .  American   Cincinnati     4-1
     1962    New York   . .  American   San Francisco  4-3
     1963    Los Angeles .   National   New York       4-0
     1964    St. Louis  . .  National   New York       4-3
     1965    Los Angeles .   National   Minnesota      4-3
     1966    Baltimore  . .  American   Los Angeles    4-0
     1967    St. Louis  . .  National   Boston         4-3
     1968    Detroit  . . .  American   St. Louis      4-3
     1969    New York   . .  National   Baltimore      4-1
     1970    Baltimore  . .  American   Cincinnati     4-1
```

CREATING TABULATED COLUMNS (With Centered Column Headings)

Notes:

- In this exercise, you will create a table with centered column headings, dot leaders and a decimal alignment column. Set the dot leader tab <u>after</u> you type the column headings. Otherwise, a dot leader will appear between the "ZIP" and "$OWED" column headings.

- The exercise was created with two spaces between all columns except between the "ZIP" and "$OWED" in which there are ten spaces between the columns.

Exercise Directions:

1. Start with a clear screen.

2. Set the left and right margins to .5".

3. Create the table on the right, setting the appropriate tab settings to align the columns and center the headings.

4. Leave two spaces between each column; leave ten spaces between the "ZIP" and "$OWED" columns.

5. Vertically center the exercise.

6. Print one copy.

7. Save the exercise; name it **ACCOUNT**.

```
                    J. V. SIDING, INCORPORATED
                    DELINQUENT ACCOUNTS

                         JUNE 199-

        NAME              ADDRESS            ZIP           $OWED

   Janice Smith       54 Jackson St.        10012  . . .$   345.23
   Thomas Renner      656 Travis St.        10044  . . . 1,366.66
   Simon Kline        444 East 86 St.       10022  . . . 1,500.00
   Henry Davis        55 East End Ave.      10077  . . .     75.99
   Dean Nevins        14 East 48 St.        10016  . . .    555.55
   Patricia Marge     231 Willowbrooke West 10323  . . .    200.96
   Scott Silver       87 Riverside Dr.      10087  . . . 4,203.09
```

CREATING TABULATED COLUMNS (With Long Column Headings)

Notes:

- In this exercise, the column headings are longer than any of the items in the columns. To determine tab settings when the column heading is longer than any item in the column, create a "reference line" as follows:

  1. Depress **Shift + F6** (center) and type the longest line of each column (which are the headings in this exercise) including the intercolumn space.

  2. Make note of where each column heading begins (Check the "Pos" indicator on the status line).

  3. Move cursor to the first character in the first column. With the cursor arrow key, move the cursor **right** 1x for every 2 characters for the longest line (the column heading). Using the cursor arrow, move the cursor **left** lx for every two characters for the longest line *in the column.* Make note of where the longest line in the column begins (check the "Pos" indicator on the status line).

  4. Repeat step 3 for each column.

  5. Access the tab ruler (**Shift + F8, L, T**) and set your tabs <u>for the items in the column</u> at your noted positions according to how you want the text in the column to be formatted (Left, Right or Decimal-Aligned).

  6. Return to your document (**F7**).

  7. Space to your noted position for each column heading and type it.

  8. Tab to each tab setting within the column and type the items within the column.

  9. Delete the reference line.

  10. Vertically center the exercise.

Exercise Directions:

1. Start with a clear screen.

2. Use the preset margins.

3. Using the method of calculating tab settings for tables with long column headings, create the table on the right, setting appropriate tab settings to align the columns and center the headings.

4. Leave four spaces between columns.

5. Vertically center the exercise.

6. Print one copy.

7. Save the exercise; name it **EMPLOYEE.**

```
                    ACME ELECTRICAL GROUP
                       PERSONNEL LIST
                     Union Membership


    LAST NAME      FIRST NAME     EMPLOYEE NO.     UNION MEMBER

       ALLEN          JOHN            2676             YES
       SMITH          ROBIN           6000             NO
       JONES          SAM             8211             YES
       ROBBIN         MARTIN          4110             YES
       LASAR          SALLY           1220             NO
       JOHNNS         JAMAL           6767             YES
```

CREATING TABULATED COLUMNS (With Long Column Headings)

Notes:

- In this exercise, the column headings are longer than any of the items in the columns. The second column contains a decimal alignment tab and the third column contains a right-alignment tab. The exercise was created using eight spaces between the columns.

- To determine tab settings when the column heading is longer than any item in the column, follow the procedures described in Exercise 88.

Exercise Directions:

1. Start with a clear screen.

2. Use the preset margins.

3. Create the table on the right, setting appropriate tabs.

4. Leave eight spaces between columns.

5. Vertically center the exercise.

6. Print one copy.

7. Save the exercise; name it **STOCK**.

```
                        PORTFOLIO OF
                       HARRY S. AHRENS
                          As Of
                        June 199-


    NAME OF STOCK          PURCHASE PRICE          NO. SHARES PURCHASED

       R & L                  $60.00                     100
       TECH LABS               45.35                       80
       ASTEC IND.              14.85                      250
       X-MATION                 2.50                      800
       IDM                     50.00                    1,000
```

CREATING TABULATED COLUMNS (With Long Column Headings)

Notes:

- In this exercise, you will create a memorandum with an inserted table. Note that the items in the memo heading are aligned at the colon. This will require you to change your alignment character. After the first paragraph is typed, you will create the table using the procedures outlined in Exercise 88.

Exercise Directions:

1. Start with a clear screen.

2. Set left and right margins for .5".

3. Create the memo on the right, centering the inserted table.

4. Change the alignment character to a colon (:) and set the appropriate tab to align the colon in the memorandum side headings.

5. Justify your document for **WP5.0** (full justify for **WP5.1**).

6. Reset the appropriate tab settings for the inserted table. Use the colon to align hours/minutes in the third column. Leave four spaces between each column in the table.

7. Print one copy.

8. Save the exercise; name it **COURSES.**

```
        TO:       GUIDANCE PERSONNEL

      FROM:       Cynthia Greenkill, Chairperson

        RE:       Fall Computer Offerings

      DATE:       Today's
```

Listed below is a tentative schedule of computer classes that our department will be offering in the fall. Please be sure to use the correct code when registering students for the courses listed.

COURSE TITLE	COURSE CODE	TIME OF CLASS	INSTRUCTOR
Database	DB3	10:00 A. M.	Winston
Spreadsheets	SS101	9:20 A. M.	Rosen
Basic	BC1	11:00 A. M.	Simms
Desktop	DTP1	12:40 P. M.	Pilgrim
Word Proc.	WP3	1:50 P. M.	Gold

If you have any questions regarding the above, please call me. Preliminary scheduling will begin on Monday of next week.

cg/

CREATING TABULATED COLUMNS (With Mixed-Length Column Headings)

Notes:

- In this exercise, you will create a full-block letter with an inserted table. The table includes mixed-length column headings. This exercise was created using four spaces between the columns.

- The procedures for formatting mixed-length column heading tables are a combination of those reviewed in Exercises 83 and 88. The first step is to create a "reference line" as you did in previous exercises:

  1. Depress **Shift + F6** (center) and type the longest line of each column (which may include a combination of headings and/or longest item(s) in the column) including the intercolumn space.

  2. Note where each column begins (check the "Pos" indicator on the status line).

  3. If the column heading is shorter than the items in the column, follow steps 3-7 outlined in Exercise 84; if the column heading is longer than the column items, follow steps 3-8 outlined in Exercise 88.

Exercise Directions:

1. Start with a clear screen.

2. Use the preset margins.

3. Create the full-block letter on the right, centering the inserted table.

4. Justify your document for WP5.0 (full justify for WP5.1).

5. Leave four spaces between columns in the table.

6. Print one copy.

7. Save the exercise; name it **RECEIPT.**

Today's Date

Mr. Wilson Smith
Upjohn Foods, Inc.
546 Market Lane
Bronx, NY 10456

Dear Mr. Smith:

I received my order yesterday and found that the following items
were missing. Robert Phillips, our order clerk, indicated to me
that these items were included on the order form he sent to you.
Whatever the reason for the mix-up, I would appreciate it if you
would send the items listed below as quickly as possible.

QUANTITY	DESCRIPTION	UNIT PRICE	AMOUNT
25	Cans Tomato Paste	.25	6.25
10	Cases Potato Chips	8.45	84.50
3	Cases Pop Corn	2.00	6.00
14	Turkeys	6.85	95.90
12	Pkgs. Hot Dogs	3.65	43.80
8	Boxes Sugar Cubes	.85	6.80

The prices for each item should be correct. If there is a problem,
please call me at 212-965-5433 between 9:30 a.m. and 5 p.m.

Sincerely,

Barbara Yussim
Manager

by/

CREATING TABULATED COLUMNS
(With Multiple Mixed-Length Column Headings)

Notes:

• In this exercise, you will create multiple-line, mixed-length column headings. This exercise was created using six spaces between the columns.

• To center one heading above the other:

1. Create your "reference line" as indicated in Exercise 91.

2. Place your cursor on the first character of the longer heading. With the cursor arrow key, move the cursor **right** 1x for every two characters in the longest line. Then, using the cursor arrow, move the cursor **left** lx for every two characters in the shorter column heading. Note where the shorter line in the heading begins (check the "Pos" indicator on the status line).

3. When you are ready to type the exercise, space to the noted positions to type the shorter part of the column heading.

Exercise Directions:

1. Start with a clear screen.

2. Set the left and right margins to .5".

3. Create the full-block letter on the right, centering the inserted table.

4. Justify your document for WP5.0 (full justify for WP5.1).

5. Leave three spaces between columns in the table.

6. Print one copy.

7. Save the exercise; name it **WORK.**

Today's Date

Mr. Avram Issey
ABC Computer Company
785 Lighthouse Road
Portland, OR 98138

Dear Mr. Issey:

Listed below is our projected delivery schedule for the items you ordered.
We agreed that it normally takes approximately six weeks from the day of
purchase to receive your order. We are trying to make every effort to
deliver on time.

We like for you to know when shipments will be arriving so that someone in
your company is there to accept them.

ITEM	YOUR ORDER NO.	EXPECTED DELIVERY DATE	QUANTITY SCHEDULED
Computer Paper	7651-988	April 21	220
Computer Ribbons	2787-000	May 1	130
Printers	8861-243	May 15	89
Monitors	0098-123	May 16	10
Keyboards	3450-344	June 1	108
Disk Drives	8890-220	July 1	199

If there is a problem with any of the delivery dates, please be sure to phone
me as soon as possible. We will phone you several days in advance if we
expect there to be a problem with delivery time.

Sincerely,

Jackson Kellogg
Distribution Manager

jk/

CALCULATING COLUMNS (Procedure 1)

Notes:

- WordPerfect's columnar math feature allows you to calculate numbers in columns and rows. (Calculating rows and using math formulas for addition, subtraction, multiplication and division will not be covered in this book. Refer to software documentation for instruction.)

- To use the math feature, numbers must be arranged in columns which were established with tab settings.

- When the math feature is accessed, WordPerfect considers all alphabetic text entered in columns to be numeric. If you try to enter alphabetic text in a numeric column, the text will move to the left (like a decimal column); if you enter a decimal point, the text will move to the right. Therefore, do not use a tab set for alphabetic text; space to an alphabetic column or use the left margin for entering alphabetic text. Be sure to set numeric column tabs for the decimal location (or end of column if there is no decimal point--not the beginning of the column.) NOTE: Since this exercise contains only one column of text and one column of numbers to be calculated, Procedure I outlined below may be used. In subsequent exercises, Procedure II will be introduced.

- A math operator, or symbol, must be entered in the column to indicate the type of total desired. The math operator and the result of the calculation appear below:

MATH OPERATOR	RESULT	ACTION
+	subtotal	adds numbers above it
=	total	adds subtotals above it
*	grand total	adds totals above it

- In this exercise, you will create two columns and enter math operators in the numeric column to get total, subtotal and grand total results. The procedures for completing this exercise are:

1. Center the longest line in each column, plus the intercolumn space (reference line).

2. Note where the columns/column headings begin; SET A TAB(S) ONLY FOR THE NUMERIC COLUMN(S). Set numeric column tabs for the decimal location (or end of column if there is no decimal point--not the beginning of the column).

3. Delete the reference line.

4. Type column headings (if applicable).

5. Turn **on** the math feature.

6. **a**. Space to the noted location for the first column and type the text. **b**. TAB to the second column and type the numeric text. Repeat steps 6a and 6b until all text is entered.

Exercise Directions:

1. Start with a clear screen.
2. Use the preset margins.
3. Create the two-column table on the next page using a decimal tab setting for the numerical column.
4. Leave ten spaces between the columns.
5. Insert the math operator indicated and calculate the column.
6. Vertically center the exercise.
7. Print one copy.
8. Save the exercise; name it **TOTAL**.

continued...

```
Region 1 Sales
     Zone 1              $25,000.00
     Zone 2               15,000.00
     SUBTOTAL                +

Region 2 Sales
     Zone 1               10,000.00
     Zone 2               45,000.00
     SUBTOTAL                +

     TOTAL                   =

Region 3 Sales
     Zone 1               18,000.00
     Zone 2               20,000.00
     SUBTOTAL                +

Region 4 Sales
     Zone 1               22,000.00
     Zone 2               14,000.00
     SUBTOTAL                +

     TOTAL                   =
     GRAND TOTAL             *
```

TO CALCULATE SUBTOTAL, TOTAL, GRAND TOTAL (Procedure 1)

* Use when there are few or no text columns. (Math without define feature.)

WP5.0

1. Set tabs FOR NUMERIC COLUMNS ONLY (See Ex. 75).

2. Press **Alt + F7** (math/columns menu).......................**Alt** + **F7**

3. Select **M** (math on)....................**M**
   NOTE: Math message appears at the bottom of screen.

4. **TAB** (to each numeric column and type column data)...................**TAB**

5. **TAB** (to bottom of numeric column to be calculated)....................**TAB**

6. Type + (to create subtotal)........**+**
   or
   or = (to create total).................**=**
   or
   or * (to create grand total)........*****
   (Repeat steps 5 & 6 for all columns to be calculated.

---

7. Press **Alt + F7** (math / column menu) ....**Alt** + **F7**

8. Select **A** (calculate)....................**A**
   NOTE: The result of calculation column will be displayed.

9. Press **Alt + F7** (math/column menu) ....**Alt** + **F7**

10. Select **M** (math off).....................**M**

WP5.1

1. Set tabs FOR NUMERIC COLUMNS ONLY (See Ex. 75).

2. Press **Alt+F7** (columns/tables/math)..........................**Alt** + **F7**

3. Select **M** (math)..........................**M**

4. Select **O** (on)..............................**O**
   NOTE: Math message appears at the bottom of screen.

5. **TAB** (to each numeric column and type column data)...................**TAB**

---

6. **TAB** (to bottom of numeric column to be calculated)....................**TAB**

7. Type + (to create subtotal)........**+**
   or
   or = (to create total).................**=**
   or
   or * (to create grand total)........*****
   (Repeat steps 6 & 7 for all columns to be calculated.

8. Press **Alt + F7** (columns/tables/math)..........................**Alt** + **F7**

9. Select **M** (math)..........................**M**

10. Select **C** (calculate).....................**C**
    NOTE: The result of calculation column will be displayed.

11. Press **Alt + F7** (columns/tables/math)..........................**Alt** + **F7**

12. Select **M** (math)..........................**M**

13. Select **F** (off)..............................**F**

CALCULATING COLUMNS (Procedure I)

Notes:

- In this exercise, you will create a three-column table with left-justified column headings. After creating the table, enter the appropriate math operator(s).

- Review steps for creating a math calculation table in Exercise 93.

Exercise Directions:

1. Start with a clear screen.
2. Use the preset margins.
3. Vertically center the exercise.
4. Create the table on the right, setting tabs where necessary.
5. Leave five spaces between each column.
6. Insert the appropriate math operators and calculate the money columns.
7. Print one copy.
8. Save the exercise; name it WEEK.

```
                    WEEKLY SALES AND SALARIES
                   FOR PART-TIME SALESPERSONS
                      Week of January 22


        NAME                SALES          SALARY

        Daniel Levin       $1,234.00     $    685.00
        John Imperio          865.99          290.00
        Rachael Simson      2,775.45          888.35
        Corey Modeste         553.12          578.55
        Patricia Nunez        923.34          571.00
        Hubert Attale         654.00          355.50

        TOTALS
```

CALCULATING COLUMNS (Procedure I)

Notes:

- In this exercise, you will create a two-column table and enter appropriate math operators to calculate the numeric column.

- Review steps for creating a math calculation table in Exercise 93.

Exercise Directions:

1. Start with a clear screen.
2. Use the preset margins.
3. Vertically center the exercise.
4. Create the table on the right, setting tabs where necessary.
5. Leave ten spaces between columns.
6. Insert the appropriate math operators to calculate the column.
7. Print one copy.
8. Save the exercise; name it **SALESRPT.**

```
              ACE COMPUTER COMPANY
              SALES REPORT - 199-


    FIRST QUARTER
    January                    81,825.64
    February                   72,987.43
    March                      65,012.97
         Subtotal

    SECOND QUARTER
    April                      79,821.34
    May                        78,123.23
    June                       63,455.91
         Subtotal

    FIRST HALF TOTAL

    THIRD QUARTER
    July                       83,888.22
    August                     74,122.45
    September                  95,305.08
         Subtotal

    FOURTH QUARTER
    October                   100,797.53
    November                  110,834.17
    December                  105,009.36
         Subtotal

    SECOND HALF TOTAL

    GRAND TOTAL
```

CALCULATING COLUMNS (Procedure II)
Notes:

- In this exercise, the first two columns are text, while the last three are numeric and require calculation. When several text columns are included in a math calculation table, it is not efficient to space to the text column and tab to the numeric column.

- To tell WordPerfect that the first two columns are **text** and the last three columns are **numeric** and will be calculated, you must access the "math definitions menu" which is illustrated below. (Procedure II).

- Note that columns are indicated by A, B, C, D, etc. Below the columns are the "Type" of columns. They are all defaulted with the number "2" -- indicating numeric columns.

- To tell WordPerfect that the first two columns in this exercise are text, you must set columns A & B to "text" columns before turning on the math feature.

- After settings are made on the math definitions menu and data has been entered after tabbing <u>to each column</u>, you can then tab to each numeric column and insert the plus (+) symbol where the answer should appear. Then, calculate the columns.

- In this exercise, you will create a five-column table with left-justified column headings and you will total the money columns. First, type column headings; then, access the math definitions menu, set columns A and B to "text," and turn on the math feature. Follow keystroke procedures outlined.

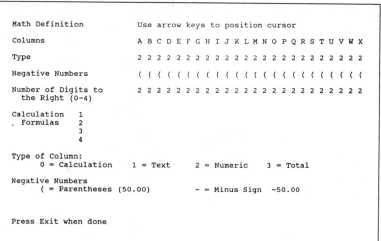

```
Math Definition           Use arrow keys to position cursor

Columns                   A B C D E F G H I J K L M N O P Q R S T U V W X

Type                      2 2 2 2 2 2 2 2 2 2 2 2 2 2 2 2 2 2 2 2 2 2 2 2

Negative Numbers          ( ( ( ( ( ( ( ( ( ( ( ( ( ( ( ( ( ( ( ( ( ( ( (

Number of Digits to       2 2 2 2 2 2 2 2 2 2 2 2 2 2 2 2 2 2 2 2 2 2 2 2
  the Right (0-4)

Calculation       1
. Formulas        2
                  3
                  4

Type of Column:
   0 = Calculation    1 = Text      2 = Numeric    3 = Total

Negative Numbers
   ( = Parentheses (50.00)       - = Minus Sign  -50.00


Press Exit when done
```

Exercise Directions:

1. Start with a clear screen.

2. Use the preset margins.

3. Vertically center the exercise.

4. Create the table on the next page, setting tabs where necessary. Leave three spaces between each column.

5. Access the math definitions menu; change the first two column types to "text."

6. Total each money column.

7. Print one copy.

8. Save the exercise; name it **JUNE.**

continued...

```
                    MICRO ELECTRONICS
              WEEKLY SALES BY SALESPERSON
                         JUNE


WEEK ENDING      TERRITORY     W. EMERY      A. RIVERA     J. THOMPSON

JUNE 5           EASTERN     $ 3,456.00    $ 2,345.22    $ 3,478.25
JUNE 12          WESTERN       2,455.23      5,321.95      5,190.75
JUNE 19          NORTHERN      2,100.77      4,165.20        900.87
JUNE 26          SOUTHERN      1,222.12      6,871.54        965.75

TOTALS
```

TO CALCULATE SUBTOTAL, TOTAL, GRAND TOTAL
Procedure II *

* Use when there are several text columns. (With math define menu).

WP5.0
1. Set tabs for all columns (See Ex.75).
2. Press **Alt + F7** (math/columns menu)........................ `Alt` + `F7`
3. Select **E** (math define)............... `E`
4. Move cursor to "Type" line.
5. Move cursor under column to be defined as text (A,B,C, etc.).
6. Type **1** (Text)........................ `1`
7. Repeat steps 5 & 6 until all desired columns are changed.
8. Press **F7** (to exit math definition).................................. `F7`
9. Select **M** (math on).................... `M`

   NOTE: Math message appears at the bottom of screen.

10. **TAB** to each column and type data.................................... `TAB`

11. **TAB** to bottom of numeric column to be calculated....... `TAB`

12. Type + (to create subtotal)......... `+`
    or   or
    = (to create total)........................ `=`
    or   or
    * (to create grand total)............. `*`

(Repeat steps 11 & 12 for all columns to be calculated.

13. Press **ALT + F7** (math/column menu)........................ `Alt` + `F7`
14. Select **A** (calculate)..................... `A`

    NOTE: The result of calculation column will be displayed.

15. Press **Alt + F7** (math/column menu)........................ `Alt` + `F7`
16. Select **M** (math off).................... `M`

WP5.1
1. Set tabs for all columns (See Ex. 75).
2. Press **Alt + F7** (columns/tables/math)........................ `Alt` + `F7`
3. Select **M** (math)..................... `M`
4. Select **D** (define)..................... `D`
5. Follow steps 4-8 above.
6. Select **O** (on)............................. `O`

   NOTE: Math message appears at the bottom of screen.

7. **TAB** to each column and type data.................................... `TAB`

8. **TAB** to bottom of numeric column to to be calculated..................... `TAB`

9. Type + (to create subtotal)......... `+`
    or   or
    = (to create total)........................ `=`
    or   or
    * (to create grand total)............. `*`

(Repeat steps 8 & 9 for all columns to be calculated.

10. Press **Alt + F7** (columns/tables/math)........................... `Alt` + `F7`
11. Select **M** (math)..................... `M`
12. Select **C** (calculate)..................... `C`

    NOTE: The result of calculation column will be displayed.

13. Press **Alt + F7** (columns/tables/math)........................... `Alt` + `F7`
14. Select **M** (math)......................... `M`
15. Select **F** (off)............................. `F`

TO DEFINE MATH DECIMAL PLACES TO BE DISPLAYED

1. Follow steps 1-3 (WP5.0) or steps 1-4 (WP5.1).
2. Move cursor to "number of digits" to the right (0-4) line.
3. Move cursor to column to change.
4. Type number of decimal places to be displayed.
5. Repeat steps 2-4 until all desired columns are changed.
6. Follow remaining steps above to calculate subtotal, total and grand total.

CALCULATING COLUMNS (Procedure II)

Notes:

- In this exercise, you will create a memorandum with an inserted table and total the money columns.

- To center column headings, cursor forward 1x for every two characters/spaces in longest line in the first and second columns and intercolumn, cursor back 1x for every two characters in column heading.

- To tell WordPerfect that the first and third columns are text, access math definitions menu and set columns A and C to "text." To tell WordPerfect that there are no decimals in the numeric columns, set "number of digits to the right" to "0" for columns B and D. (See Exercise 96.) After exiting the math definitions menu, turn on the math feature.

Exercise Directions:

1. Start with a clear screen.

2. Set left and right margins for .75"

3. Create the memo with an inserted table as indicated on the right. (Be sure to change the first and third column types to "text.")

4. Begin the exercise on Ln 2".

5. Justify your document for WP5.0 (Full justify for WP5.1).

6. Leave four spaces between columns.

7. Total each money column.

8. Print one copy.

9. Save the exercise; name it **EXTRA**.

TO: Shari Roberts, Personnel

FROM: Matt Romano, Sales

RE: EMPLOYEE BONUSES

DATE: Today's

Listed below are employees and their bonuses for the first and second
quarters of this year. These bonuses are based on the sales made in
their respective divisions. The total bonuses paid for the quarter are
also indicated. You will note that Joseph Monte and Moon Young were the
only employees that received bonuses in both the first and second
quarters.

↓3×

FIRST QUARTER		SECOND QUARTER	
Kenneth Shewitzz	$ 1,100	Chia-Jung Yen	$ 2,456
Joseph Monte	450	Joseph Monte	1,367
Kristin Schmit	2,345	Chris Sikora	861
Moon Young	920	Moon Young	3,677
Linda Malacuso	1,690	Lois Lane	224

↓2×

TOTAL BONUSES PAID

↓3×

If you need further information or have any questions, please let me
know.

yo

CALCULATING COLUMNS (Procedure II)

Notes:

- In this exercise, you will create a letter with an inserted table and total the money columns. Note that the first and second columns are text columns and that column headings are left aligned.

Exercise Directions:

1. Start with a clear screen.
2. Use the preset margins.
3. Create the letter with an inserted table as indicated on the right. (Be sure to change the first and second column types to "text".)
4. Begin the exercise on Ln 2.5".
5. Justify your document for WP5.0 (Full justify for WP5.1).
6. Leave three spaces between columns.

   NOTE: Column headings are left-aligned.
7. Total each money column.
8. Retrieve the standardized paragraph, CLOSING, where indicated.
9. Print one copy.
10. Save the exercise; name it **EXPENSES**.

Today's date

Freed, Frank & Mulligan, Inc.
Attention Mr. Weston Freed
543 Main Street
Detroit, MI 48236

Ladies and Gentlemen:

We have reviewed Alison Jackson's expenses for September. We find
that all is in order. The following is a summary:

DATE	CITY/STATE	LODGING	AUTO	FOOD	MISC.
9/1	Los Angeles, CA	1,000.00	195.00	189.00	118.00
9/7	New York, NY	450.00	45.00	215.00	35.00
9/14	Springfield, IL	189.50	87.45	105.65	25.56
9/21	Harrisburg, PA	175.00	80.00	125.50	45.00
9/28	Newton, MA	250.80	105.00	85.00	116.00

TOTALS

We will file all the necessary end-of-quarter papers as we have in
the past. I think we should get an earlier start next year in
preparation of an audit. We should discuss how to proceed at our
next meeting.

RETRIEVE
CLOSING

Lesson 8
Summary Exercise A

Exercise Directions:

1. Create the "GLOSSARY OF WORD PROCESSING TERMS" below using a parallel-column format.
2. Justify your document (for WP5.0); (full justify for WP5.1).
3. Begin the document 1" from the top of the paper.
4. Print one copy.
5. Save the exercise; name it **WP.**

AUTOMATIC RETURN
See "Wordwrap"
BOILERPLATE
Standardized or repetitive text which is saved for use in assembling documents.
BOLD PRINT
Printing of characters to look larger and darker.
CENTERING
Automatic positioning of text between margins and/or around a point.
DECIMAL TAB
Automatic alignment of columns of decimal figures at the decimal point.
DOCUMENT ASSEMBLY
Combining selections from prerecorded text to form a new document.
FORMAT
Layout of text on a page. Includes page size, tab and margin settings, line spacing, pitch and justification. Once the format is set, it may be recorded and recalled for future use.
HARD RETURN
Depressing the return key at the end of the line.
HEADERS/FOOTERS
Text placed at the top (header) or bottom (footer) of each document.
INDENT
Setting a temporary left or right margin where text will align.
JUSTIFICATION (FULL)
Text printed with an even right and left margin.
MERGE
Combining a standard document with a variable document to create new documents.
SAVE
The process of storing text on media for later retrieval.
SEARCH AND REPLACE
Searching for repeated occurrences of a character string and replacing it with another character string. This may be done automatically or by operator-instructed replacement.
WORDWRAP
Automatic placement of text onto the next line (without depressing the return key) when text reaches the end of the right margin. Also referred to as <u>AUTO WRAP</u>, and <u>AUTOMATIC RETURN</u>.

Lesson 8
Summary Exercise B

Exercise Directions

1. Create the table below, setting appropriate tab settings and using any desired intercolumn space.

2. Total the "STAFF" and "SALES" column.

3. Vertically center the exercise.

4. Print one copy.

5. Save the exercise; name it **BRANCH**.

BALIWANE SPORTSWEAR
New Branches/Locations/Gross Sales
As of January 31, 199 –

BRANCH	CITY	STATE	STAFF	SALES
Paramount	New York	NY	18	$ 350,000
Sunview	Hollywood	CA	12	125,000
Seaview	Portland	ME	8	100,000
Cornielle	Providence	RI	20	450,000
Astro Center	Houston	TX	19	99,000
Mountainaire	Troy	NY	6	95,000
5⎤ TOTALS				

LESSON 9:
USING GRAPHICS; CHANGING FONTS AND ATTRIBUTES;
USING LINE DRAW.

USING GRAPHICS (Creating a "Figure Box")

Notes:

- WordPerfect's graphics feature allows you to include pictures and images in a document. The ability to combine graphics and text in a document will enable you to create newsletters, brochures, flyers or other documents where pictures are needed.

- The graphics feature enables you to create four different boxes into which you can place a graphic image or text. The size and location of the box can be adjusted as desired.

- The WordPerfect 5.0 and 5.1 programs each contain 30 predesigned graphic pictures. The images that are available on WP5.0 and WP5.1 are shown on pages 290 - 292 (Appendix A.) You can, however, purchase graphics disks containing other images and access these images into the "box".

- In order to use the graphics feature, your computer must contain a "graphics card" and your printer must support graphics. You can still create graphics without a graphics card; however, you will not be able to view them. If you were able to view your document in earlier exercises, your machine has a graphics card.

- When you access the Graphics command (**Alt + F9),** you will need to select the box type you wish to create (1 Figure). The next menu will ask what you wish to do with the "figure." Since you want to "Create" a figure, you would then select

"C" (Create). The next menu contains information which will allow you to select the image or text you want to insert into the box (Filename), and the size and horizontal position of the graphic. **Other menu items will be covered as they become relevant to the exercise at hand.**

- If you are inserting a graphic image contained in WordPerfect, you must use the filename shown below the graphic. (See pages 290 - 292.) Note that each graphic filename has a ".WPG" extension.

- The **horizontal** placement of the figure can be aligned at left, at right or it can be centered when the "Type/Anchor Type" (WP5.1) is set at "Paragraph" (the default for this setting).

- The **size** selection allows you to change the width and height of your graphic.

- In this exercise, you will learn how to create one of the four box types -- a "figure box" -- and insert a graphic into it. You will create three different images, each sized differently and placed in separate horizontal positions. A figure box is generally used to create graphic images, diagrams and charts.

- After you create each graphic, you will notice that the word "figure" is displayed and a number follows it. Each new figure is given a new number by WordPerfect (the numbers will not print). This is done so that when you wish to make changes or edit your graphic box, you have a way to identify which graphic you want to edit.

Exercise Directions:

1. Start with a clear screen.

2. With the cursor at the top of the screen, create a "figure box" and insert a graphic, using any desired image.

3. Horizontally **center** the graphic; size the graphic to 1" wide x 1" high. Return as many times as necessary to bring your cursor to 2.5".

4. View the exercise at 100%.

5. Create a second graphic, positioning it **left** on the page and changing the size to 2" wide x 2" high. Return as many times as necessary to bring your cursor to 5".

6. View the exercise at 100%.

7. Create a third graphic, positioning it **right** on the page and changing the size to 3" wide x 3" high.

8. View the graphic at 100%.

9. Print one copy.

10. Save the file; name it **PICTURE**.

CENTERED GRAPHIC
1" x 1"

LEFT GRAPHIC
2" x 2"

RIGHT GRAPHIC
3" x 3"

TO CREATE A GRAPHIC BOX

1. Press **Alt + F9**............`Alt` + `F9`

2. Select one of the following box types:

   F (figure).................................`F`

   T (table....................................`T`

   B (text box)..............................`B`

   U (user box...)..........................`U`

   E (equation) (WP5.1 only).......`E`

3. Select **C** (create) ....`C`

4. Select **F** (filename)....................`F`

5. Type name of WordPerfect graphic file.

NOTE: If filename is not known, access "list files" (**F5**, **ENTER**), highlight a file with a ".WPG" extension and retrieve it.

6. **ENTER**....................................`↵`

TO CHANGE SIZE OF GRAPHIC

7. Select **S** (size)........................`S`

8. Select **B** (both width and height)..................................`B`

9. Type desired width.

10. **ENTER**..................................`↵`

11. Type desired height.

12. **ENTER**..................................`↵`

TO CHANGE HORIZONTAL POSITION OF GRAPHIC

13. Select **H** (horizontal position)...`H`

14. Select desired position:

    L (left)..............................`L`

    R (right).............................`R`

    C (center)..........................`C`

15. **ENTER**..................................`↵`

231

USING GRAPHICS (Creating a Letterhead)

Notes:

- In this exercise, you will combine text with a graphic to create a letterhead. To do this, you will first create the graphic as described in Exercise 96 and position it on the right of the page. You will then type the text on the left.

- After accessing the graphics command (**Alt + F9, 1, C**), it is important to note the menu item "Type/Anchor Type" (WP5.1) especially when combining text and graphics. The menu is defaulted to "paragraph" which means that the graphic will move with the text or paragraph surrounding it. If you want the graphic fixed at a particular location on a page, you must change the setting to "Page". If you want the graphic to be handled as part of text on a line, you must change the setting to "Character."

- In this exercise, you will use the default setting (Paragraph) for the "Type/Anchor Type" selection.

Exercise Directions:

1. Start with a clear screen.

2. With your cursor at the top of the screen, create a graphic, using a picture that relates to the letterhead. (See pages 290 - 292 for graphic choices.)

3. Place the graphic on the right of the page; size the graphic to 1" wide x 1" high.

4. Type the text as shown.

5. View the exercise at 100%.

6. Print one copy.

7. Save the file; name it **PARTY.**

PARTY BALLOONS, INC.

234 Riverside Drive

New York, NY 10098

USING GRAPHICS (Creating a Letterhead)

Notes:

- In this exercise, you will combine text with a graphic to create a letterhead. The graphic will be positioned on the left, while the text will be positioned flush right.

- You will note that while the graphic box is sized 2" wide x 1" high, the image is positioned in the middle of the box. It is possible to have the image "stretched" (referred to as "scaling") to fit the box. "Scaling a graphic" will be covered in the next exercise.

Exercise Directions:

1. Start with a clear screen.

2. With your cursor at the top of the screen, create a graphic, using the CLOCK.WPG graphic file.

3. Place the graphic on the left of the page; size the graphic to 2" wide x 1" high.

4. Using the flush right command (**Alt + F6**), type the text as shown.

5. View the exercise at 100%.

6. Print one copy.

7. Save the file; name it **CLOCK.**

TICK-TOCK SHOP
"Timepieces from Around the Globe"

157 East 68 Street
New York, NY 10087
212-123-TIME

USING GRAPHICS (Scaling a Graphic; Creating a Caption)

Notes:

- In this exercise, you will combine text with a "stretched" graphic containing a caption to create another letterhead.

- A **caption** is text that appears below the graphic which sometimes explains or details the graphic image. When you select "caption" from the menu, the screen will become blank for you to type the desired caption. The margins of the caption screen correspond to the margins of the box. The box number will appear in the caption screen automatically. To delete the box number, press backspace and then type your caption.

- The **scale** option allows you to expand or contract the graphic image horizontally or vertically (to have the graphic fill the box) by percentages. You will have to indicate to WordPerfect what percentage you wish to "stretch" the graphic horizontally (X-axis) or vertically (Y-axis). For example, to stretch a square image into a rectangular image, you might set the X-axis to 200% while not increasing the y axis at all. The image will immediately be rescaled to your directions. The box, however, will not change in size. The examples below show an image in which the X and Y axes have been scaled by various percentages.

SCALING SAMPLES

X-AXIS - 100
Y-AXIS - 100

X-AXIS - 140
Y-AXIS - 80

X-AXIS - 50
Y-AXIS - 100

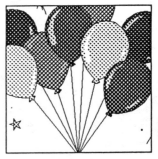

X-AXIS - 200
Y-AXIS - 200

Exercise Directions:

1. Start with a clear screen.

2. With your cursor at the top of the screen, create a graphic using the USAMAP.WPG (WP5.0) or BKGRND-1.WPG (WP5.1) graphic file.

3. Place the graphic on the left of the page; size the graphic to 3" wide x 1" high.

4. Insert a caption that reads, "Fun and Relaxation Await You".

5. Scale the X-axis to 300% and the Y-axis to 100% (the default).

6. Using the flush right command, type the text as shown.

7. View the exercise at 100%.

8. Print one copy.

9. Save the file; name it **FUN**.

EQUINOX TRAVEL & TOURS
19877 20th Avenue SE
Bothell, WA   98041

Fun and Relaxation Await You

TO CREATE A GRAPHIC BOX WITH A CAPTION AND SCALED GRAPHIC

1. Press **Alt + F9**........... `Alt` + `F9`
2. Select one of the following box types:

    F (figure)................................ `F`

    T (table)................................. `T`

    B (text box)............................ `B`

    U (user box)........................... `U`

    E (equation) (**WP5.1 only**)....... `E`
3. Select **C** (create)..................... `C`
4. Select **F** (filename).................. `F`

5. Type name of WordPerfect graphic file.

    NOTE: If filename is not known, access "list files" (F5), highlight a file with a ".WPG" extension and retrieve it.
6. **ENTER**...................................... `↵`

TO INCLUDE A CAPTION

7. Select **C** (caption)...................... `C`
8. **Backspace** (to erase word

    "figure #").................. `Backspace`
9. Type caption.
10. Press **F7**.............................. `F7`

TO SCALE GRAPHIC

11. Select **E** (edit)........................... `E`
12. Select **S** (scale)........................ `S`
13. Type **X-axis** percentage.
14. **ENTER**.................................... `↵`
15. Type **Y-axis** percentage.
16. **ENTER**.................................... `↵`

    NOTE: PgUp and PgDn keys may also be used to change scale of graphic.
17. Press **F7** to return to graphic menu.................................... `F7`
18. Press **F7** to return to document............................ `F7`

USING GRAPHICS (Scaling a Graphic; Creating a Caption)

Notes:

- In this exercise, you will create a newsletter. After you create the graphic, insert the caption and scale the graphic according to exercise directions. Return 2x to begin typing the text.

Exercise Directions:

1. Start with a clear screen.

2. With your cursor at the top of the screen, create a graphic using the NEWS.WPG (WP5.1) or NEWSPAPR.WPG (WP5.0) graphic file.

3. Place the graphic in the center of the page (select **Full** in WP5.1); size the graphic to 6.5" wide x 4.7" high.

4. Insert a caption that reads, "Alumni News Brief."

5. Scale the X-axis to 180% and the Y-axis to 120%.

6. Return 2X.

7. Type the text.

8. View the exercise at 100%.

9. Print one copy.

10. Save the file; name it **ALUMNI.**

Alumni News Brief

ALUMNI ASSOCIATION TO USE DESKTOP

The Washington High School Alumni Association has decided to use desktop publishing to create their newsletters. Michael Griffith and Melanie McKinley have volunteered to desktop future editions of the newsletter.

DR. MARTIN BROWN RETIRES

Dr. Martin Brown, Business Education Department Chair, has retired after 40 years as an educator. The Alumni Association wishes him good health and good luck in his new endeavors.

CLASS OF '75 REUNION PLANNED

Mr. Robert Wascher, 1975 Class President, is organizing a reunion for the graduating class of 1975. The reunion will be held on September 29, 1991 at the Ritz-Carlton Hotel in Laguna Beach, California. Those interested in attending should send a check for $75.00 per person to the Alumni Association. Tickets will be mailed to you.

USING GRAPHIC LINES (Horizontal)

Notes:

- WordPerfect's graphic lines feature allows you to include horizontal and vertical lines in your document. The graphic line feature allows you to adjust the width and darkness of lines. The "Line Draw" feature, which will be covered in a later exercise, does not allow for these adjustments.

- When working with horizontal lines, you may position the line against the **Left** or **Right** margin, or **Center** it between the left and right margins, or start it at a **Set Position** from the left edge of the page, or have a "**Full**" line fill the area from the left to the right margin. You may specify the length of your line as well as the thickness (width) of the line on the line menu. The default setting for the width of a line is 0.013". To increase the thickness of a line, you must enter a number higher than 0.013". See sample lines and width measurements on the right.

Exercise Directions:

1. Start with a clear screen.

2. With your cursor at the top of the screen, create a horizontal line between the existing margins (Left/Right for WP5.0; Full for WP5.1). Use the default width (.013).

3. Return 2x.

4. Create a graphic using the PC.WPG (WP5.0) or PC-1.WPG (WP5.1) graphic file; size the graphic to 1" wide x 1" high.

5. Scale the X-axis to 150% and the Y-axis to 150%.

6. Type the text at the left margin.

7. Return 2x.

8. Create another horizontal line between existing margins; set width to .1".

9. View the exercise at 100%.

10. Print one copy.

11. Save the file; name it **LINE**.

Numbers represent portions of an inch.

.01
.02
.03
.04
.05
.06
.07
.08
.09
.1
.15
.2
.25
.3
.4
.5

```
COMPUTSTORE, INC.
12 Turbo Chip Circle
Annadale, VA  22033
703-987-98122
```

TO CREATE A HORIZONTAL LINE

1. Press **Alt + F9**............... **Alt** + **F9**
2. Select **L** (line)............................ **L**
3. Select **H** (horizontal line)........... **H**
4. Select **one or more** of the following options:
   a. **H** (horizontal position)........... **H**
      Select one:
      L (left)..................................... **L**
      R (right)................................. **R**

     C (center)............................ **C**
     F (full) - WP5.1 only................ **F**
     B (both left/right) - WP5.0 only. **B**
     S (set position)....................... **S**
     - type position
     - **ENTER**................................ ↵
   b. **L** (length of line)...................... **L**
     - Type length
     - **ENTER**................................... ↵

   c. **W** (width of line)........................ **W**
     - Type width
     - **ENTER**................................. ↵
5. Press **F7** (to return to document)................................ **F7**

USING GRAPHIC LINES (Horizontal)

Notes:

- In this exercise, you will create a letterhead which contains lines of varying lengths and widths and includes a graphic (which will be scaled). In addition, this letterhead contains footer text which includes a short horizontal line on the left and right of the text.

- Since a letterhead should generally begin 1/2" from the top of the page and the footer should be placed I/2" up from the bottom of the page, it will be necessary for you to change the top and bottom margins of your paper. (**Shift + F8, P, M,** set margins to .5" top and bottom).

- If you should make an error, reveal your codes, delete the code that is in error and continue. If you correctly created this exercise, the codes for the top part of the letterhead should look like the illustration below.

```
{                                                      }
[T/B Mar:0.5",0.5"][HLine:Full,Baseline,6.5",0.013",100%][HRt]
[HRt]
[Center][HLine:Left,Baseline,1",0.013",100%]THE BICYCLE SHOPPE[HLine:Right,Basel
ine,1",0.013",100%][HRt]
[HLine:Left,Baseline,1",0.03",100%][HLine:Right,Baseline,1",0.03",100%][HRt]
[HRt]
[HLine:Left,Baseline,1",0.1",100%][HLine:Right,Baseline,1",0.1",100%][Fig Box:1;
BICYCLE.WPG;][HRt]
[HRt]
[HRt]
```

Exercise Directions:

1. Start with a clear screen.

2. With your cursor at the top of the screen, set top and bottom margins to .5". (See page 59.)

3. Create a horizontal line between the existing margins (Left/Right for WP5.0; Full for WP5.1). Use the default width (.013).

4. Return 2x.

5. Create a **left** horizontal line 1" in length, using the default width (.013").

6. Center the text, THE BICYCLE SHOPPE (WP5.1) or FLAG SHOPPE (WP5.0).

7. Create a **right** horizontal line 1" in length using the default width (.013").

8. Return 1x.

9. Create a **left** horizontal line 1" in length setting the width to 0.03"; set a **right** horizontal line using the same measurements.

10. Return 2x.

11. Create a **left** horizontal line 1" in length, setting the width to .1".

13. Create a **centered** graphic using BICYCLE.WPG (WP5.1) or FLAG.WPG (WP5.0) graphic file. Size the graphic to 3" wide x .5" high. Scale the x-axis to 400%; use the default y-axis.

14. Create a **right** horizontal line 1" in length, setting the width to .1".

15. Return as many times as necessary to bring your cursor to Ln 10.31".

16. Create a **left** horizontal line .5" in length, using the default width; center the footer text; create a **right** horizontal line using the same measurements.

17. View your document.

18. Print one copy.

19. Save your file; name it **RIDES**.

THE BICYCLE SHOPPE

123 Wheel Avenue*Ann Arbor, MI 48187*313-987-3245

USING GRAPHIC LINES (Vertical)

Notes:

- WordPerfect allows you to create vertical lines of varying lengths and widths. You may adjust the Horizontal Position of the line slightly to the Left of the margin or slightly to the Right of the margin. If you are creating a document containing columns, you may include vertical lines Between columns. You may also adjust the Vertical Position of the line by indicating whether you want the line to start at the Top or Bottom margin, Center it between the top and bottom margins, or Set the position of the line by indicating how far down from the top of the margin it should begin. If you want the line to extend from the top to the bottom margin, you may select the Full page option. When you indicate that you would like a vertical line to start at the top or bottom margin, you can specify how long you would like the line to be.

- The Width of Line is adjusted using the same measurements as the horizontal lines.
- In this exercise, you will create a flyer with a left and right vertical line which extends the full length of the page. Also included are two graphics, one of them scaled.

Exercise Directions:

1. Start with a clear screen.
2. With your cursor at the top of the screen, create a **left** vertical line extending the full length of the page, setting a 1" width.
3. Create a **right** vertical line extending the full length of the page, setting a 1" width.
4. With the cursor at the top of your screen, center the first six lines of text as indicated.
5. Return as many times as necessary to bring the cursor to Ln 3.5".
6. Create a **centered** graphic using the ARROW-22.WPG (WP5.1) or NO1.WPG (WP5.0) graphic file. Use the default height and width to size the graphic.
7. Return as many times as necessary to bring the cursor to Ln 7". Center the next three lines of text as indicated.
8. At Ln 7.83", center the same graphic. Size the graphic to 3" wide x 1" high. Scale the X-axis to 300%; use the default scale for the Y-axis.
9. View the exercise.
10. Print one copy.
11. Save the file; name it **EAT**.

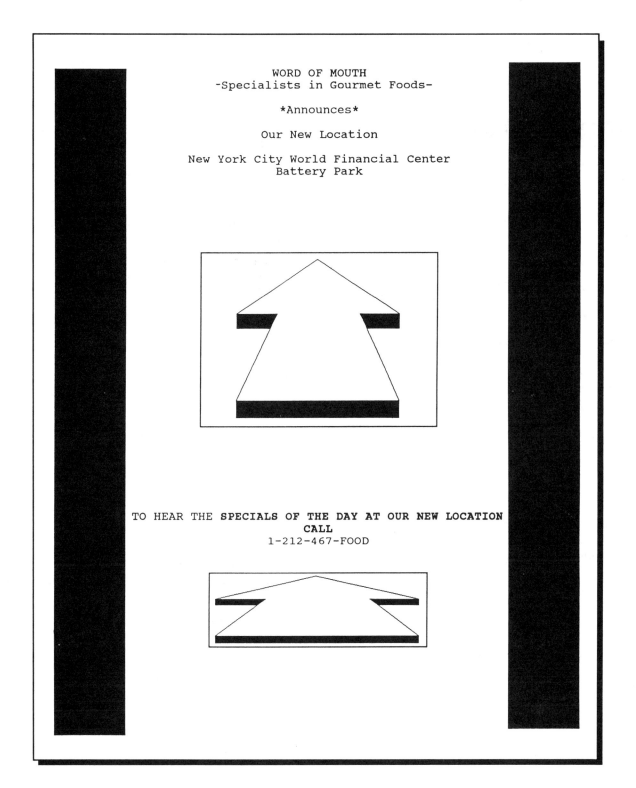

TO CREATE A VERTICAL LINE

1. Press **Alt + F9**.......... `Alt` + `F9`
2. Select **L** (line)..................... `L`
3. Select **V** (vertical line)........ `V`
4. Select **one or more** of the following options:
  a. **H** (horizontal position)........ `H`
    Select one:
    L (left)................................. `L`
    R (right)............................... `R`
    B (between columns)............... `B`

S (set position)........................... `S`
  - type position
  - **ENTER**............................ `↵`
b. **V** (vertical position)............. `V`
  Select one:
  F (full page)...................... `F`
  T (top)................................ `T`
  C (center)............................ `C`
  B (bottom)........................... `B`
  S (set position)................... `S`
    - type position

ENTER................................ `↵`
c. **L** (length of line)................... `L`
  - Type length
  - **ENTER**............................ `↵`
d. **W** (width of line)................. `W`
  - Type width
  - **ENTER**............................ `↵`
5. Press **F7** (to return to document).............................. `F7`

USING GRAPHIC LINES (Vertical)

Notes:

- In this exercise, you will create a vertical line on the left, on the right and between columns. To position the vertical line between columns 1 and 2, position your cursor in column one, access the graphics feature (**Alt + F9**) and select "Vertical Lines". Then, select the option "Horizontal Position" which allows you to place the line **B**etween the Columns." You must enter a column number to position the line between that column and the one to the right. For example, if you have a two-column document and you wish to insert a vertical line between columns 1 and 2, you would enter column number 1; the line would then be inserted between columns 1 and 2.

- To create the vertical line on the right, the cursor must be positioned in the right column.

- Remember, the line will not display on the screen, but may be viewed (**Shift + F7, V**) and will print.

Exercise Directions:

1. Start with a clear screen.

2. With your cursor at the top of the screen, create a left horizontal line 3" long and .25" wide. Return 2x.

3. Type WORD OF MOUTH. Return 2x.

4. Create a left horizontal line 2" long and .5" wide.

5. Return as many times as necessary to bring the cursor to Ln 3.83".

6. Create two-columns (**Alt + F7**).

7. Create a left vertical line using the default width and setting the vertical position to 3.83"

8. Create a vertical line between the columns setting the width to .02" and the vertical position to 3.83".

9. View the exercise.

10. Type the first column of text. (Flush right the prices and double indent the sandwich descriptions.)

11. Move the cursor to the top of the second column (CTRL + ENTER).

12. Create a right vertical line using the default width and setting the vertical position to 3.83."

13. Type the second column of text same as the first column.

14. View the exercise.

15. Print one copy.

16. Save the file; name it **HUNGRY**.

WORD OF MOUTH

MEATY SANDWICHES

Tuna Salad
    Made with white-meat
    tuna.
	$2.50

Turkey Breast	$3.50

Chicken Salad
    Chicken with apples,
    celery and walnuts.
	$3.50

Roast Beef	$3.50

Club Special
    Turkey, ham, roast
    beef, swiss,
    cheddar.
	$4.50

Club Italian
    Salami, ham,
    provolone,
    anchovies, peppers.
	$5.00

Salami Grilled or plain.	$3.00

California Club
    Turkey, avocado,
    cheddar, bacon.
	$4.50

Pastrami
    Hot, spicy, lean
    slices of beef.
	$5.00

VEGIE SANDWICHES

*Four Cheeses
    Swiss, cheddar,
    provolone, cream
    cheese.
	$3.25

Garden Club
    Sprouts, lettuce,
    tomatoes, cucumbers,
    jack cheese.
	$3.50

Vegie Delight
    Avocado, sprouts,
    mushrooms, swiss,
    peppers.
	$4.00

Club Dill
    Dill cream cheese,
    cucumbers, sprouts.
	$3.25

Peanut Butter
    Peanut butter,
    bananas, cucumbers.
	$3.00

Olive Delight
    Cream cheese,
    chopped black and
    green olives.
	$3.50

Summer Salad
    Red-leaf lettuce,
    cucumbers, olives,
    feta cheese, on pita
    bread.
	$4.50

TO CREATE A VERTICAL LINE to the Left and Right of the Margins and Between Columns

1. Press **Alt** + **F9**.............. **Alt** + **F9**
2. Select **L** (line).................... **L**
3. Select **V** (vertical line)................ **V**
4. Select **H** (horizontal position)..... **H**
   Select one:
   L (left)........................... **L**
   R (right)......................... **R**
   B (between columns)............... **B**

NOTE: Be sure column feature has been turned on <u>before</u> you complete this procedure.
   - Type column #, to position line to the right of it.
   - **ENTER**............................. ↵
5. Select **V** (vertical position).......... **V**

Change options below as desired:
   Type **S** (set position).............. **S**
   - Type position where line is to begin.
   - **ENTER**................................. ↵

Select **L** (length of line)................ **L**
   - Type length
   - **ENTER**.................................... ↵
Select **W** (width of line).................. **W**
   - Type width
   - **ENTER**.................................... ↵
6. Press **F7** (to return to document.......................... **F7**

USING ATTRIBUTES (Changing the Appearance of Printed Text)

Notes:

- WordPerfect's **Attribute** feature allows you to change the appearance of printed text. There are basically two types of attributes: "size" and "appearance."

- The "Size" attributes enable you to change the height and width of a character. Selections include: superscript, subscript, fine, small, large, very large or extra large. Examples of each appear below.

With a base font of Courier 10:

SIZE ATTRIBUTES

This is an example of fine.

This is an example of small.

This is an example of large.

This is an example of very large.

This is an example of extra large.

This is an example of superscript.

This is an example of subscript.

- The "Appearance" attributes enable you to change the appearance of your text for emphasis. Selections include: bold, underline, double underline, italic, outline, shadow, small caps, redline or strikeout. Examples of each appear below.

APPEARANCE ATTRIBUTES

This is an example of *italic*.

This is an example of outline.

This is an example of shadow.

This is an example of SM CAP.

This is an example of redln.

This is an example of ~~stkout~~.

This is an example of bold.

This is an example of double underline.

This is an example of underline.

- Bold and underline may be accessed using F6 and F8, as learned in earlier exercises.

- A **font** is a set of characters available in a particular **typeface, typestyle** and **typesize.** Therefore, a font has three parts: the typeface is the design of the character (Roman, Sans Serif, Helvetica, CGTimes, Universal and Courier); the typestyle is how the character is emphasized (bold, underline, italic, etc.); the typesize is the way the character is measured. Font size is measured in points or pitch. Note the examples below of CGTimes and Universal type-faces in bold typestyle and 12 pitch. Compare it to the example of Courier in 10 pitch.

TYPEFACE, TYPESTYLE AND TYPESIZE

This is an example of Courier 10cpi.

This is an example of CGTIMES bold 12cpi.

This is an example of UNIVERSAL bold 12cpi.

- In order for you to use a variety of fonts, your printer must have these fonts available.

- Your printer can print in at least one font (usually Courier -10-pitch). The "base font" is the basic font in which normal text is printed. All size and appearance font changes refer to the base font. For example, if your base font is Courier 10 cpi (characters per inch) and you select the "large" size font, WordPerfect looks for a larger version of Courier 10. If it doesn't find one, it retains the base font. If you include italics and there is an italicized version of the base font, WordPerfect uses it; otherwise, it retains the base font.

- To determine what fonts are available, depress the font command (**Ctrl + F8, F**). The asterisk indicates the current font. The base font may be changed as often as necessary throughout a document.

- In this exercise, you will retrieve a previously created exercise and change the size and appearance of some of the text. You will use the default base font. **Remember, sizes are relative to the base font and depend on what fonts are available for the printer. If a size is unavailable, the closest available size will be substituted.**

Exercise Directions:

1. Retrieve **LINE.** (See next page)

2. Use the default base font.

3. Change the size of the text in the heading, COMPUTSTORE, INC. to "extra large."

4. Set the address, city, state, zip and phone number to "italics."

5. View your document.

6. Print one copy.

7. Resave your file.

   NOTE: If your printer does not support italics or the size change, the heading in the printed copy will remain the same and the address, city, state, zip and phone number may appear underlined.

continued...

set to
extra large

set to
italics

COMPUTSTORE, INC.
12 Turbo Chip Circle
Annadale, VA   22033
703-987-98122

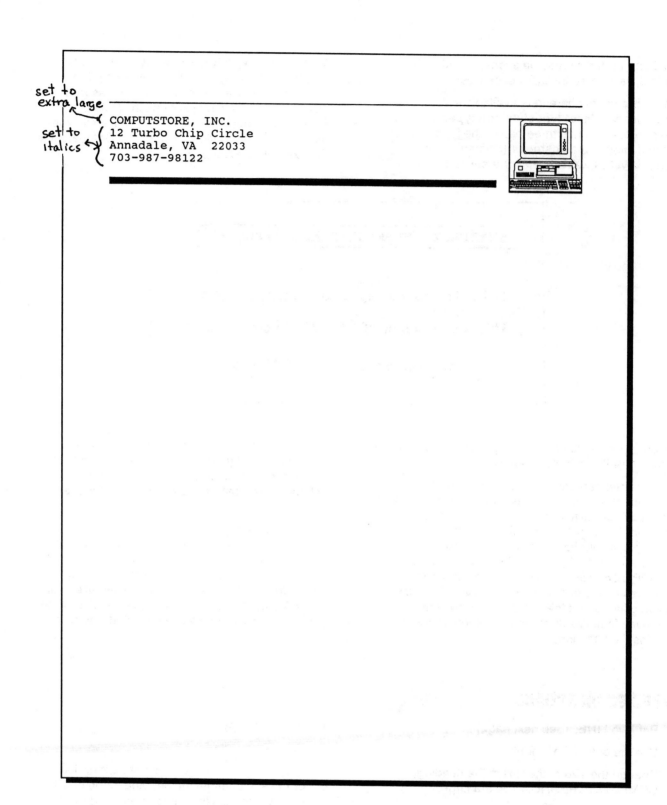

TO CHANGE FONT SIZE

- Before typing text

1. Place cursor where font size change will begin.
2. Press **Ctrl + F8** (font).. `Ctrl` + `F8`
3. Select **S** (size)............................. `S`
4. Select one of the following sizes:

    P (superscript)...................... `P`

    B (subscript)......................... `B`

    F (fine)................................ `F`

    S (small).............................. `S`

    L (large).............................. `L`

    V (very large)....................... `V`

    E (extra large)...................... `E`
5. Type text.
6. Press **right arrow** (to restore original font setting)...................... `→`

- Existing text

1. Place cursor on first character of text to be changed.
2. Press **Alt + F4** (block).. `Alt` + `F4`
3. Highlight text to be changed.
4. Press **Ctrl + F8** (font)... `Ctrl` + `F8`
5. Follow steps 3-6 on left.

TO CHANGE APPEARANCE OF FONT

- Before typing text

1. Place cursor on line where font appearance change will begin.
2. Press **Ctrl + F8**.......... `Ctrl` + `F8`
3. Select **A** (appearance)............... `A`
4. Select one of the following:

    B (bold)... `B`

    U (underline).............................. `U`

    D (double underline)................. `D`

    I (italic).................................... `I`

    O (outline)................................ `O`

    A (shadow).............................. `A`

    C (small caps)......................... `C`

    R (redline)............................... `R`

    S (strikeout)............................ `S`
5. Type text
6. Press **right arrow**(to restore original setting)................................. `→`

- Existing text

1. Place cursor on first character of text to be changed.
2. Press **Alt + F4** (block).. `Alt` + `F4`
3. Highlight text
4. Press **Ctrl + F8**.......... `Ctrl` + `F8`
5. Follow steps 3-6 above.

USING ATTRIBUTES / CHANGING THE BASE FONT
Notes:

- In the exercise, you will retrieve a previously created exercise and change the base font as well as the size of the font. If your printer does not support more than one font, you will not be able to change the base font. (See NOTES in Exercise 108 to review base font information.)

Exercise Directions:

1. Retrieve **RIDES.**

2. Change the current base font to another one that is available.

3. Change the size of the text in the heading THE BICYCLE SHOPPE to "very large" as indicated.

4. Change the size of the text in the footer to "fine" as indicated.

5. View your document.

6. Print one copy.

7. Resave your file.

THE BICYCLE SHOPPE]— *set to "very large"*

123 Wheel Avenue*Ann Arbor, MI 48187*313-987-3245

set to "fine"

TO CHANGE THE BASE FONT

1. Place cursor where font change will begin.
2. Press **Ctrl + F8** (font).. **Ctrl** + **F8**
3. Select **F** (base font).................**F**
4. Use cursor keys to highlight desired font.
5. Select **S** (select)...........................**S**

USING ATTRIBUTES/CHANGING THE BASE FONT

Notes:

- In this exercise, you will retrieve a previously created exercise and change the base font as well as change the size and appearance of the font. (See NOTES in Exercise 108 to review base font information.)

Exercise Directions:

1. Retrieve **HUNGRY.**

2. Change the current base font to another one that is available.

3. Change the size of the text in the heading WORD OF MOUTH to "extra large"; change the size of MEATY AND VEGIE SANDWICHES to "large"; change sandwich types to bold; change sandwich descriptions to "fine" as indicated.

4. Add "Sliced Steak" and its description to the "Meaty Sandwiches" column and "Cottage Delight" and its description to "Vegie Sandwiches" column as indicated.

5. View your document.

6. Print one copy.

7. Resave your file.

WORD OF MOUTH]- set to "extra large"

set sandwich descriptions to "fine"

MEATY SANDWICHES]- set to "large"		**VEGIE SANDWICHES**] set to "large"	
Tuna Salad	$2.50	*Four Cheeses	$3.25
Made with white-meat tuna.		Swiss, cheddar, provolone, cream cheese.	
Turkey Breast	$3.50	*Garden Club*	$3.50
Chicken Salad	$3.50	Sprouts, lettuce, tomatoes, cucumbers, jack cheese.	
Chicken with apples, celery and walnuts.		*Vegie Delight*	$4.00
Roast Beef	$3.50	Avocado, sprouts, mushrooms, swiss, peppers.	
Club Special	$4.50	*Club Dill*	$3.25
Turkey, ham, roast beef, swiss, cheddar.		Dill cream cheese, cucumbers, sprouts.	
Club Italian	$5.00	*Peanut Butter*	$3.00
Salami, ham, provolone, anchovies, peppers.		Peanut butter, bananas, cucumbers.	
Salami	$3.00	*Olive Delight*	$3.50
Grilled or plain.		Cream cheese, chopped black and green olives.	
California Club	$4.50	*Summer Salad*	$4.50
Turkey, avocado, cheddar, bacon.		Red-leaf lettuce, cucumbers, olives, feta cheese, on pita bread.	
Pastrami	$5.00		
Hot, spicy, lean slices of beef.		* Cottage Delight*	$4.00
* Sliced Steak*		Chunks of cottage cheese with fresh vegetables on pita bread.	
Slices of tender sirloin.	$6.50		

USING GRAPHICS (Creating a Text Box)

Notes:

- In earlier exercises, you created a figure box for graphic images. In this exercise, you will create a two-column newsletter in which a "Text Box" is positioned in the middle of the page. It may not be possible for you to create a document to look exactly like the illustration since the fonts available to your printer may vary.

- Text boxes may be used for setting off special text from the rest of the document by inserting the text into a box. The box may be horizontally positioned to the left, right or center of the document and may be positioned vertically on the page and sized as desired. The procedure is similar to that used in creating a figure box.

- The text that will be used in the box can either be saved as a separate file and retrieved into the box or it can be typed into the box. Both procedures are outlined on the right.

- In this exercise you will create the text that appears in the box as a separate file and then retrieve it into the box.

Exercise Directions:

1. Start with a clear screen.

2. Type the text that appears in the middle of the box exactly as shown (each line should be centered). Save this text as a file; name it CHOC.

3. Clear your screen.

4. Create a horizontal line .05" wide. Return 3x.

5. Center and bold the word CHOCOLATE; change the size of the font to "extra large." Return 3x.

6. Create another horizontal line .05" wide. Return 2x.

7. Create a centered text box inserting the CHOC file. Set the horizontal position to "Center"; set the vertical position to 2.5". Use the default size.

8. Create a two-column table (**Alt + F7**).

9. Type the document text as shown (the text will wrap around the box).

10. View your document.

11. Print one copy.

12. Save your file; name it **COCOA**.

CHOCOLATE

CHOCOLATE is probably the world's favorite food. You can drink it hot or cold, or eat it as a snack or as part of a meal. It is made into pies, cakes, cookies, candy, ice cream and even breakfast cereal. Chocolate comes in lacy Valentine boxes and in survival kits. It is nourishing, energy-giving and satisfying.

Chocolate came to us from Mexico, by way of Europe. When the Spanish explorer Cortez arrived at the court of Montezuma, the Aztec Emperor, he found him drinking a cold, bitter drink called Chocolatl. It was made from seeds of the cacao tree, ground in water and mixed with spices. Montezuma gave Cortez the recipe and some cacao and vanilla beans. Cortez took them back to Spain, where the Spanish king and queen quickly improved the drink by adding sugar and having it served hot.

For about a hundred years, chocolate was exclusively a royal Spanish treat. But once the secret leaked out, the upper classes in most of the European capitals were soon sipping hot chocolate. From Amsterdam, the Dutch settlers brought chocolate to the American colonies, and in 1765 a man named Baker started a chocolate mill near Boston. By this time, people had figured out how to make powdered cocoa by extracting some of the cocoa butter and adding it to the ground beans to make solid chocolate.

A hundred years later a man in Switzerland found a way to make solid sweet milk chocolate, and a great candy business was born. Chocolate companies like Nestle and Hershey need a lot of cacao beans. About one-third of the supply, over 350 thousand tons, is imported each year from the African country of Ghana. Ghana is the world's largest supplier of cacao beans. For many years, chocolate was made by hand. Now, machines do most of the work.

THE CHOCOLATE FACTORY has been specializing in the finest chocolate products for over 50 years. Stop in and sample some of our outstanding chocolate delights.

THE CHOCOLATE FACTORY

SPECIALIZING IN CHOCOLATE CAKES, COOKIES, CANDY AND OTHER MOUTH-WATERING DELIGHTS.

754 Riverbend Drive
San Francisco, CA 94107

415-987-4333

HOURS: 9-7 DAILY.

TO CREATE A TEXT BOX

1. Press **Alt + F9** .... `Alt` + `F9`
2. Select **B** (text box) .... `B`
3. Select **C** (create) .... `C`

TO RETRIEVE A TEXT FILE INTO BOX:

4. Select **F** (filename) .... `F`
5. Type name of text file to be inserted into box.
6. ENTER .... `↵`

OR

TO TYPE TEXT INTO BOX:

4. Select **E** (edit) .... `E`
5. Type text to be inserted into box.

6. Press **F7** .... `F7`

OPTIONS:

Select **V** (to set vertical position). `V`
- Type number of inches from top to place box.
- **ENTER** .... `↵`

Select **H** (to set horizontal position) .... `H`
- Type **L** (left) .... `L` or
  C (center) .... `C` or
  R (right) .... `R`

- ENTER .... `↵`

Select **S** (to size the box) .... `S`
- Type **W** (width) .... `W` or
  H (height) .... `H` or
  B (both width and height)
  .... `B`

- Type desired inches for width/height

- ENTER .... `↵`

6. Press **F7** .... `F7`
   to return to document.

USING GRAPHICS (Creating a Text Box); ROTATING A GRAPHIC

Notes:

- In this exercise, you will retrieve a previously created two-column document and add a title created as a text box and rotate a graphic (see explanation below).

- Unlike Exercise 111 in which you created a file and then retrieved it into the box, in this exercise you will type the text into the box. It is possible, however, to create the title as you did in the last exercise (by creating two horizontal lines with a title in the middle). The text box gives you an added dimension --it is shaded.

- A graphic can be rotated--that is, it can be pivoted by moving it clockwise or counter-clockwise. Images may be rotated counter-clockwise using the plus (+) key or clockwise using the minus (-) key, or they may be rotated by a specific amount of degrees. After you select the rotate option, you will be asked if you wish to "mirror-image" the graphic. You might think of a mirror-imaged graphic as one that has been flipped over. Examples of rotated and mirror-imaged graphics appear on the right.

 0°

 300°

 100°

 MIRROR-IMAGED

 200°

Exercise Directions:

1. Start with a clear screen.

2. Retrieve **PROCESS**.

3. With your cursor at the top of the screen, create a centered text box; use the default size and vertical position.

4. Select Edit in the Text Box Menu. Return 2x. Center and bold the words THE COMPUTER. Return 2x. Return to your document.

   (See procedures, Exercise 111.)

5. Create a graphic at the end of the second column using the PC (WP5.0) or PC-1 (WP5.1) graphic file; place it on the right and size it to 3" wide x .75" high. Create the caption that appears below the graphic. Scale the X-axis to 200%; scale the Y-axis to 100%. Rotate the graphic 180°.

6. View your document.

7. Print one copy.

8. Resave your file.

The computer is an electronic device that can process vast amounts of facts and numbers and perform calculations at very high rates of speed. While a computer can accomplish many things, IT CANNOT THINK. A computer has to be "told" what to do with the information it receives. **Programs** are machine-language instructions which tell a computer what to do with information. Programs are developed by computer programmers.

Computers come in various sizes. Some computers are so large they fill an entire room, while others are so small, they can be held in your hand. No matter what their size, computers contain the same basic parts. Every computer has a way through which the operator can enter instructions and information. A keyboard is an "input" device which is common to all computers. The "storage" device (sometimes called memory) receives the information from the input device and holds it until it is needed. A "processing" device selects the instructions from the storage unit and processes the information as it has been directed. The "output" device translates the processed information into readable form. A typical output device would be a printer or a visual display.

......Will Turn Your Office Right Side Up............

1. Follow keystroke steps 1-10 in Exercise 102, page 237 for **CREATING A FIGURE BOX AND A CAPTION.**

TO ROTATE A GRAPHIC

2. Select **E** (edit)............**E**
3. Select **R** (rotate)............**R**
4. Type desired rotation percentage.
5. **ENTER**............↵

OPTION:

6. To MIRROR IMAGE, type **Y**........**Y**
7. Press **F7** to return to graphics menu............**F7**
8. Press **F7** to return to document............**F7**

EDITING A GRAPHIC or TEXT BOX

Notes:

• It is possible to edit a graphic or text box after it has been created. To do this, you must retrieve the document containing the box and access the graphics menu (**Alt + F9**). When the menu appears, you must indicate what type of box you wish to edit (figure, text, etc.) After making the selection, you will select "Edit." It is then necessary for you to indicate the figure or box number you wish to edit. Remember, as you created each box, a number was assigned to it by WordPerfect so that you could later identify it for editing purposes. The menu relating to the box you created earlier appears on the screen. You can now make the changes you wish.

Exercise Directions:

1. Start with a clear screen.
2. Retrieve **ALUMNI.**
3. Change the height of the graphic to 2.5".
4. Rotate the graphic 324°; scale the X-axis to 150%.
5. Change the font size for each headline to "very large."
6. Add the last paragraph.
7. View the exercise.
8. Print one copy.
9. Resave the file.

change
size,
Scale and
rotate
(see
directions)

Alumni News Brief

change
font
to
"very
large"

ALUMNI ASSOCIATION TO USE DESKTOP

The Washington High School Alumni Association has decided to use desktop publishing to create their newsletters. Michael Griffith and Melanie McKinley have volunteered to desktop future editions of the newsletter.

DR. MARTIN BROWN RETIRES

Dr. Martin Brown, Business Education Department Chair, has retired after 40 years as an educator. The Alumni Association wishes him good health and good luck in his new endeavors.

CLASS OF '75 REUNION PLANNED

Mr. Robert Wascher, 1975 Class President, is organizing a reunion for the graduating class of 1975. The reunion will be held on September 29, 1991 at the Ritz-Carlton Hotel in Laguna Beach, California. Those interested in attending should send a check for $75.00 per person to the Alumni Association. Tickets will be mailed to you.

ALUMNI SCHOLARSHIP FUND ESTABLISHED
The Alumni Association has voted to establish a scholarship fund.
Each year, the Association will award a $200 savings bond
to a graduating senior who demonstrates outstanding
scholarship and service. Mr. Theodore Bates, class of '73,

will present this year's award at the graduation
awards ceremony to be held on Monday, June 3
at 7:30 p.m.

TO EDIT A GRAPHIC

1. Retrieve document containing graphic to be edited.
2. Press **Alt + F9**.......... `Alt` + `F9`
3. Select type of box to be edited:

   F (figure).................................... `F`

   T (table)..................................... `T`

   B (text box)................................ `B`

   U (user box)............................... `U`

   E (equation) (WP5.1 only).......... `E`

4. Select **E** (edit)............................. `E`
5. Type number of graphic to be edited.
6. Make desired changes in menu.
7. **ENTER**.. `↵`
8. Press **F7**.................................... `F7`
   to return to document.

EDITING A GRAPHIC or TEXT BOX

Notes:

* In this exercise, you will edit the graphic by changing its horizontal position (placing it on the left), scaling and rotating it. In addition, you will change the font size to "very large" and include a horizontal line below the address.

Exercise Directions:

1. Start with a clear screen.

2. Retrieve **PARTY.**

3. Place graphic on the left.

4. Scale the X-axis to 200% and the Y-axis to 200%. Rotate the graphic 36°.

5. Change the font size for the company name to "very large."

6. Create a .1" line below the address as indicated.

7. View the exercise.

8. Print one copy.

9. Resave the file.

PARTY BALLOONS, INC.] Change font to "very large"

234 Riverside Drive

New York, NY 10098

add a .1" horizontal line

scale +
rotate
graphic
(see directions)

USING BORDERS AND SHADING

Notes:

- WordPerfect allows you to change the border style and/or shading of the graphics (or text) boxes you create.

- Through the Graphic Options menu, you may select any one of the following border styles for any side of your graphics box.

SINGLE   THICK   DOUBLE   EXTRA THICK

DASHED   TOP-SINGLE LEFT-SINGLE RIGHT-EXTRA THICK BOTTOM-EXTRA THICK   DOTTED   TOP-THICK LEFT-THICK RIGHT-DOUBLE BOTTOM-DOUBLE

- Also through the Graphic Options menu, you may shade your graphics box by selecting the percentage of black you wish to create. Note the examples below:

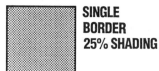 SINGLE BORDER 25% SHADING

 DASHED BORDER 75% SHADING

 DOUBLE BORDER 50% SHADING

 DOTTED BORDER 100% SHADING

- In order for the options to work on your graphics or text box, the options code must appear before the graphics or text box code. (If the changes do not occur as desired, reveal your codes (Alt + F3) to check the code order.) Therefore, set your options before you create the box.

- When a graphic image is used in a shaded box, some printers will shade inside the image while some printers leave a white inside image.

- Shading percents may vary depending on the type of printer used.

- In this exercise, you will create the same graphic with various borders and shading.

Exercise Directions:

1. Start with a clear screen.

2. Create each graphic, including the caption, indicated to the right. Use any desired image. Change the borders and shading as directed in the caption.

3. Position boxes 1 and 3 left and boxes 2 and 4 right; size each graphic to 2" x 2".

4. View the exercise.

5. Print one copy.

6. Save the exercise; name it **BORDERS**.

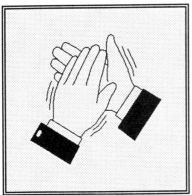

Double Line Border
10% Shading

Dashed Border
20% Shading

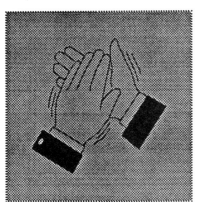

Dotted Border
40% Shading

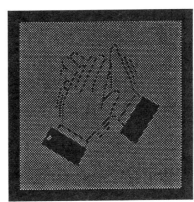

Extra Thick Border
60% Shading

CHANGE BORDER STYLE/ SHADING

NOTE: Border style / shading change code must appear before graphic code to be affected. Reveal codes to check code placement.

1. Press **Alt + F9** (Graphics).....
   ....`Alt` + `F9`
2. Select box type to be used:
   F (Figure)....................................`F`
   T (Table)....................................`T`
   B (Text Box)..............................`B`

U (User Box)...............................`U`
E (Equation)..**[WP5.1 only]**........`E`
3. Select **O** (Options).....................`O`

TO CHANGE BORDER STYLE

- Select **B** (Border Style).........`B`
- Select **one** of the following borders for **each** side of the box:
  N (None)...............................`N`
  S (Single)..............................`S`
  D (Double)............................`D`
  A (Dashed)...........................`A`

O (Dotted)...........................`O`
T (Thick)..............................`T`
E (Extra Thick).....................`E`

TO CHANGE SHADING

- Select **G** (Gray Shading.......`G`
- Type percentage
- **ENTER**..............................`↵`
4. Press **F7** (to return to document)..`F7`

USING BORDERS AND SHADING

Notes:

• In this exercise, you will create a border around a sized graphic, shade it, and type text within the graphic. The procedures for accomplishing this exercise are:

1. Access graphics (Alt + F9).

2. Select box type.

3. Select "Options."

4. Make desired changes to the border style and shading.

5. Create a figure box and select an image.

6. To type text within the graphic, change the "WRAP TEXT AROUND BOX" option to "No."

7. Determine approximately where on the page the text should be typed so that it fits within the graphic. Use the view feature to see where adjustments must be made.

Exercise Directions:

1. Start with a clear screen.

2. Access graphics. Change the border style (for figure box) for the <u>bottom</u> and <u>right</u> sides of the box to "extra thick"; change shading to 10%.

3. Create a figure box and use the PRESNT- 1.WPG (WP5.1) or PC.WPG (WP5.0) graphic; center and size it to 6.33" wide x 8.83" high.

4. Change "WRAP TEXT AROUND BOX" option to "No."

5. If using the PRESNT-1.WPG graphic, begin typing text on about Ln. 3.5", Pos. 3.5" and set font to Extra Large and Large as indicated; if using the PC.WPG graphic, begin typing text on Ln. 3.3", Pos 3" and omit the last paragraph.

6. View the exercise.

7. Print one copy.

8. Save the exercise; name it **LESSON.**

TODAY'S LESSON:
Portable PCs are as functional
as Desktop PCs.

Call 1-800-765-6666
for more information
about portable PCs.

**You've just learned an
important fact.**

USING BORDERS AND SHADING

Notes:

- In this exercise, you will create two figure boxes, one inside the other. Neither figure box contains a graphic. When a graphic is not inserted into a figure box and the border style and/or shading is changed, you can create the effect shown in the exercise.

- In order to type text into the "empty box(es)", you must change the "WRAP TEXT AROUND BOX" option for each figure box to "No."

Exercise Directions:

1. Start with a clear screen.

2. With your cursor at the top of the screen, access graphics. Change the border style (for figure box) to "extra thick."

3. Create a figure box, but **do not insert a graphic file**; center and size it to 6.33" wide x 8.83" high.

4. Change "WRAP TEXT AROUND BOX" option to "No."

5. Return 4x.

6. Access graphics. Change the border style (for figure box) for the top and left sides of the box to "double line"; change the border style for the right and bottom sides of the box to "thick"; change shading to 20%.

7. Create a figure box, but **do not insert a graphic file**; center and size it to 3" wide x 2" high.

8. Change option, "WRAP TEXT AROUND BOX," to "No."

9. Center all typed text; change fonts to "large" and "italics" as indicated. Begin typing text within the shaded box at Ln. 2.5"; begin typing remainder of text at Ln. 4.33".

10. View the exercise.

11. Print one copy.

12. Save the exercise; name it **TEACH.**

FACULTY POSITION
YALE LAW SCHOOL

Attorney/teacher sought for Faculty position
at Yale Law School. Responsibilities include
classroom teaching and supervision of students.
Experience in practice required and prior
teaching desirable.
Send resume, references and writing sample to:

Professor Harold Johns
Yale Law School
New Haven, CT 06520-7497

FACULTY POSITION
POLY PREP HIGH SCHOOL

Teacher of Mathematics sought for position
at Poly Prep High School. Responsibilities include
classroom teaching of Algebra, Geometry and Calculus.
Candidate must possess a Master's Degree in mathematics.
Prior teaching experience desired but **not** required.
Send resume, including references to:

Dr. Joanna Newman
Department Chair
Poly Prep High School
New Haven, CT 06520-7496

USING LINE DRAW

Notes:

- WordPerfect's Line Draw feature allows you to use the four cursor arrow keys to draw charts, boxes, graphs, or do line drawings around existing text.

- If you make an error, you can erase it by selecting the erase feature and retracing your lines.

- If you wish to draw lines around text, first type the text, then turn on the Line Draw feature. However, if you wish to add text to a Line Draw box, use TYPEOVER. (Press "Ins" key once.)

- The Line Draw feature gives you three options to select a draw character: option 1 - a single line, option 2 - a double line, option 3 - defaults to an asterisk but can be changed, using option 4, to a shaded line or any character you wish.

- Sometimes it becomes necessary to suspend the Line Draw feature temporarily so that you can move the cursor to another location without drawing. You can do this by accessing the Line Draw feature and selecting "Move."

- You can use the Line Draw feature with the RE-PEAT KEY function. Therefore, if you wanted to draw a line 35 characters long, you would depress ESC and indicate 35 before you drew the line.

- When using Line Draw, unjustify your document for (WP5.0); (Left- justify for WP5.1.)

- Some printers do not support the Line Draw feature.

- You may wish to combine Graphics Lines, Text Boxes and Line Draw features. The Line Draw feature does not enable you to vary the thickness of the lines as you can with the Graphics Line feature. Select the feature(s) that best accomplishes your task.

- Line Draw cannot be used with centered text; use it on left-justified text only.

- In this exercise, you will recall a previously created table and use the Line Draw feature to box the table. However, because this feature does not work on centered text, you will need to make modifications to the exercise to create the boxed text.

Exercise Directions:

1. Start with a clear screen.
2. Retrieve **EMPLOYEE.**
3. To use Line Draw to box the heading, ENTER before the headings to insert a blank line. Note the "Pos" of the first letter in the first line of the of the heading. Delete the center command and space the heading to the noted "Pos." Repeat for the second and third lines of the heading.

4. Using the Line Draw feature, box the table on the right as indicated.
5. Print one copy.
6. Resave your file.

```
┌─────────────────────────────────┐
│        ACME ELECTRICAL GROUP     │
│          PERSONNEL LIST          │
│          Union Membership        │
└─────────────────────────────────┘
```

LAST NAME	FIRST NAME	EMPLOYEE NO.	UNION MEMBER
ALLEN	JOHN	2676	YES
SMITH	ROBIN	6000	NO
JONES	SAM	8211	YES
ROBBIN	MARTIN	4110	YES
LASAR	SALLY	1220	NO
JOHNNS	JAMAL	6767	YES

TO USE LINE DRAW:

1. Place cursor where drawing is to begin.
2. Press **Ctrl + F3**.......... `Ctrl` + `F3`
3. Select **L**...................................... `L`
4. Type number of desired option:

    1 (single line)............................ `1`

    2 (double line)........................... `2`

    3 (asterisk *)............................... `3`

C (Change character).................. `C`

  Select desired option:

    1. ░   2. ░

    3. ▒   4. █

    5. ■   6. ▐

    7. ▌   8. ▪

  9. (other) enter desired
     character

E (erase)...................................... `E`

M (move)....................................... `M`

5. Use arrow keys to create drawing.
6. Press **F7** (to exit Line Draw)...... `F7`

USING LINE DRAW

Notes:

- In this exercise, you will create an organizational chart using the Line Draw feature. An organizational chart lists the hierarchy or ranking/reporting order of people in an organization.

Exercise Directions:

1. Start with a clear screen.

2. Using the Line Draw feature, create the organizational chart on the right. HINT: Center the words "House of Representatives," note the "Pos" indicator, delete the center command and space it back to the correct "Pos." Then, draw the box around it. Draw all other boxes, then insert the words within them. REMINDER: When inserting words within a box, be sure the TYPEOVER mode is on.

   Use your judgment for establishing box sizes.

3. Print one copy.

4. Save the exercise; name it **RANK**

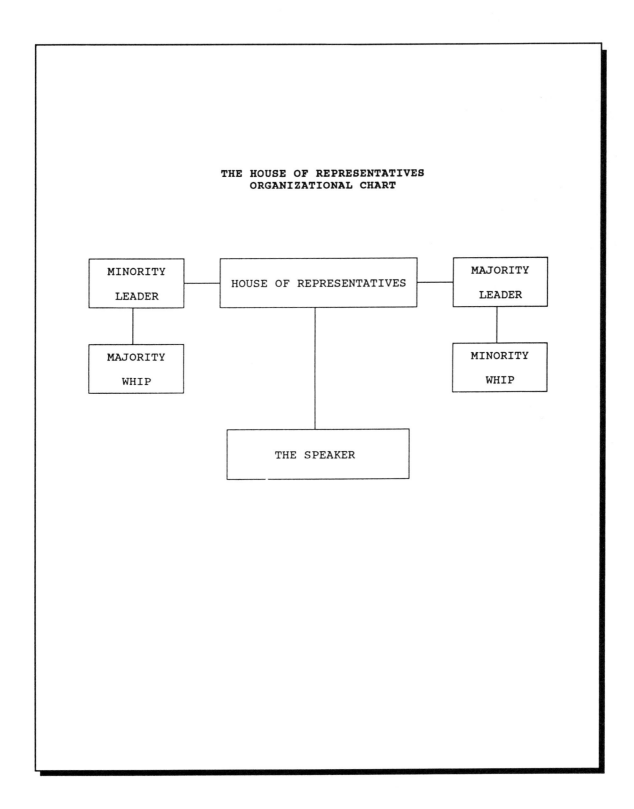

**THE HOUSE OF REPRESENTATIVES
ORGANIZATIONAL CHART**

| MINORITY LEADER | — | HOUSE OF REPRESENTATIVES | — | MAJORITY LEADER |

MAJORITY WHIP

THE SPEAKER

MINORITY WHIP

USING LINE DRAW

Notes:

* In this exercise, you will use the Line Draw
  feature to draw a bar graph. To draw the vertical
  bars, you must change the draw character. After
  accessing Line Draw (Ctrl + F3), select
  "Change." This selection will present several
  lines in various shades. Select any one that you
  desire (it should be dark to be effective).

Exercise Directions:

1. Start with a clear screen.

2. Create the memo on the right using the Line
    Draw feature to create the bar graph.

3. Use a centered text box for the memo heading.

4. Print one copy.

5. Save the exercise; name it **AIRLINE.**

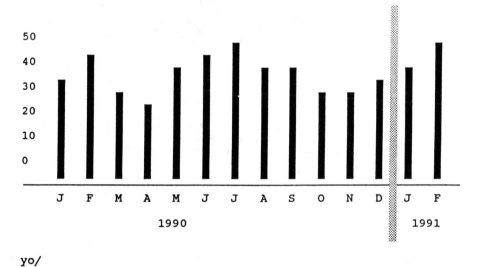

```
        M*E*M*O*R*A*N*D*U*M


   TO:        Tour Operators

   FROM:      R. Johnson

   RE:        Airline Travel Increase

   DATE:      March 14, 199-


   As you can see by the chart below, air travel significantly
   increased in the summer months last year and continued to increase
   early this year.  If the increase in travel continues, it is a
   clear sign that the recession may be over.

   All managers should begin aggressive marketing campaigns for the
   coming months.  We have been told that airlines will be cutting
   fares again and we should, therefore, expect people to book hotels
   early.

   I would like to meet with all managers next Tuesday at 10:00 a.m.
   in my office to discuss marketing strategies.


   50
   40
   30
   20
   10
    0
        J  F  M  A  M  J  J  A  S  O  N  D  J  F

              1990                      1991


   yo/
```

TO CHANGE DRAW CHARACTER:

1. Place cursor where drawing is to begin.
2. Press **Ctrl + F3**........ **Ctrl** + **F3**
3. Select **L**..................................... **L**
4. Select **C** (change character)..... **C**

5. Select desired draw character option:

   1.   2.

   3.   4.

   5.   6.

   7.   8.

   9. **O** (other) - type desired character.

6. Select **3** (to access new draw character)................................. **3**
7. Use arrow keys to create drawing.
8. Press **F7** (to exit Line Draw)...... **F7**

Exercise Directions:

1. Start with a clear screen.

2. Retrieve **EXTRA.**

3. Make the changes indicated using the graphics and attributes features. (It may not be possible to create an exact copy since this will depend on the graphics and printer capabilities that are available to you.) HINT: To create the centered text in the text box, access the text-box menu, select "Edit" and center the text indicated in "large" type.

4. Measure the figure box to determine the size.

5. View the exercise.

6. Print one copy.

7. Resave the file.

} create box

MEMORANDUM

italics {

TO: Shari Roberts, Personnel

FROM: Matt Romano, Sales   create Graphic →

RE: **EMPLOYEE BONUSES** ← bold

DATE: Today's

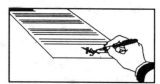

Listed below are employees and their bonuses for the first and second quarters of this year. These bonuses are based on the sales made in their respective divisions. The total bonuses paid for the quarter are also indicated. You will note that Joseph Monte and Moon Young were the only employees that received bonuses in both the first and second quarters.

FIRST QUARTER ← set to large → SECOND QUARTER   create horizontal lines

Kenneth Shewitz	$ 1,100	Chia-Jung Yen	$ 2,456
Joseph Monte	450	Joseph Monte	1,365
Kristin Schmit	2,345	Chris Sikora	861
Moon Young	920	Moon Young	3,677
Linda Malacuso	1,690	Lois Lane	224

bold → **TOTAL BONUSES PAID** $6,505 $8,583 ↓

If you need further information or have any questions, please let me know.

yo

Lesson 9
Summary Exercise B

Exercise Directions:

1. Create the magazine cover below as shown using the graphics and attributes features.

2. Change the left and top borders to extra thick; change the right and bottom borders to double line. Shade the graphic 20%. (It may not be possible to create an exact copy since this will depend on the graphics and printer capabilities that are available to you.)

3. View the exercise.

4. Print one copy.

5. Save the file; name it **MAGAZINE**.

VACATIONING

JUNE 199-   VOLUME 16 NUMBER 3

IN THIS ISSUE:

* Dining in the Bahamas
* Deep-Sea Fishing Vacations
* Safaris Anyone?
* Shopping Tips in Florence
* Top Spas in the Northeast

FIND YOUR PLACE IN THE SUN

Lesson 9
Challenge Exercise C

Exercise Directions:

1. Create the document on the next page as shown using the graphics and attributes features. (It may not be possible to create an exact copy since this will depend on the graphics and printer capabilities that are available to you.)

2. View the exercise.
3. Print one copy.
4. Save the file; name it **WINNER**.

C*O*N*N*E*C*T*I*O*N*S

AWARD WINNERS

This year's achievement awards were presented by David Roberts, Director of Personnel, during a magnificent ceremony at the Long Island Marriot Hotel. HAPPY TOURS is committed to recognizing and honoring achievements above and beyond normal expectations in all areas of employment.

Thanks to everyone for such an outstanding

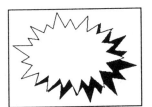

effort. **Sales Awards** are based on the number of tours that were organized by an employee. Best overall performance by a branch will be judged by total sales increases, operating efficiency, and returning customers. **CONGRATULATIONS** to Marietta Davis for winning the Sales Award. Marietta is employed in our Washington, D.C. branch. GREAT WORK!

NEWS BITES

Mohamed Samee comes to HAPPY TOURS as Public Relations Director. **Anita Jackson, Peggy Stovall** and **Corey Daniels** are learning the ropes in the Marketing Division of the Los Angeles Branch. GOOD LUCK!!!

> ## LESSON 10:
> BASIC SORTING; USING LIST FILES OPTIONS: RENAMING DOCU-
> MENTS, DELETING DOCUMENTS, WORD/NAME SEARCHING

BASIC SORTING (by Line)

Notes:

- WordPerfect's Sort feature allows you to arrange text alphabetically or numerically by line, para- graph or record (the secondary file used during the merge process).

- When sorting by line, text or numbers may be arranged in ascending order (from A to Z; 1 to 25) or decending order (Z to A or 25 to 1). <u>WordPerfect is defaulted to sort by line in ascending order.</u>

- A line sort should be used to arrange lists or columns of text and/or numbers.

- In order to use line sort, you must create tabulated columns, setting tabs for text and decimal columns for numbers as you did in Lesson 8. However, you can type a list at the left edge of the screen and sort it.

- To begin the sort, **place your cursor on the first column to be sorted** and follow the keystroke procedures on the next page. Some of the screen prompts are described below:

    The message, "Input file to sort: (Screen)" requires that you indicate the name of the file you wish to sort. Since the file is already on the screen, you simply press Enter.

    The message, "Output file for sort: (Screen)" requires that you indicate the name of the file where you wish to save the sorted text. If you want the sorted text to be saved to another document, enter the document name. If you want the sorted text to appear on the screen, press Enter.

- Note the "Sort by Line" menu below. When it ap- pears on the screen, select (**K**)eys to give WordPerfect information about how you want the material sorted: the type of sort, the field to use, and the word to use. "Key" refers to the "item" (field and word in the field). Key one is the primary sort item. Key two is the secondary sort item, for example. "Typ" refers to the kind of data to be sorted: (**a**)lphabetic or (**n**)umeric.

- In a line sort, a "field" is a column of text. In tabulated data, the first field is the left margin, the second field is the first tab stop, the third field is the second tab stop, etc.

- "Word" refers to what word in the field (column) you wish to sort on--first (1), second (2), third (3), last (-1), second from last (-2), etc.

```
----------------------------- Sort by Line -----------------------------

Key Typ Field Word        Key Typ Field Word        Key Typ Field Word
 1  a    1     1           2                          3
 4                         5                          6
 7                         8                          9
Select


Action                    Order                     Type
Sort                      Ascending                 Line sort

1 Perform Action; 2 View; 3 Keys; 4 Select; 5 Action; 6 Order; 7 Type: 0
```

- To activate the sort, you must select "Perform Action" from the selections on the bottom of your screen.

- In this exercise, you will sort the names in ascending order (alphabetically A-Z). Be sure to set tabs for each column.

Exercise Directions:

1. Start with a clear screen.

2. Use the preset margins.

3. Set the appropriate tabs and type the columns on the right.

4. Center the exercise vertically.

5. Save the exercise; name it **SORT. DO NOT EXIT THE DOCUMENT.**

6. Sort the first word in the name column alphabetically (ascending order).

7. Save the sorted text to a new file; name it **SORT1.**

8. Sort the second column alphabetically.

9. Save the sorted text to a new file; name it **SORT2.**

10. Retrieve SORT1.

11. Print one copy.

12. Retrieve SORT2.

13. Print one copy.

```
Watson, Patricia          Publicity
Tracey, Frank             Ethics
Brittany, Margaret        Policy/Action
Harrison, George          Convention
Cooper, Kevin             Newsletter
Zarin, William            Convention
Aronson, Julie            Awards
Izzary, Oscar             Membership
```

TO SORT (BY LINE)

1. Place cursor on first line to be sorted.
2. Press **Ctrl + F9**.......... `Ctrl` + `F9`
3. Select **S** (sort)............................ `S`
4. **ENTER** (if input file is on the screen)................................ `↵`

   or
   - Type name of document to be sorted (input file).
   - **ENTER**................................ `↵`

5. **ENTER** (to sort document to screen.)................................ `↵`

   or
   - Type name of document where sorted file is to be saved. (output file).
   - **ENTER**................................ `↵`

6. Select **K** (Keys)............................ `K`
7. Enter **Type** of sort:

   A (alphabetic)............................ `A`
   or
   N (numeric)................................ `N`
8. Enter **Field** number to be sorted.
9. **ENTER**................................ `↵`
10. Type **Word** number to be sorted.
11. Press **F7** (exit Keys menu)...... `F7`
12. Select **P** (Perform Action)............ `P`

BASIC SORTING

Notes:

- In this exercise, you will create a two-column table and sort the second column numerically in ascending order and then in descending order.

- Note that this exercise contains a centered heading. If you were to sort the second column of this exercise, WordPerfect would include the heading in the sort.

- To sort columns containing other text, you must first block the text to be sorted and then perform the sort. Place your cursor at the beginning of the second column, block the text (Alt + F4); then sort the column (Ctrl + F9).

- When you are in the "Line Sort Menu," remember that you are sorting "Field 3." WordPerfect considers the left margin field one, the first tab, field two, and the third tab, field three.

Exercise Directions:

1. Start with a clear screen.

2. Use the preset margins.

3. Set the appropriate tabs and type the columns on the right.

4. Center the exercise vertically.

5. Save the exercise; name it **DEBT. DO NOT EXIT THE DOCUMENT.**

6. Sort the second column numerically in ascending order.

7. Save the sorted text to a new file; name it **DEBT1.**

8. Sort the second column numerically in descending order.

9. Save the sorted text to a new file; name it **DEBT2.**

10. Retrieve DEBT1.

11. Print one copy.

12. Retrieve DEBT2.

13. Print one copy.

```
                    OUTSTANDING ACCOUNTS
                         OCTOBER


         ABC Carpets                    4,456.87
         R & R Jewelers                   786.77
         Alison's Sweet Shoppe           234.56
         Harrison Taylor, Ltd.         2,192.33
         P & A Brands, Inc.              456.99
         Jolson Brothers               1,443.98
```

TO BLOCK SORT/TO CHANGE SORT ORDER

1. Place cursor on first line to be sorted.
2. Press **Alt + F4** (block). `Alt` + `F4`
3. Highlight text to be sorted.
4. Press **Ctrl + F9** .... `Ctrl` + `F9`
5. Select **K** (keys) .... `K`
6. Enter **Type** of sort:

   A (alphabetic) .... `A`
   or   or
   N (numeric) .... `N`
7. Enter **Field** number to be sorted.
8. **ENTER** .... `↵`
9. Type **Word** number to be sorted.
10. Press **F7** (exit Keys menu) .... `F7`

TO CHANGE SORT ORDER

11. Select **O** (order) .... `O`
12. Select
    A (ascending) .... `A`
    or   or
    D (descending) .... `D`
13. Select **P** (Perform Action) .... `P`

BASIC SORTING

Notes:

- In previous exercises, you sorted one column of records alphabetically or numerically in ascending or descending order. In other words, you sorted on one "key" field.

- It is possible to sort one column of records (Key 1 field) and then sub-sort another column (Key 2 field) within the first column.

- For example, in this exercise, you are asked to create a membership list. Suppose you wanted to sort the records by "CITY" and then sub-sort the records by "LAST" name. The Key 1 field would be "CITY" and the Key 2 field would be "LAST". The "Sort-by Line Menu" appears on the right. Note the Key 1 entries: since "CITY" is the fifth column (the left margin is considered the first column), the Field number to be sorted is "5", and since there is only one word in the field, the Word to be sorted is "1". Note the Key 2 entries: since "LAST" is the third column, the Field number to be sorted is "3", and since there is only one word in the field, the Word to be sorted is "1". Since sort and sub-sorts will be alphabetical, the Typ is entered as "a" in both cases.

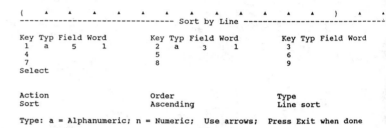

```
(    ^    ^    ^    ^    ^    ^    ^    ^    ^    ^    )    ^    ^
----------------------------- Sort by Line ---------------------------------
Key Typ Field Word        Key Typ Field Word        Key Typ Field Word
 1   a    5    1           2   a    3    1           3
 4                         5                         6
 7                         8                         9
Select

Action               Order                Type
Sort                 Ascending            Line sort

Type: a = Alphanumeric; n = Numeric;  Use arrows;  Press Exit when done
```

- Note the result of the sort below--the records are in alphabetical order by city and in alphabetical order by last name within each city.

ASTOR ASSOCIATION MEMBERSHIP LIST
SPRING 1992

FIRST	LAST	ADDRESS	CITY	ZIP	PHONE
Michael	Griffen	2345 Albee St.	Bronx	10456	212-544-091
Pamela	Johns	234 Davis Dr.	Bronx	10434	212-987-432
Miles	Brown	1640 Ocean Ave.	Brooklyn	11234	718-665-432
Rose	Casen	710 Linden St.	Brooklyn	11234	718-666-443
Leah	Davis	54 Wilmer St.	Brooklyn	11234	718-234-876
Natasha	Alesi	545 Prince St.	Manhattan	10032	212-123-346
David	Asher	61 Chambers St.	Manhattan	10003	212-345-555
Janice	Paoli	150 Broadway	Manhattan	10011	212-432-122
Robert	Payne	34 W. 68 St.	Manhattan	10011	212-432-467
Roy	Porter	500 E. 78 St.	Manhattan	10023	212-654-654
Edwin	Case	2 Imperial Way	Queens	11433	718-432-987
Sharon	Walker	376 Jewel Ave.	Queens	11414	718-432-910

- In this exercise, you will perform several sorts and sub-sorts. Remember, since there is other text in the exercise beside the columns (column headings and centered headings), be sure to block highlight the text to be sorted before performing the sort procedure. **Do not include the column headings in your highlighting of the column.**

Exercise Directions:

1. Start with a clear screen.

2. Set left and right margins to 0".

3. Create the table on the right using left-aligned columns and column headings. Leave two spaces between columns.

4. Center the exercise vertically.

5. Save the exercise; name it **JOIN. DO NOT EXIT THE DOCUMENT.**

6. Sort the records in alphabetical order by LAST name.

7. Save the sorted text to a new file; name it **JOIN1.**

8. Sort the records in numerical order by ZIP.

9. Save the sorted text to a new file; name it **JOIN2.**

10. Sort the records in numercial order by PHONE.

11. Save the sorted text to a new file; name it **JOIN3.**

12. Sort the records in alphabetical order by CITY and sub-sort in alphabetical order by LAST name.

13. Save the sorted text to a new file; name it **JOIN4.**

14. Sort the records in numercial order by ZIP and sub-sort in alphabetical order by LAST name.

15. Save the sorted text to a new file; name it **JOIN5.**

16. Retrieve each file and print one copy: **JOIN1, JOIN2, JOIN3, JOIN4, JOIN5.**

```
          ASTOR ASSOCIATION MEMBERSHIP LIST
                   SPRING 1992

FIRST     LAST     ADDRESS           CITY       ZIP     PHONE

Leah      Davis    54 Wilmer St.     Brooklyn   11234   718-234-8765
Pamela    Johns    234 Davis Dr.     Bronx      10434   212-987-4322
Roy       Porter   500 E. 78 St.     Manhattan  10023   212-654-6543
Edwin     Case     2 Imperial Way    Queens     11433   718-432-9872
David     Asher    61 Chambers St.   Manhattan  10003   212-345-5555
Janice    Paoli    150 Broadway      Manhattan  10011   212-432-1222
Michael   Griffen  2345 Albee St.    Bronx      10456   212-544-0912
Rose      Casen    710 Linden St.    Brooklyn   11234   718-666-4438
Miles     Brown    1640 Ocean Ave.   Brooklyn   11234   718-665-4324
Sharon    Walker   376 Jewel Ave.    Queens     11414   718-432-9104
Robert    Payne    34 W. 68 St.      Manhattan  10011   212-432-4670
Natasha   Alesi    545 Prince St.    Manhattan  10032   212-123-3466
```

USING LIST FILES (For Deleting/Renaming/Copying)

Notes:

- By accessing the List Files feature (F5) you can:

  - delete a file (Delete)

  - rename a file (Move/Rename)

  - print a file (Print)

  - view a file without retrieving it (Look)

  - retrieve a file (Retrieve)

  - copy a file (Copy)

  - change the subdirectory displayed on the screen or create new subdirectories (Other Directory)

  - search for a word in all files in a subdirectory (Word Search-WP5.0) or (Find WP5.1)

  - search the directory for a particular file (Name Search)

  - change the display format (Short/Long Display- WP5.1) [See documentation for explanation.]

- List Files is accessed by depressing **F5, ENTER**. This will display all the files in the default directory. If you wish to see files in another directory, you must depress F5 and enter the directory name, and then press ENTER.

- To delete many files at one time, you must mark the files for deletion with an asterisk. Use your cursor arrow keys to highlight a file and press **Shift + 8** to place an asterisk next to that file. When all files have been marked for deletion, press **2** or **D** to delete the marked files. If you wish to delete one file, highlight that file and press **2** or **D**.

- A file may be moved or renamed through the List Files feature.

- When the List Files feature is accessed and the "Rename" option is selected, you can move the file to another directory or subdirectory by specifying a different path and keeping the same name. **Or,** you can give the file a new name and keep the file in the current directory.

- To prevent loss of data, it is recommended that backup files be made. The "Copy" option may be used for this purpose. If you are saving your data on a hard drive or a network, you can use "Copy" to copy your data to an external disk by indicating the drive where the disk is residing. After highlighting the file on the List Files screen to be copied, a message will display, "Copy this file to:" Type "A:" and Enter.

- In this exercise, you will use the List Files feature to delete single files and groups of files, and rename files.

Exercise Directions:

1. Access List Files.

2. Mark the files indicated on the right for deletion.

3. Delete the files.

4. Rename the files indicated on the right.

```
DELETE:                          RENAME:

CONGRATS                         WAGES  - MONEY
COMPANY                          WEEK  - 7DAYS
TRYAGAIN                         WORK  - TOIL
TRY                              DOCUMENT - VOUCHER
VOYAGE
UPNDOWN
```

TO DELETE/RENAME/COPY A FILE

1. Press **F5** (List Files)............... `F5`

   NOTE: Type drive if other than default.

2. **ENTER**.. `↵`

3. Press arrow keys to highlight file to be deleted/renamed/copied.

4. Select an option:

   D (delete)................................... `D`

- Press **Y** (to confirm)............... `Y`

or   or

M (Move/Rename)...................... `M`

- Type new document name

- **ENTER**.................................. `↵`

or   or

C (Copy).................................... `C`

- Type drive letter/colon (A:) where file will be copied.

- ENTER.................................... `↵`

5. Press **F7** to return to document..... `F7`

TO DELETE A GROUP OF FILES

1. Follow steps 1-3 above.

2. Press **Shift + 8** to insert asterisk next to each file to be deleted......

   .... `Shift` + `F8`

3. Select **D**..................................... `D`

4. Press **Y** (to delete marked files)....

   .... `Y`

5. Press **Y** (to confirm)................... `Y`

USING LIST FILES (For Word Search/Name Search)

Notes:

- Through List Files, the Word Search (WP5.0) or Find (WP5.1) option allows you to search all files in a subdirectory for a particular word. This is particularly helpful if you forget the name of a file but remember some of its contents, or if you are gathering information about a particular topic and want a listing of all files containing that topic. When the search is complete, a new List Files screen is displayed with only those files which contain the particular word that was searched.

- When the Word Search or Find option is selected, you are given a menu. The menu for WP5.1 (WP5.0 contains the same menu except for the Name and Undo selections) consists of the following:

  Name - allows you to search the current directory for a filename that meets certain conditions.

  Doc Summary - allows you to search document summary screens associated with a particular file. The document summary (WP5.1) or document contents (WP5.0) screen allows you to further identify your document by inserting a non-printing comment in a document.

  First Pg - allows you to search only the first page of each document.

  Entire Doc - allows you to search the entire document.

  Conditions - allows you to add a condition when searching for a word. For example you might want to indicate that you are searching for files containing the word "computer" but only if the word "OCR" is that file.

  Undo - allows you to clear a previously entered condition.

- The Name Search option is used to search for the name of a file in a subdirectory. You may have forgotton how you named the file but remember the first three letters. Using the Name Search option, you can enter the first three letters or a filename and WordPerfect will highlight all files with those letters or the particular file you are looking for.

- In this exercise, you will search for files containing specified words and quickly locate a file using the Name search option.

Exercise Directions:

1. Access List Files.

2. Using the Word Search/Find option, search all files on your data disk for those which contain the word "computer." Make note of them.

3. Search all files for those which contain the word "Trinitron." Make note of them.

4. Search all files for a letter addressed to Ms. Elizabeth DeKan. Make note of it.

5. Using the Name Search Option, find the file STOCK.

TO SEARCH FOR A WORD IN A FILE/OR A FILE IN THE DIRECTORY

1. Press **F5** (List Files)................. `F5`

   NOTE: Type drive if other than default.

2. **ENTER**..................................... `↵`

3. Select **F** (WP5.1)...................... `F`

   or   **or**

   W (WP5.0).............................. `W`

4. Select an option:

   N (name) [**WP5.1** only]............... `N`

   Type word pattern

   - **ENTER**................................ `↵`
   - Press **F7** to exit List Files..... `F7`

   D (document summary)

- Type word pattern
- **ENTER**.................................. `↵`
- Press **F7** to exit List Files

P (First Pg) [**WP5.1**].................... `P`

or   **or**

F (First Page) [**WP5.0**]................. `F`

- Type word pattern
- **ENTER**.................................. `↵`
- Press **F7** to exit List Files.... `F7`

E (Entire Doc)............................ `E`

- Type word pattern
- **ENTER**.................................. `↵`
- Press **F7** to exit List Files

C (Conditions)........................... `C`

- Select options.
- **ENTER**.................................. `↵`
- Press **F7** to return to List Files.... `F7`

U (Undo) [**WP5.1** only]............... `U`

TO SEARCH FOR A FILE IN THE DIRECTORY

N (Name Search)........................ `N`

- Type document name
- Press **F7** .... `F7`
- Press **F7** to return to document.......................... `F7`

APPENDIX A

WP5.0 GRAPHIC IMAGES

AIRPLANE.WPG

AND.WPG

ANNOUNCE.WPG

APPLAUSE.WPG

ARROW1.WPG

ARROW2.WPG

RPTCARD.WPG

AWARD.WPG

BADNEWS.WPG

BOOK.WPG

BORDER.WPG

PRESENT.WPG

QUILL.WPG

CHECK.WPG

CLOCK.WPG

CONFIDEN.WPG

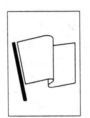

FLAG.WPG

GAVEL.WPG

THINKER.WPG

USAMAP.WPG

GOODNEWS.WPG

HAND.WPG

HOURGLAS.WPG

KEY.WPG

MAPSYMBL.WPG

NEWSPAPR.WPG

NO1.WPG

PC.WPG

PENCIL.WPG

PHONE.WPG

...continued

APPENDIX A

WP5.1: GRAPHIC IMAGES

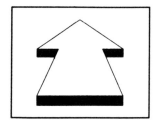

ARROW-22.WPG

BALLOONS.WPG

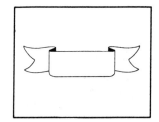

BANNER-3.WPG

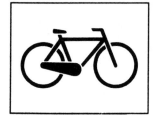

BICYCLE.WPG

BKGRND-1.WPG

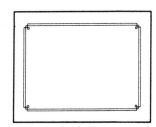

BORDER-8.WPG

BULB.WPG

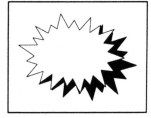

BURST-1.WPG

BUTTRFLY.WPG

MAILBAG.WPG

NEWS.WPG

PC-1.WPG

PRESNT-1.WPG

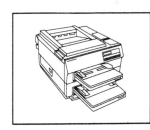

PRINTR-3.WPG

SCALE.WPG

STAR-5.WPG

TELPHONE.WPG

TROPHY.WPG

...continued

APPENDIX A

**WP5.1:
GRAPHIC
IMAGES**

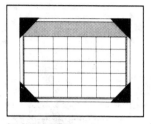

CALENDAR.WPG

CERTIF.WPG

CHKBOX-1.WPG

CLOCK.WPG

CNTRCT-2.WPG

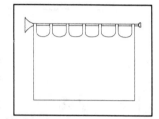

DEVICE-2.WPG

DIPLOMA.WPG

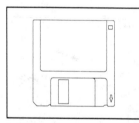

FLOPPY-2.WPG

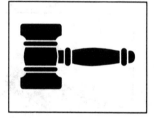

GAVEL.WPG

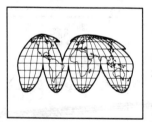

GLOBE2-M.WPG

HANDS-3.WPG

MAGNIF.WPG

APPENDIX B
PROOFREADER'S MARKS

SYMBOL	MEANING	EDITED	CORRECTED
⟋	Transpose	(brochure enclosed)	enclosed brochure
∧	Insert	rte (a)	rate
#	Insert space	onthe ∧	on the
⌣	Close up	peȓcent	percent
ℓ	Delete	the great many	the many
⟋	Change word	We carry (stock)	We stock
stet or	Do not delete	this service will	this service will
5⌐ or .5⌐	Indent number of spaces or inches shown	5⌐Each year we	Each year we
→ or ⊐	Move to the right or tab	→ it is	it is
← or ⊏	Move to the left	← We should	We should
/	Change capital letter to lowercase	in your Ȼompany	in your company
≡	Change lowercase letter to capital	if he comes ≡	If he comes
☰	Change to all capitals	Business ☰	BUSINESS
ss	Use single spacing	ss { I think he / will be there.	I think he will be there.
ds	Use double spacing	ds { She will not go / if you go also	She will not go / if you go also.
___	Underscore	This is <u>not</u> correct.	This is <u>not</u> correct
═══	Double Underscore	This is <u>not</u> correct.	This is <u>not</u> correct.

continued…

APPENDIX B
PROOFREADER'S MARKS

SYMBOL	MEANING	EDITED	CORRECTED
∿∿∿	Use bold	This is <u>not</u> correct.	This is **not** correct
◯	Spell out	Send ③ people.	Send three people.
◯↰	Move as shown	Try to find the (document) word in the long.	Try to find the word in the long document.
¶	New paragraph	The note was past due as of last week. ¶ We know this to be true.	The note was past due as of last week. We know this to be true.
⊐⊏	Center	⊐ Meeting Agenda ⊏	Meeting Agenda
⟨ ⟩	Use thesaurus to replace word	The meeting was ⟨noisy⟩	The meeting was boisterous.

APPENDIX C

INDEX OF KEYSTROKES FOR WORDPERFECT FUNCTIONS

continued...

APPENDIX C

INDEX OF KEYSTROKES FOR WORDPERFECT FUNCTIONS

continued...

APPENDIX C

INDEX OF KEYSTROKES FOR WORDPERFECT FUNCTIONS

APPENDIX D

SUMMARY OF WORDPERFECT COMMANDS

BLOCK	Alt + F4
BOLD	F6
BOTTOM MARGIN	Shift + F8, P, M
CANCEL	F1
CANCEL PRINT	Shift + F7, C, C
CENTER	Shift + F6
CENTER PAGE	Shift + F6
(Top to Bottom)	Shift + F8, P, C
COLUMNS	Alt + F7, D
COPY (List Files)	F5, ENTER, C
DATE	Shift + F5, T or C
DELETE	
(Character)	DEL
(To end of Line)	Ctrl + End
(To end of Page)	Ctrl + PgDn
(File-List Files)	F5, ENTER, D
(Word)	Ctrl + Backspace
DOUBLE INDENT	Shift + F4
DOUBLE SPACE	Shift + F8, S
DOUBLE UNDERLINE	Ctrl + F8, A, D
ENDNOTE	Ctrl + F7, E
ESCAPE	ESC
EXIT	F7
FLUSH RIGHT	Alt + F6
FONT	Ctrl + F8, A
FOOTNOTE	Ctrl + F7, F
GRAPHICS	Ctrl + F9
HARD PAGE BREAK	Ctrl + ENTER
HARD RETURN	ENTER
HARD SPACE	Home + Spacebar
HEADERS/FOOTERS	Shift + F8, P
HELP	F3
HYPHENATION	Shift + F8, L, Y
INDENT	F4
INDENT Left/Right	Shift + F4
JUSTIFICATION	Shift + F8, L, J
LINE DRAW	Ctrl + F3, L
LINE SPACING	Shift + F8, S

LIST FILES	F5, ENTER
MACRO	Alt + F10
MARGINS	Shift + F8,1, M
MATH	Alt + F7, M
MERGE	Ctrl + F9
MOVE	Ctrl + F4
NAME SEARCH	F5, ENTER, N
NUMBER OF COPIES	Shift + F7, N
PAGE NUMBERING	Shift + F8, P, P
PAGE PRINT	Shift + F7, P
PAPER SIZE/TYPE	Shift + F8
PRINT DOCUMENT	Shift + F7, F
PRINT PAGE	Shift + F7, P
PRINT (List Files)	F5, ENTER, P
PRINT MENU	Shift + F7
RENAME	F5, ENTER, M
REPLACE	Alt + F2
RESTORE	F1, R
RETRIEVE	Shift + F10
RETRIEVE	
(List Files)	F5, ENTER, R
REVEAL CODES	Alt + F3
SAVE	F10, F7
SEARCH	F2
SORT	Ctrl + F9, S
SPELL	Ctrl + F2
STOP PRINT	Shift + F7, C, S
SUPER/SUBSCRIPT	Ctrl + F8, S
TAB SET	Shift + F8, L, T
TABLES	Alt + F7
THESAURUS	Alt + F1
TOP MARGIN	Shift + F8, P, M
TYPEOVER	INS
UNDELETE	F1, R
UNDERLINE	F8
WIDOW/ORPHAN	Shift + F 8, L, W
WORD SEARCH	F5, F (WP5.1) F5, W (WP5.0)
TEMPLATE REVEAL	F3, F3